ORGANIZATION
A GUIDE TO PROBLEMS AND PRACTICE

John Child
Professor of Organizational Behaviour
University of Aston Management Centre

Harper & Row Publishers

London New York Hagerstown San Francisco

First published 1977
Reprinted 1979
Published by Harper & Row Ltd
28 Tavistock Street, London WC2E 7PN

British Library Cataloguing in Publication Data
Child, John
Organization.
1. Management
I. Title
658.4 HD38

ISBN 0-06-318040-5
ISBN 0-06-318036-7 Pbk

Designed by Richard Dewing 'Millions'
Typeset by Blackmore Press, Gillingham, Dorset
Printed and bound by A. Wheaton & Company, Ltd, Exeter

Contents

Preface

Having been engaged on research and consultancy into organization for a number of years, I have felt that there is a need for a book which draws from available findings some guidelines for the analysis of practical problems. The problem with most books on organization is that they are written by academics for academics, and their material is presented in a way that enlightens purely academic themes.

This book is grounded on the belief that research is of great significance for the improvement of practical affairs. Research studies are in themselves usually directed to the refinement of theories, but as an eminent psychologist, Kurt Lewin, once observed, 'there is nothing so practical as a good theory'. What I have attempted here is to examine problems which practitioners will recognize as theirs. I have drawn upon my knowledge of relevant research, including my own. The book is, however, written in a straightforward non-academic manner. Each chapter closes with a short summary of its main themes. These summaries are followed by suggested further reading on the topics which have been covered. There are no academic footnotes.

This is an introduction to the field of organization. It delineates the main problems which arise in designing structures and jobs. It does not cover the field of organizational behaviour as a whole, although the interfaces between structure and behaviour are examined. Frequent reference is also made to the context in which decisions on organization have to be made.

The readers I have had in mind when writing this book include both those who are practising management and administration and those who are engaged in its study. I have had the benefit of valuable comment from my students, many of whom have been practitioners attending an advanced course of study. My personal belief, however, is that the subject of organization cannot be treated simply as a technical matter. It has a wide social relevance, affecting access to decision-making in society and the quality of life of all who work in, or have dealings with, social institutions. The more widely it is appreciated that there are many choices available to us in the organization of public, industrial and other institutions, the closer we should move towards a truly democratic society. In this light, the present book is offered to all. We should each and every one of us be concerned with how our fellow human beings and our scarce economic resources are managed.

Increasing difficulties are being placed in the way of giving time to reflection in British universities today, and it has not been an easy matter to write this book. I am therefore all the more grateful to colleagues who have both helped to relieve me of additional burdens and also found time to exchange ideas and comment—particularly John Berridge and Diana Pheysey. My debt to students is a heavy one, especially to members of the

1974/75 and 1975/76 Master in Business Administration courses at the Aston Management Centre. Miss Katie Talbot worked wonders in typing from untidy manuscripts. Above all my wife, Elizabeth, inspired perseverance and lent a critical faculty which will perhaps offset some of the faults in this work for which I alone bear responsibility.

John Child
July 1976.

PART I

Introduction

CHAPTER 1

THE CONTRIBUTION OF ORGANIZATION STRUCTURE

'Structure is a means for attaining the objectives and goals of an institution.' Peter F. Drucker, 'New Templates for Today's Organizations'. *Harvard Business Review,* Jan-Feb 1974, p.52.

The design of its organization is one of management's major priorities. This entails creating a structure which suits the need of the particular enterprise or institution, achieving consistency between the various aspects of the structure, and adapting it over time to changing circumstances. As Drucker points out, the function of an organizational structure is to assist the attainment of objectives, and it can do this in three main respects.

First, structure contributes to the successful implementation of plans by formally allocating people and resources to the tasks which have to be done, and by providing mechanisms for their co-ordination. This is sometimes called the *basic structure*. It takes the form of job descriptions, organization charts and the constitution of boards, committees and working parties.

Second, it is possible to indicate to the members of an organization more clearly what is expected of them by means of various structural *operating mechanisms*. For example, devices such as standing orders or operating procedures can set out the ways in which tasks are to be performed. In addition, or perhaps as an alternative when the manner of doing tasks cannot be closely defined, standards of performance can be established incorporating criteria such as output or quality of achievement. These would be accompanied by procedures for performance review. As well as control procedures such as these, other operating mechanisms include reward and appraisal systems, planning schedules and systems for communication.

Third, the ambit of structure encompasses provisions for assisting decision-making and its associated information processing requirements. These may be called *decision mechanisms*. They include arrangements for relevant intelligence to be collected from outside the organization, partly through specifying these among the duties of specialist jobs. Procedures can be established whereby information is collated, evaluated and made available to decision-makers on a regular basis and/or in response to some new development outside of the organization. The process of decision-making itself can be assisted, where appropriate, through programming, specification of stages in the process, indication of decision rules and provision of procedures for post-audit.

The allocation of responsibilities, the grouping of functions, decision-making, co-ordination and control—all these are fundamental requirements for the continued operation of an organization. The quality of an organization's structure will affect how well these requirements are met.

Components of structure

The structure of an organization is often taken to comprise all the tangible and regularly occurring features which help to shape its members' behaviour. This encompasses what used misleadingly to be called formal and informal organization. The way in which those terms have generally been used is misleading because it fails to distinguish between the degree of formality in a structure and the separate dimension of whether it is officially sanctioned or not. The degree of formality in structure is a dimension of design which will be considered in a later chapter. On the other hand, a book like this naturally lays emphasis on structural arrangements which managers can design and which are therefore official by definition. Unofficial practices have to be recognized as part of the context of organizational design, and they often point to a deficiency in the official structure. But organizational designers do not implement unofficial structures.

There has also been a long standing confusion as to whether the term 'organization' refers to the structure of an organized body, institution or enterprise, or whether it describes the total entity *per se*. In this book I shall use the term 'structure' whenever the sense of 'organization' would be ambiguous. Otherwise, I have conformed with popular expression and used organization to refer to structural attributes (as in 're-organization' or 'the organization of a company'), and the term '*an* organization' or similar to refer to institutions or units as a whole.

Some idea of the components of an organization structure has already emerged. Major dimensions are:

1 The allocation of tasks and responsibilities to individuals, including discretion over the use of resources and methods of working. Structural features concerned here are the degree of job specialization and definition.

2 The designation of formal reporting relationships, determining the number of levels in hierarchies and the spans of control of managers and supervisors.

3 The grouping together of individuals in sections or departments, the grouping of departments into divisions and larger units, and the overall grouping of units into the total organization.

4 The delegation of authority together with associated procedures whereby the use of discretion is monitored and evaluated.

5 The design of systems to ensure effective communication of information, integration of effort, and participation in the decision-making process.

6 The provision of systems for performance appraisal and reward which help to motivate rather than to alienate employees.

If any of these structural components is deficient, there can be serious consequences for the performance of an organization.

Consequences of structural deficiencies

Among the features which so often mark the struggling organization are low motivation and morale, late and inappropriate decisions, conflict and lack of co-ordination, rising costs and a generally poor response to new opportunities and external change. Structural deficiencies can play a part in exacerbating all these problems.

1 Motivation and morale may be depressed because:

(a) Decisions appear to be inconsistent and arbitrary in the absence of standardized rules.

(b) People perceive that they have little responsibility, opportunity for achievement and recognition of their worth because there is insufficient delegation of decision-making. This may be connected with narrow spans of control

(c) There is a lack of clarity as to what is expected of people and how their performance is assessed. This is due to inadequate job definition.

(d) People are subject to competing pressures from different parts of the organization due to the absence of clearly defined priorities, decision rules or work programmes.

(e) People are overloaded because their support systems are not adequate. Supervisors, for instance, have to leave the job to chase up materials, parts and tools as there is no adequate system for communicating forthcoming requirements to stores and tool room.

2 Decision-making may be delayed and lacking in quality because:

(a) Necessary information is not transmitted on time to the appropriate people. This may be due to an over-extended hierarchy.

(b) Decision-makers are too segmented into separate units and there is inadequate provision to co-ordinate them.

(c) Decision-makers are overloaded due to insufficient delegation on their part.

(d) There are no adequate procedures for evaluating the results of similar decisions made in the past.

3 There may be conflict and a lack of co-ordination because:

(a) There are conflicting goals which have not been structured into a single set of objectives and priorities. People are acting at cross purposes. They may, for example, be put under pressure to follow departmental priorities at the expense of product or project goals.

(b) People are working out of step with each other because they are not brought together into teams or because mechanisms for liaison have not been laid down.

(c) The people who are actually carrying out operational work and who are in touch with changing contingencies are not permitted to participate in the planning of the work. There is therefore a breakdown between planning and operations.

4 An organization may not respond innovatively to changing circumstances because:

(a) It has not established specialized jobs concerned with forecasting and scanning the environment.

(b) There is a failure to ensure that innovation and planning of change are mainstream activities backed up by top management through appropriate procedures.

(c) There is inadequate co-ordination between the part of an organization identifying changing market needs and the research area working on possible technological solutions.

5 Costs may be rising rapidly, particularly in the administrative area because:

(a) The organization has a long hierarchy with a high ratio of 'chiefs' to 'indians'.

(b) There is an excess of procedure and paperwork distracting people's attention away from productive work and requiring additional staff personnel to administer.

(c) Some or all of the other organization problems are present.

Organizational choices

All the components of organization structure can be designed to take different forms, and they in fact vary considerably in practice. As Jay W. Lorsch of the Harvard Business School has put it, 'the structure of an organization is not an immutable given, but rather a set of complex variables about which managers can exercise considerable choice' (G. W. Dalton, P. R. Lawrence and J. W. Lorsch, *Organizational Structure and Design* 1970, p.1).* There is no single way of organizing and therein lies the dilemma facing managers, or indeed anyone else participating in organizational design decisions.

The one model of organization with which we are most familiar is bureaucracy. Bureaucracy not only has a long history, its genesis reaching back to the administration of ancient civilizations, but it is in a more advanced form the type of structure commonly adopted by large organizations today. For several thousand years, bureaucracy has been widely accepted as the most efficient, equitable and least corruptable basis for administration. Despite some early social criticism by novelists such as Balzac and sociologists like Max Weber, it is only during the past few decades that bureaucracy has been attacked as an inefficient model of organization in the conditions of unprecedented change, complex technology and an ethos of personal individuality which prevail today.

Bureaucratic structures are characterized by an advanced degree of specialization between jobs and departments, by a reliance on formal procedures and paperwork, and by extended managerial hierarchies with clearly marked status distinctions. In bureaucracies there tends to be a strictly delimited system of delegation down these hierarchies whereby an employee is expected to use his discretion only within what the rules allow.

---

*Full references to any sources cited in the text are given along with suggested further reading at the end of each chapter.

The bureaucratic approach is intended to provide organizational control through ensuring a high degree of predictability in people's behaviour. It is also a means of trying to ensure that different clients or employees are treated fairly through the application of general rules and procedures. The problem is that rules are inflexible instruments of administration which enshrine experience of past rather than present conditions, which cannot be readily adapted to suit individual needs, and which can become barriers behind which it is always tempting for the administrator to hide. This is why bureaucracy today has come under increasing attack on the grounds of its inability to innovate, its demotivating effects on employees and its secrecy. The search for alternative forms of organization serves to remind us that bureaucracy is only one organizational design and that other choices are available. The fundamental question is what form of organization should be selected and on what basis? The following are some of the decisions that have to be made.

1 Should jobs be broken down into narrow areas of work and responsibility, so as to secure the benefits of specialization? Or should the degree of specialization be kept to a minimum in order to simplify communication, and to offer members of the organization greater scope and responsibility in their work? Another choice arising in the design of jobs concerns the extent to which the responsibilities and methods attaching to them should be precisely defined.

2 Should the overall structure of an organization be 'tall' rather than 'flat' in terms of its levels of management and spans of control? What are the implications for communication, motivation and overhead costs of moving towards one of these alternatives rather than the other?

3 Should jobs and departments be grouped together in a 'functional' way according to the specialist expertise and interests that they share? Or should they be grouped according to the different services and products which are being offered, or the different geographical areas being served, or according to yet another criterion?

4 Is it appropriate to aim for an intensive form of integration between the different segments of an organization or not? What kind of integrative mechanisms are there to choose from?

5 What approach should a management take towards maintaining adequate control over work done? Should it centralize or delegate decisions, and all or only some decisions? Should a policy of extensive formalization be adopted in which standing orders and written records are used for control purposes? Should work be subject to close supervision?

When thinking about these organizational choices, there are certain more general questions which help to place one's analysis in a more dynamic context. These are:

6 What are the structural requirements posed by the growth and development of an organization? What practical conclusions can be drawn from research into the association between structure and performance in general?

7 What are the pressures which force managements to change organization structures, and what problems commonly arise with re-organization? How can these be tackled?

8 Finally, in the light of contemporary changes in social and industrial circumstances, what kinds of structural arrangements are we likely to see in the future? In what ways are our present approaches to organization going to become inadequate or un-acceptable?

These are the main issues which a manager faces when thinking about the design of his organization. They constitute the subject matter of this book. It is not possible to offer any precise answers to problems of organization structure in abstraction from the particular institution we are talking about, and from the conditions it is facing. As Drucker has also said in the article cited, 'organization is organic and unique to each individual business or institution'. What one can do, however, is to provide the reader with a constructive way of analysing his organizational problems and to alert him to the kind of alternatives he has available when designing a structure.

A full consideration of structural design has to be informed by the objectives which are selected for the organization. It is in this respect a political rather than a purely technical question. If the members of an organization value its present culture and way of doing things, then the preservation of these features will enter into the range of objectives of that organization. I wish to stress this point at an early stage because most of the literature on organizational design treats it as a purely technical matter, a question of adjusting structures to suit prevailing contingencies. These contingencies are, of course, significant and they will be discussed shortly. A recognition that organizational design should have regard to contin-gencies is important in drawing attention to the need to select an appropriate structure and to avoid the fallacy of thinking that there is any 'best' general model of administration. My point is, however, that in reality this choice goes even further. It incorporates the preferences of decision-makers for a particular approach to management, preferences which are ultimately derived from their philosophies of man. Consensus over such preferences and its embodiment in an accepted culture can itself have a powerful positive motivating effect, and goes some way towards explaining a phenomenon analysed in Chapter 7, whereby successful enterprises operating under similar contingencies are found to utilize different types of organizational design.

The objectives selected for an organization are embodied in a strategy. Strategy refers to the policies and plans through which a management attempts to realize the objectives it has set (or has been given) for its organization. The implementation of strategies over the course of time will determine the tasks an organization performs, its areas of location, the diversity of its activities and the kind of people it seeks to employ. The degree of success it attains will influence its growth and its latitude to pursue policies of its management's own choosing, as will also the decisions of external bodies to which it may be responsible. If factors such as these bring about contingencies for the design of organization structure, they do so largely as a product of strategy and its degree of realization against external constraint. Decisions on the type of structure to be adopted themselves represent major items of policy which may in practice be weighed against other strategic considerations. This is increasingly likely to be the case as in contemporary societies the design of organization has to satisfy political expectations such as those embodied in demands for the extension of participation. Nevertheless, the impact of existing contingencies upon structure is substantial enough, and warrants some consideration at this point.

Structural contingencies

Decisions to follow a particular policy will usually have some direct implications for organizational design. For example, if primacy is given in a business company to a policy of growth via acquisition then the experience of American firms indicates that the establishment of specialized acquisition teams is normally required to carry out a thorough search for and evaluation of opportunities. If greater emphasis comes to be placed upon cost reduction and cash budgeting in order to improve profitability and use of funds, then an elaboration of financial control procedures and an expansion of financial departments may logically follow. The success with which policies have been achieved will contribute to the amount of surplus resources ('slack') available to an institution, or conversely to the degree of pressure its management feels itself to be under. A pressure situation almost invariably leads to a greater centralization of decision-making, as well as to reductions in the scale of some activities which may in turn reduce numbers of departments and the level of specialization within the organization.

The overall size of an organization has been shown in many research surveys to be closely associated with the type of structure adopted, particularly in the range from about 100 to about 5000 employees.

Institutions in many fields of business, public service, trade unionism and so forth have grown steadily larger, with the aim of expanding their fields of activity, taking advantage of economies of large-scale operation and supporting the overheads of advanced research and development or a wider range of specialist support services. As the numbers employed in an organization grow so does its complexity. The number of levels of management increases, bringing additional problems of delegation and control at each level. The increase in size makes it economically possible to utilize specialist support services which must be slotted in to the organization structure. The spread of separate groups and departments across the organization also increases with growth. Additional procedures are then required for co-ordination and communication between these different units, while the contribution of new specialists has to be integrated with the activities of line management.

Size in these ways has very significant implications for organizational design, a theme which will be illustrated at many points later on. It creates so many administrative and behavioural problems that many organizations are divided into semi-autonomous units upon reaching a certain scale, especially if this coincides with diversification into different fields of activity. Hence, the relative impact of size on an organization's structure may in practice be progressively reduced beyond this stage in its development.

Many large organizations, business companies in particular, have diversified their activities into a number of distinct fields or industries. Large companies will also quite often be selling and manufacturing in several different regions of the world. Diversification is an important means of growth, through which firms move into expanding fields and avoid the constraint of legislation which discourages overconcentration in any one industry. When an organization's operations in a new field have attained a certain maturity and scale, it is normally appropriate for its structure to be divisionalized. This permits suitable personnel and resources to be allocated specifically to what is now a distinctive field of operation and for their activities to be integrated closely around it. If the proportion of a company's business in a particular geographical area reaches a significant scale, then a similar logic may justify the establishment of area divisions. Depending on the balance between product and area diversification, area divisions may be an alternative to product divisions or may be established concomitantly with them. Divisionalization is an organizational response to diversification, though it is also encouraged by the growing administrative problems of large scale. As divisions themselves grow large, and possibly diversified, pressures towards further sub-division are activated both to achieve smaller units of management and to reflect the distinctiveness of separate business areas.

Diversification extends the range of different environments in which an organization operates. These environments may also vary in their characteristics, especially the rate of change experienced in market and technological features, the rate at which they are expanding, types of competitive pressure and the degree of dependence on other institutions. These factors will serve to generate different levels of managerial uncertainty regarding new developments to which the organization has to adapt. The greater its dependence on other organizations for custom, supplies, governmental sanction or other necessary support, the more that uncertainty will be reinforced because management's ability to ignore new developments or to control them will be correspondingly reduced. Uncertainty and dependence together place a premium upon an organization's capacity to secure and rapidly disseminate intelligence about the outside world, and to operate in a flexible manner which permits any necessary reactions to new developments that have been forecast. The conglomerate ITT, which had been operating in a climate of chronic uncertainty about the future of its telephone business in countries such as Chile, felt it necessary to build up a highly developed system of political intelligence in order to provide this capacity to anticipate and adapt. Environmental conditions have important implications for the type of organization structure to be adopted.

The kinds of environment in which an organization is operating determine the tasks and production it undertakes, and these have implications for its structural design and choice of personnel. For example, a firm may be operating in a high-technology science-based industry. It will have to give special attention to organizing its research and development activities so as to encourage inventiveness while also retaining control over expenditures and commercial relevance. Seeking to utilize advanced technical knowledge, it will probably employ a broad range of occupational specialists who must be adequately co-ordinated. If a company can place its operations onto a mass-produced basis, this will speak for a different form of production organization than if it happens to be producing for a small batch or one-off market. Much attention was paid in pioneering studies of organization to the physical technology of production as a contingent influence on effective organization, and the practical implications of these studies will be considered later on. By and large, the technology of an organization reflects the kind of environment in which its management has chosen to operate. Some complex technological processes may also only be available on an economic basis to organizations which have attained a given size.

The purpose of some institutions will reflect the nature of their membership. This is obviously true of a voluntary association like a trade union. The character of other institutions such as hospitals or universities will attract certain types of employees, most notably in these cases staff who expect to work to their own professional standards free from close administrative control. A science-based company will employ a significant body of scientists who similarly are likely to have strong preferences about how they wish to work. The proportion of the total working population accounted for by professional and highly trained personnel such as these is steadily rising. In contrast, a mass-production car assembly plant will tend to attract semi-skilled workers who place more emphasis on relatively high pay than conditions of work. These instances go to show that the kind of job design and working environment which is in tune with the expectations of an organization's members will vary according to who they are and why they have joined the institution. Both from a managerial viewpoint of securing motivation and a social viewpoint of raising people's quality of working life, the type of membership and workforce an institution has provides a further important contingency to be satisfied in the design of jobs, operating procedures, career opportunities and so forth.

This brief discussion of structural contingencies permits three further points to be made at the outset of this book. The first point is that the attainment of an organization's objectives will be facilitated if two conditions are satisfied:-

(a) the policies it adopts are realistic in the light of prevailing conditions, and (b) its structure is designed to satisfy these policies. A simple example can illustrate this point.

The management of a small company producing good quality and rather expensive confectionery wished to expand out of its limited markets by supplying a new low-price quality line to a chain store. This line would consist of simply produced and wrapped sweets which were made from standard ingredients and varied only in flavouring. The company proved unable to supply the store at a sufficiently high rate of production, and it lost the contract.

Its structure was such that it had a director in charge of quality control ('Technical Director') as well as a director of production. Quality control was rigorously applied at various stages of production and to wrapping. The company was sufficiently small to mean that initial production of the new line used existing mixing, boiling and other plant. Also no change was made to quality control procedures or to the system of production control. Considerable conflict arose between production management and quality control who attempted to apply the normal procedures to the new line, including rules such as the placing of trays at certain distances from walls. (The higher level of volume generated pressures on storage space.) Production was seriously disrupted by batches being rejected or delayed, and by batches of traditional products holding up those of the new. At this stage, then, the company had not modified its structure to suit its new growth-oriented policies.

At a later date the company was successful in securing and fulfilling another high volume contract. This time it revised its quality requirements for the new line, held discussions between quality control and production about the new operation, and after a short while placed inspectors under the day-to-day control of production management. It also set up a formal procedure whereby decisions on conflicting batch priorities were referred to the sales manager as opposed to merely following traditional practice on the sequencing of batches. The structure had now been amended to support the shift in objectives.

The second point is that contingencies such as environment, size, type of work, and personnel employed are not the same in different divisions and departments within an organization. Accounting tasks and the kind of personalities carrying them out are not very similar to research tasks and personnel. An electronics division of a conglomerate like ITT operates in quite different conditions to its hotel chain. This means that within an institution one should expect to find variations in structure to suit its different parts. There is no merit in imposing a common form of structure on the diverse sections of an organization. That would merely represent a misplaced sense of administrative tidiness. Structural diversity, however, does mean that the integration of sections is a problem. As we see in Chapter 5, the more an organization is internally differentiated, the more its management will have to pay special regard to integrative mechanisms.

Thirdly, structural contingencies are themselves interrelated; for instance, larger companies are generally the more diversified. The particular combination of objectives and contingencies found in an organization gives it a unique character. The set of contingencies which are peculiar to that organization may also in some degree conflict, which poses a policy and structural dilemma for its management. For instance, the firm which has based its commercial success on low cost mass-production technology may today be beginning to reap severe costs of employee alientation in the form of disruption to production, high absenteeism and turnover. Local authorities in Britain have been amalgamated in pursuit of scale economies but this is at the expense of their ability to maintain close involvement with local people.

The implication of this is not that we should give up any hope of designing structures which will cope, or even forget about considering any general guidelines at all. The unique character of an institution can be identified in terms of component dimensions which can be compared with the experience of other organizations along the same dimensions. Managers in practice have to take account of a multiplicity of details and attempt to reconcile the pressures of conflicting contingencies. This really means that improvements in organizational design can only proceed through a process of organizational development, which entails a painstaking working through of details with the managers and employees concerned. As I wrote a few years ago, the guidelines which can be derived from our present knowledge will assist managers in working through their organizational problems. 'But, in the present state of knowledge, this working through is necessary. Particular cases have to be assessed, that is researched, virtually from scratch.' This is, of course, what managers often attempt to do by trial and error. In many organizations today, structures are constantly being adjusted, partly as operating conditions and contingencies change, partly in response to the changing balance of managerial politics.

Limitations to the contribution of structure

I have so far put forward the view that the design of organization structure must make reference to a complexity of different requirements, and that it cannot proceed on an *a priori* basis. At certain times one of those requirements may be given priority over the others, but it will not be fruitful to ignore them completely. In this section, I shall mention some of the reasons why structure, however well designed, can only be expected to make a limited, though nonetheless significant, contribution to an organization's effectiveness. Effectiveness is first discussed in economic terms from the standpoint of the whole organization, and then from the standpoint of the individual employee.

The performance of an organization is influenced by many factors apart from its structure. For instance, an organization structure may be quite effective in guiding people to perform the right tasks, in co-ordinating their efforts and in processing information, but this will not be reflected in overall performance if strategies are being followed that are not in tune with desired objectives or prevailing circumstances. Nor can a mere structure of organization support an appropriate pattern of behaviour if there is not the will or competence among managers and employees to perform in that manner. If skills are lacking or the climate of morale is bad, then an otherwise appropriate structure will have relatively little effect.

Certain structural features can come to be regarded as ends in themselves, whether or not they contribute to a higher level of performance. Provisions to allow employees or their representatives to have a greater say in decision-making are today under serious discussion in Europe. The argument for these lies not so much in their possible contribution to economic efficiency (which could nevertheless be quite real) as in the way they can satisfy other aspirations. Family-controlled firms have often been known to persevere with a centralized system of decision-making long beyond the stage of growth at which delegation to non-family members came to be required on grounds of effectiveness. Some organizations may temper their pursuit of economic goals with social policies which cause their organization structures to be other than the most efficient. I know of one large group of companies in which a policy of plant rationalization coupled with one of declaring few managerial redundancies has led to extended hierarchies within which surplus managers are lodged. These not only embody excess manpower costs but give rise to communication problems.

Organization structure cannot be expected to resolve political problems within an institution. There are deep-seated conflicts in many fields about the legitimate objectives of institutions, and concerning the correctness of the methods by which they are run. If objectives are in dispute between managers and employees, managers and groups outside the organization or between managers themselves, a formal structure cannot of itself resolve these differences in a way that integrates people's actions in an effective manner. At best, it can be designed to provide mechanisms, such as discussion meetings, which bring conflicts into the open and so offer some chance of reconciling them.

Structure itself often becomes victim to politics, and indeed it will not be allowed to operate effectively if it does not reflect political forces within the organization. A department, for instance, will tend to ignore a restrictive procedure if it has the power to do so. Political ambitions are frequently a driving force behind structural changes. Recently a major programme of organizational development was initiated in the division of a large British company partly because a newly appointed production manager felt he was not occupying a viable job and wished to make his mark in time to succeed the divisional director due to retire in eighteen months hence. The development involved the re-grouping of various functional support activities under his command.

Structure cannot resolve conflicts over objectives. It can, however, be shaped in a way that more closely accords with changing views on the correct manner of conducting relationships at work. Traditional norms of authority are being challenged from many quarters today and effective structures of organization have to change accordingly. Whether in fact the organization of any units above the primary group size can be designed in such a way as completely to eliminate formal authority relationships is a moot point. Therein probably lies an inevitable source of conflict between managers and others which is heightened by contemporary notions of the freedom and responsibility necessary to the achievement of personal fulfilment. Organization structure in this respect will always appear potentially coercive to the employee. In business firms and other institutions where there is a cash nexus with their members, this coercion of formalized authority will be reinforced by economic conflicts of interest. Organizational design and development can only help to resolve this conflict with the individual to a limited extent, by exploring more satisfactory means of reconciling the different interests involved.

Plan of the book

In Part II, five chapters examine different organizational choices in turn. The choice of structural alternatives is discussed in the light of relevant contingencies. Much of the research literature on organization divides up the field in terms of these contingences, since they to a large extent define the different academic interests involved. From a practitioner's point of view it is more useful to concentrate upon the specific structural choices with which he will have to deal, though at the same time bearing in mind their interdependent nature.

Chapter 2 considers the micro-level of structuring individual jobs, including developments in job design and job enrichment. Chapter 3 discusses the hierarchical distribution of jobs in terms of management levels and spans of control. This chapter addresses the problem of vertical differentiation which is one of finding an appropriate balance between tall and flat structures. The subject of Chapter 4 is horizontal differentiation—the ways in which jobs and departments can be grouped together and the basis on which such groupings should be divided. An important consideration in grouping people together is that this should be done in accordance with major co-ordination requirements. Chapter 5 is concerned with co-ordination and integration, and attempts to set out the main structural mechanisms which can help. The last chapter in Part II, Chapter 6, addresses the problem of control and considers the use of delegation, formalization and direct supervision. The main area of organizational design which is not considered at length is the specialized field of reward systems, on which an ample literature is already available.

Part III contains three chapters which attempt to place the field of organization structure into perspective. This entails giving particular attention to changes which managers are facing or are likely to experience. Chapter 7 in a sense sums up the work of Part II by reviewing evidence on how organizational design relates to performance, with particular reference to contingencies created by expansion. As successful organizations develop, their managers naturally have to cope with various accompanying changes. Chapter 8 looks at signs which point to a need for structural change, and it also considers practical problems of implementing change. Chapter 9, finally, is concerned with longer-term currents of social change which may seriously call into question our familiar methods of organizing, and which certainly provide a challenge to our ability to adapt the structures we currently employ. Possibilities for breaking away from the familiar bureaucratic model are considered.

Summary

Organizational design aims to devise appropriate structural arrangements. Organization structure is a means for allocating responsibilities, providing a framework for operations and performance assessment, and furnishing mechanisms to process information and assist decision-making. Deficiencies in structure can give rise to serious problems.

There are many alternative structural designs to choose from. This choice is not simply a technical matter but also reflects the preferences embodied in an institution's dominant culture. In addition, contingencies such as the organization's scale, environment, diversity and type of membership need to be considered. Too much should not, however, be asked of structure and even a well-conceived organizational design cannot be expected to cope with problems such as deep-seated conflicts. Nonetheless, the way a structure is designed makes a contribution to an organization's performance, and a book such as this can present useful guidelines which inform both practising managers and students of the subject.

Suggested further reading

There is at the time of writing no single text which adequately covers the whole field of organizational design. Jay W. Lorsch provides an 'Introduction to the Structural Design of Organizations' in Gene W. Dalton, Paul R. Lawrence and J. W. Lorsch (editors), *Organizational Structure and Design* (Irwin-Dorsey 1970). Lorsch and Lawrence have also edited a useful set of papers in *Studies in Organizational Design* (Irwin-Dorsey 1970). Another book which will be referred to in later chapters is Jay Galbraith, *Designing Complex Organizations* (Addison-Wesley 1973). Peter M. Blau and Marshall W. Meyer, *Bureaucracy in Modern Society* (Random House, 2nd edition 1971) provides a readable guide to bureaucracies, how they operate and their significance in society.

All the books mentioned here are by American authors. A British writer Peter A. Clark has produced *Organizational Design: Theory and Practice* (Tavistock 1972) which is a case study of how behavioural scientists worked with a company team on the design of a new factory.

PART II

Organizational Choices

CHAPTER 2

SHAPING THE JOBS PEOPLE DO

'The work under our labour grows luxurious by restraint.' Milton, *Paradise Lost*.

It would be difficult to imagine organizations in which there is not some specification of the functions their members perform. The very notion of organization implies that there is an understanding among a collectivity of people as to what their respective responsibilities shall be. This is not to deny that people stamp their own personalities on what they do and how they do it, but it does mean that organizations possess a structure of jobs which can be thought about in addition to the people who might be filling them at any moment of time. Thinking about jobs means considering both the work that has to be done and the people who are available to do it. Decisions are required on the range of tasks which a job should encompass, on the ways in which the job should be defined and on the freedom of action people should have in carrying out their jobs. These decisions involve questions of specialization, definition and discretion.

Jobs can be shaped in various ways along these dimensions. Some idea of the available choice is provided by the contrasting answers one is given in different organizations when asking how a particular task is tackled, such as dealing with a customer's complaint. In one organization the reply may be that 'Peter Jones from Quality or one of his team, and a chap from Engineering—quite often Phil Bond or Jim Dankworth usually get together on that one. They will sort it out, and call in anyone else, as they think best.' In another organization, you might be referred to page 23 of the procedures manual where it states that 'customer complaints are the responsibility of the Assistant Quality Control Manager—Warranty and Complaints.' This man, you are told, 'has a job description which lays down quite specifically the way he should deal with a complaint, including the maximum amount of expenditure he can incur. Should he wish to spend more, or involve anyone from another department, he must first refer to the Quality Control Manager.'

The different ways in which management in these two organizations has gone about coping with the task of customer complaints reveals the kind of decisions that have to be made about people's jobs. One major decision is how specialized should jobs be? In the first organization, jobs appeared to be less specialized in two significant respects: (a) people took on additional tasks such as dealing with a customer complaint when they felt it appropriate to do so—their jobs were not tightly and narrowly bounded as to which tasks they were to cover; (b) they also had some control over how the task was to be tackled—there was not such a tight boundary in discretion between themselves and management as in the second organization.

There was also a considerable difference between the two organizations in the extent to which people's jobs were being formally defined. In the first case, two departments—Quality and Engineering—had been given the responsibility for dealing with customer complaints and that was just about as far as formal definition went. It was left to members of the departments to decide who would be involved with any complaint that arose and how best to deal with it. In other words, their jobs were not closely defined by management. In the second organization the method for dealing with complaints was precisely laid down as were various constraints on the way the job was to be done.

Specialization and definition are two main dimensions of job design and they are closely tied to a third, namely the degree of discretion or autonomy allowed. In the first example, where specialization and definition were relatively low, the discretion people had in carrying out their work was quite high. Given that some degree of overall managerial control has to be exercised in any organization, this would probably be done indirectly through periodic reviews of expenditures and performance. In the second case control was exercised more directly through the limits imposed by high specialization and definition (both reducing discretion). A third approach to control which limits employee discretion in a very direct manner is through close personal supervision.

This chapter considers the decisions which have to be made on job specialization and job definition. The question of discretion will also be central to the discussion. Choices on specialization and on definition are themselves linked because specialization will normally require that a job is precisely defined in respect of the limits to its responsibilities and jurisdiction, though not necessarily the manner in which its duties are to be carried out. While our main focus will be on operative level jobs, some attention is given to higher level positions. The wider organizational implications of decisions on the shape of jobs also have to be considered, and they remind one that job design forms part of organizational design as a whole.

Variations in jobs

The extent to which in practice jobs are shaped differently—even jobs at approximately the same hierarchical level—serves to indicate how major a decision area this is. It is readily apparent that operative jobs vary considerably in the degree to which they are specialized and defined. We can contrast in our mind the man on the assembly line in his highly specialized and defined job of, for example, fastening on one windscreen seal after another with the craft electrician who has a wide range of tasks including machine installation, dealing with breakdowns and preventative maintenance. While his job is specialized in terms of the skilled knowledge it requires, it is far less specialized than the assembly line job in terms of tasks performed and far less closely defined either by management or by technology.

What is perhaps less well appreciated is how much administrative and managerial jobs also vary. A study which the writer carried out of nearly 800 British managers drawn from companies of different sizes and industries indicated that those in charge of departments and divisions concerned with finance, production or equivalent, and general administrative duties, tended to have jobs which were not formally defined by job descriptions, organization manuals and so forth. At the other end of the scale, managers in charge of specialized departments such as purchasing, quality control, personnel and production support activities, such as production control, tended to have jobs which were more highly defined in a formal manner. These functional differences in formal job definition remained fairly consistent across companies, though other factors such as the size of the company and its technology also appeared to have an effect. That is, in larger companies jobs as a whole tended to be more highly defined (and more specialized), while in routine production situations, such as process production, production managers' jobs were found to be more closely defined than in less routine production sites.

Rosemary Stewart, who has spent much of her research career investigating managerial jobs, has advanced a classification of such jobs which recognizes their intrinsic variety. Writing in the Winter 1974 issue of *Organizational Dynamics*, she expressed the view that 'our language for describing the difference among managers' jobs is not sufficiently developed for our needs. We have paid far too much attention to the common aspects of management and far too little to the great differences that exist among managers' jobs.' Her classification of managerial jobs is a behavioural one which takes into account not so much how specialized and defined the job is, as how it is carried out in regard to use of time, the relationships it involves, whether these relationships extend to people outside the organization, how much uncertainty is involved in performing the job, the responsibility the job holder carries for the use of an organization's resources and so on. Using this classification, Miss Stewart has been able to contrast jobs such as a branch bank manager and an area manager of a retail chain store.

From the point of view of our present interest, research which has demonstrated the differences between jobs serves to remind us that a range of alternatives is available for the way in which jobs are shaped. In addition, it suggests that jobs are in practice sensibly varied to suit the demands of the situation as well as the capacity of the individuals who hold them. In other words, from a managerial perspective, decisions on the design of jobs have to be made and there is a choice between alternatives each having certain pros and cons. The weight given to these plus and minus factors will vary with different circumstances. This choice can now be examined more systematically, starting with the question of specialization.

What degree of specialization?

Throughout the process of industrial development there has been a steady increase in the specialization of jobs. Two factors have been involved, the first affecting knowledge-based jobs, the second affecting operative jobs.

There has been an explosive growth of new knowledge and techniques, which has given rise to many new occupations within organizations such as the computer programmer, the electronics engineer, the market researcher and the corporate planner. One finds an increasing number of employees in organizations whose work is specialized in the sense of being confined to a limited range of problems, but who nevertheless enjoy a continually expanding fund of know how upon which to draw. Specialization has in fact been encouraged by the need to utilize such knowledge within the limits of our personal capacities as individuals to do so. This specialization of knowledge-based jobs may have brought with it a narrowing of vision on the part of many specialists, but not usually greater routine, less challenge or less discretion in the work they do.

That cannot be said of the other type of specialization which has developed in many manual and clerical jobs. The source of this specialization at the 'operative' level of work is a different one. It derived from a recognition that if operative jobs were broken down into simpler elements, these could be standardized to a supposedly optimum pattern through method study, and quite possibly be mechanized or machine-aided. Operatives could through training and experience become proficient in achieving a high rate of output in these standardized, simplified and specialized tasks.

In practice, the specialization of operative work often increased productivity quite dramatically. Adam Smith in *The Wealth of Nations* has provided a famous example of the enormous increase in output which followed the breaking down of pin-making into sixteen different jobs. Industrial engineers such as F. W. Taylor and Frank Gilbreth, working early this century, carried the approach further and popularized specialization within industry. Lenin saw Taylorism plus electricity as the basis for rapid industrial progress in Soviet Russia. The rate of output was speeded up through the specialization of operative tasks into smaller elements and a consequent increase in their repetitiveness, combined with closer managerial control over planning and working methods. One often-quoted rule of thumb is that for every doubling of the number of times an operation is carried out there is a reduction in the time taken per task of between 10% and 25%—subject, of course, to certain limits. An added saving was possible in that less skilled employees could be appointed at cheaper rates to perform the simpler, more repetitive and routine jobs which were established. This second form of specialization entails a devaluation of skill and responsibility; it clearly rests upon different foundations to a specialization of work on the basis of expert knowledge. The two types of specialization can therefore be considered separately.

1 Specialization of expertise

There are two major arguments for creating specialist positions filled by expert staff. The first points out that if a management wishes to make use of newly available techniques it will have to recruit employees trained in those techniques into appropriate jobs. This depends to some extent on the field of operation in which an organization functions and the tasks which follow from this. A company seeking to enter an advanced sector of electronics, for instance, will have to secure a higher degree of research and scientific expertise than will a company working in a traditional field. A specialist hospital will have to incorporate certain types of specialist jobs which a general hospital does not normally have. The more complex an organization's workflows, the more it will also require specialist assistance. For example, a manufacturing concern producing a standard product will not have so much reason, other factors being equal, to invest in a full time specialist production planner as will a company manufacturing a range of products all from the same plant.

There is a steady growth of new types of specialists whose services can be of assistance to an organization. More recent ones include systems analysts, corporate planners, organizational development specialists, and economic analysts. The management of every organization has to decide at what point it becomes worth the expense and extra complication of existing relationships and patterns of communication to appoint such experts to newly created specialist jobs. One alternative is, of course, to buy in the expertise from outside rather than to create a specialist job within one's own organization structure. This has the disadvantage that the outsider may not be well attuned to the needs of the organization in question, which can mean that one finishes up by appointing a member of staff to deal with the outside agency—in other words, creating an internal specialist post after all. The research into British companies which I carried out demonstrated that there was in fact an association between contracting out a wider range of activities to external specialist agencies and having a wider range of specialist departments and jobs.

The second argument which speaks for the adding of expert positions on to the basic structure of an organization refers to its growth. There are several considerations here. As an organization grows in scale, so its administration becomes more complex. It cannot any longer be controlled by referring every decision up to the top level—systems and procedures have to be instituted to cope with an increasing number of decisions and to provide guidelines for action. Specialist jobs then have to be created to operate these systems: planners to do the planning, personnel officers to do the recruiting and keep staff records, accountants to do the budgeting, operation researchers to design new systems and so forth. A further consideration is that as an organization grows larger it can afford to support more experts in full time specialist roles without increasing its administrative overhead above the proportion it carried as a smaller unit.

The decision-making burden of core or 'line' managers generally increases with size because more people mean more activity, and very often more diversified activity at that. The creation of specialized support roles can relieve some of that burden of decision-making. A production manager can now leave at least the more routine and non-exceptional decisions on matters such as production control, maintenance, quality and work study to specialists. Not only will new specialized jobs have been established, but the manager's own job will also have become more specialized through the narrowing in the range of his responsibilities.

It is quite usual for organizations of all types to increase the specialization of their managerial and technical jobs as they grow. Research carried out in several different countries and among different samples of organizations has produced a similar curve of overall specialization between departments, and between individual jobs, as one moves from small to large organizations. On average, an organization employing about 100 persons will have about four functions differentiated from the core function of dealing with the organization's main workflow. At the 500 employee mark, the average rises to eight or nine specialized functions with some twenty to thirty specialized jobs within them. The rate of increase in specialization generally declines as growth proceeds so that at the 3,000 employment mark one finds an average of twelve to thirteen different specialist functions, with perhaps about fifty different specialized jobs within them. The functions which tend to be differentiated first as business organizations grow are accounting, despatch, maintenance, personnel, sales or client contact, and purchasing, often in that order.

The problem arises of whether to anticipate this growth of specialization as an organization develops or whether to resist it. The argument that the line manager should shed some of his tasks to so-called staff specialists is an attractive one, so long as he is willing and able to place sufficient confidence in those staff people for him to take full advantage of the opportunity to delegate. Also a proliferation of specialist jobs and departments will only permit an organization to reap the benefits of additional expertise so long as its management has made adequate provision for those specialists to integrate their activities, a requirement that is discussed further in Chapter 5.

One of the most prevalent problems which managers face in an organization with highly specialized jobs is a narrowing and fragmentation of understanding and perspective. There is a tendency for specialists to pull in different directions, the 'strain towards functional autonomy' as one sociologist described it, and to pursue a course of action that seems appropriate in terms of their own particular values and training. The effective utilization of specialist manpower requires an integration between specialists and line management, and the alignment of their interests with objectives established for the organization as a whole. This is one of the major problems facing management today. Some degree of conflict between line and staff officers is endemic within organizations. The conflict can sometimes become acute when professional staff find their values of autonomy and service to be in conflict with a bureaucratic management system possibly pursuing purely commercial objectives. Conflict over objectives, and competition over resources, do not, however, simply arise between professionals and administrators. It is a product of specialization itself and of the identification of individuals with colleagues in 'their' group as opposed to people in 'other' groups.

2 Specialization of operative jobs

The trend towards the subdivision, simplification and standardization of manual and clerical jobs has in recent years come under increasing attack on the following grounds:

(a) Such highly specialized and routine jobs, tightly controlled by management through a machine technology or through rigid procedures, can no longer satisfy the aspirations of present day employees. In times when most people in industrialized countries have a job and an income adequate to provide for their basic material needs, they shift their aspirations upwards expecting to find some quality of meaning and personal fulfilment in their work. Many psychologists would agree that highly specialized operative jobs do not provide adequate satisfaction for workers. Research in the United States has in fact indicated that workers in machine-paced specialized assembly jobs suffer from particularly high levels of psychological strain and somatic complaints (US Department of Health, Education and Welfare, *Job Demands and Worker Health* 1975).

(b) The general level of ability in the population has been rising with educational progress, and so correspondingly have people's expectations about using their own judgement. Highly specialized, routine jobs do not make use of people's abilities much above the educationally subnormal level. They are therefore out of line with expectations people have (especially younger employees) and are frustrating. This conflict between the job as defined by the organization and by the individual can lead the latter to react by engaging in 'unproductive' activities ranging from shoddy work to literally 'throwing a spanner in the works'.

(c) The rejection by employees of highly specialized repetitive work can take various forms such as absenteeism, higher labour turnover rates, wildcat strikes and sabotage. It has also become more difficult to recruit new employees to undertake such jobs, except when unemployment forces the issue. In Sweden, these recruitment difficulties have become severe for many companies, which helps to explain their particular interest in job reform. Disruption of production and problems of recruitment can impose considerable costs on an organization which may more than offset the economies that derive from a high rate of mass production and a flow of work which is logical and economic in plant engineering terms. This situation has already arrived in many car assembly plants. For example, General Motors' infamous Lordstown Vega plant, a triumph of modern production engineering—with the average cycle time per job pared down to 36 seconds and workers facing a new but same car component 800 times in each eight-hour shift—has been plagued with official and wildcat strikes, go-slows and sabotage. At times, the line has been closed down during the second half of a day in order to remedy defects emerging from the assembly process during the first half. Most of the Lordstown workers are young, with an average age in the plant of approximately twenty-four years only.

Since the Second World War there has been a considerable amount of experimentation in various forms of job re-structuring aimed at moving away from highly specialized and de-motivating operative jobs. Sources which review the progress of these advances in redesigning jobs are given at the close of this chapter, and I shall attempt merely to highlight some of the basic developments, their effects, and the considerations management should take into account when contemplating changes in the design of operative work. The term job re-structuring refers to changes in the design of individual jobs. It will become apparent that these usually involve further changes in the organization of work—the wider context. Work organization changes may include rearrangement of workflows, provision of buffer stocks, changes in supervision and so forth.

There have been two main stages in the move away from operative specialization. The first involves a broadening of the tasks a manual or clerical worker performs, but does not retract that vertical aspect of specialization which in F. W. Taylor's words separated thinking from doing. This stage is expressed by two concepts of job enlargement and job rotation. In job enlargement two or more specialized jobs are merged so as to provide a worker with a wider range of tasks to perform and hence a longer work cycle time. Job rotation does not of itself imply a reduction in the specialization of jobs, but allows workers to achieve greater variety in work through moving at regular intervals between different jobs. The 'utility man' on motor car assembly lines has often been a sought-after position, because in substituting for absent men its occupant enjoys the variety of working at different jobs.

Pioneering experiments in job enlargement at IBM resulted both in improved productivity and greater job satisfaction. In Philips, a combination of job enlargement and job rotation instituted in the early 1960s increased morale and job satisfaction among workers, but economic factors such as productivity and scrap showed little improvement. Experience in Sweden indicates that the association between job enlargement (a lengthening of cycle times) and efficiency depends on the type of work involved and on the people concerned. In light assembly work (such as assembly of household appliances or automobile interiors) previous cycle times were generally between 1 and 3 minutes. For the great majority of people doing this type of work, cycle times can be lengthened up to 20-25 minutes with no loss in efficiency. For a few people they can be extended up to 60-90 minutes without loss of efficiency, while for some 10-20% of people efficiency drops if the original cycle times are extended at all. In heavier assembly work (such as the assembly of truck bodies or agricultural equipment) the maximum cycle time compatible with high efficiency has been found to rise for most people to 45-60 minutes. Most forms of job rotation have, however, been a failure in Sweden. The more successful schemes have either been those designed to provide multi-skill training or those cases where rotation has been organized spontaneously by work groups themselves.

Many experiments in the first stage of the move from specialization have in fact involved a shifting of responsibility for production from individuals to a group, in which jobs could be rotated or enlarged according to the group members' preferences. The formation of work groups or teams has often resulted in greater flexibility in the deployment of labour, in lower absenteeism, and sometimes in higher productivity as well. Work carried out in British coal mining, Indian textile mills and in other locations by members of the Tavistock Institute of Human Relations has largely concentrated on the transformation of individually specialized tasks into a group form of work organization. Favourable results have usually resulted from the changes.

Nevertheless many authorities, such as Frederick Herzberg, Louis Davis and Einar Thorsrud, today regard the first stage of de-specialization as quite inadequate. Basically, their criticism is that, to paraphrase Herzberg, adding one Mickey Mouse job to another does not make any more than two Mickey Mouse jobs. In other words, simply adding specialized, repetitive, routine and dreary tasks to one another, or rotating people around these, does not necessarily create a job that is satisfying and motivating. In order to meet the aspirations it is believed many people have today towards exercising judgement and assuming some responsibility, it is necessary to enlarge (or despecialize) jobs not just 'horizontally' (adding more of the same) but also 'vertically'—adding decision-making responsibilities. This vertical enlargement of jobs is expressed by the concept of job enrichment. There are commonly three main elements in job enrichment: (a) enlargement of the work cycle, (b) incorporation of indirect elements (such as routine maintenance or inspection) into direct jobs, and (c) delegation of more decision-making to employees.

Various experiments in job enrichment are now available for managers to study and evaluate. (These are more fully described in the sources given at the end of the chapter.) In Britain, for example, several groups of staff employees in ICI were given additional decision-making responsibilities—these groups included salesmen, qualified laboratory technicians, design engineers, craft foremen, and production foremen on shift work. In each case, the employees responded by increasing their performance and the quality of their work. In financial terms the company benefited at the cost of only a few days in managers' time when establishing the new arrangements.

At Philips, employee groups have been given total responsibility for assembling black-and-white TV sets and colour selectors for colour sets. The group responsible for assembling monochrone sets not only performs the entire assembly but also deals directly with service personnel such as purchasing, stores and quality control; it communicates directly with other departments too when that is necessary. There is no supervisor acting as intermediary or expediter. In the Philips case some additional costs have been involved: in re-equipment and in training. To offset these there has been a 10% reduction in manhour production costs, reduced waiting times, improved quality and greater job satisfaction.

In Air Canada maintenance shops, to cite a third example, employees were given the responsibility for deciding when and how to replace windows in DC8 aircraft. As a result productivity doubled over a 12-month period and supervisory time required dropped to a quarter of its former level.

Swedish developments in job enrichment are particularly noteworthy because they are more extensive in scale than most and have often involved the building of new plants or offices. The central feature in these new buildings has been flexibility—the attempt to become free from many of the constraints on the shape of jobs imposed by traditional technologies. In new factories built by companies such as Saab-Scania, Volvo, Holmens Bruk and Orrefors Glass, layout and facilities have been designed to permit the work to be done by operative groups with responsibilities for major stages of manufacture, which organize their work as they think best. These new developments represent a synthesis of mainly American ideas on individual job enrichment with ideas on semi-autonomous group working derived largely from Norwegian experiments initiated during the 1960s in companies such as Norsk Hydro.

A significant potential for the extension of the semi-autonomous working group approach is offered by the 'group technology' concept. This began (it is claimed in Russia) as a development intended to improve throughput times and the predictability of workflows. Most applications have been in the field of component manufacture, where group technology involves a re-organization of the shopfloor away from the grouping of machines according to function (all lathes in one section, all grinding machines in another, and so forth) in favour of their grouping by contribution to a common product, usually families of given parts such as gear wheels. This change can greatly simplify problems of co-ordinating work between different functional operations, reduce the amount of work standing idle and simplify overall workflows. In principle these are comparable advantages to those claimed for a move away from a functional structure at the whole organization level, and which are discussed in Chapter 4. The potential not only for job enlargement and rotation but also for increasing work group autonomy which group technology provides has come to be appreciated in recent years. For it sets up relatively self-contained working groups with work passing between different operations which are all within the group's own purview. This provides a natural base from which to increase the flexibility of manning within the group and to delegate decisions on this type of issue to the group itself.

The move away from the specialization of manual and clerical jobs has been concerned, then, in different ways to reconcile more effectively the requirements of production with the conditions for injecting greater personal control and meaning into work. Specialization is reduced so that (a) each employee can again see a tangible result to his labour in the form of a whole product or assembly, (b) he is made aware of the quality of this result through obtaining some direct feedback on his performance, (c) his job contains some personal challenge in the exercise of more than purely mechanical movements, and (d) he can organize his work to suit his own rhythm, pace and capabilities.

It is important for managers not to assume that a move away from job specialization among operatives which has been successful in one context will necessarily work in their own situation. There are cases, which have not been well publicized, where this policy has failed. For example, there was an attempt to enlarge (rather than to enrich) the jobs of female employees assembling the control systems of washing machines in a British plant. This failed partly because it did not suit the expectations which the women had of their jobs. They did not seek intrinsic work interest so much as the satisfaction of earning good wages and of having enjoyable social relations at work. Both these rewards were threatened by the change. The women could not reach the speed of work achieved under the specialized, repetitive system. This led to considerable pressure from management which was probably seen as threatening their pay and employment despite various guarantees. Pressure to reach target production removed the operators' freedom to leave their work places and socialize with others. Management ceased the experiment because of the reduced level of output and hostility from the operators. Management had in fact given little time to the experiment and had failed to involve supervisors in its planning at all.

Job enrichment has made slow progress. There are many minor developments masquerading under that title, but there are probably no more than about 40 European schemes that really enrich jobs significantly. According to a recent survey, relatively few job enrichment schemes are underway in the United States either. Pioneers like Philips and Saab are not extending existing schemes, which still only involve a small proportion of their labour forces. Not enough of the pioneering experimental work has been carefully evaluated to provide an assessment (a) of the overall balance between its costs and benefits and (b) of the particular conditions which made for success or failure. Evaluations which have been carried out and published are often confined to an excessively short time period. This was, for example, true of the ICI experiments among staff employees mentioned earlier.

The factors which are working against a more widespread move towards job enrichment are ones which management must weigh carefully against any decision to follow that road. In some cases, the conditions for job enrichment via autonomous group working involve capital investment which is more expensive than in traditional technologies; examples are Volvo's Kalmar automobile plant and Renault's LeMans axle factory. Successful job enrichment may require a restructuring of technologies as well as of the social aspect of work organization, and in that case managements may decide that automation is a preferable answer to the problem of dreary, repetitive, specialized jobs.

Job enrichment, and group working in particular, also requires a restructuring of pay systems away from schemes that are based on individual incentives or upon rates traditionally attached to specialized jobs and skills. This means a change over either to fixed rates or group bonuses. Changes in pay structures often meet with considerable employee and union resistance and can involve a costly 'buying out' of old schemes. In addition, Swedish experience suggests that productivity can fall off quite seriously if fixed rate payment is adopted. For example, in 1972 the Swedish Employers' Confederation published the results of a study of 73 cases where experiments involving a change from payment by results to completely fixed rates had been made. In 6% of these cases there was a slight improvement in productivity; in all the others efficiency dropped, usually by between 15% and 25%. No compensating improvements were found in regard to quality, absenteeism, labour turnover and so forth. Evidence such as this strongly suggests that an incentive element has to be retained in the payment system adopted under job enrichment, and this means that where a group system of working is adopted, group or departmental bonus schemes may be appropriate.

The conditions which make for success or failure of work restructuring schemes also require much more attention. First, there are various likely points of resistance. Junior management and supervision will normally resist job enrichment and increases in employees' autonomy which threaten their traditional roles and authority. Some, perhaps many, workers do not seek to assume greater responsibility or commitment to their work, regarding it in an instrumental way primarily as a means to an end. They are likely to regard job enrichment with little enthusiasm, the more so in periods of economic recession when every change is feared as a pretext for eliminating jobs. Under more favourable conditions, however, most workers do appear to welcome opportunities for job enrichment once they have got used to it. The initial reaction of employees to job enrichment will depend upon contextual factors such as prevailing economic circumstances, the climate of trust that prevails within the organization, and the values which employees attach to work, as well as the way in which the change is implemented.

Richard Hackman, commenting on job enrichment failures in the United States, takes the view that the way in which projects are implemented is the most frequent cause of failure. Among the common deficiencies in implementation are (a) an inadequate diagnois of existing jobs to see whether they are suited to enrichment and/or a failure to assess how receptive employees are likely to be to job enrichment; (b) a failure actually to change jobs at all, which is a more complex challenge than is sometimes anticipated; (c) development of unexpected side effects, such as supervisory resistance to change; (d) inattention to systematic evaluation which leads to the discrediting of projects in management eyes; (e) inadequate education of the managers and staff responsible for carrying out projects to redesign jobs; and (f) an eventual reassertion of bureaucratic procedure which stifles the additional discretion offered as part of job enrichment. Clearly, the successful implementation of changes in the shape of jobs requires careful planning, analysis of how the change can be located within the wider organizational system, the allocation of trained and experienced people to manage the change, some involvement of those affected by the change, and adequate arrangements for monitoring and evaluating the change throughout its whole life. These problems of bringing about organization change are considered further in Chapter 8.

A second facet of job enrichment experiments which requires more attention is the extent to which successful applications owe their success to changes of a job enrichment nature rather than to other concomitant changes. There used to be a comparable problem with the evaluation of how much increased productivity could be attributed to the introduction of incentive payment schemes as opposed to the work study which usually went with them. Many of the job enrichment schemes in the United States have been accompanied by a clearer identification of responsibility for quality and output. This is made easier when an employee is given a more visible area of responsibility, such as compiling and verifying whole sections of a telephone directory (AT & T) or assembling a whole radio receiver (Motorola). Previously highly specialized jobs, perhaps forming part of an assembly line, offered employees much more anonymity when it came to accountability for performance.

Some introductions of job enrichment have also linked pay more directly to performance through output bonuses, and most schemes have been accompanied by higher pay. This improved level of pay may have been an important incentive factor. To take a third example, in the widely quoted new General Foods petfood plant at Topeka, Kansas, there was an extremely rigorous screening of job applicants. This resulted in far from typical workforce and probably accounts in part for the plant's favourable level of performance. All these considerations suggest that factors other than the intrinsic job satisfaction motivators singled out by job enrichment theorists can help to account for the successes it has enjoyed.

Job enrichment, however, is here to stay in so far as it is a development which is consistent with long-term changes in people's capabilities and their values. It has to be viewed alongside related developments in employee participation and industrial democracy which are sustained by similar social considerations. Indeed, it is worth noting that the enrichment of jobs has already entered the range of issues which unions in Norway and Sweden bring to the negotiating table. As a managerial investment, job enrichment is high risk and offers an uncertain payback period. Much depends on the reaction of employees. While job enrichment has often received an almost immediate and favourable response from white collar and staff employees and is consonant with their expectations of work and status, it may require a long period of discussion, trial and training before it evokes a favourable response from manual operatives, especially those who do not attach so much relative importance to the intrinsic aspects of their job.

Nonetheless, an extreme specialization of manual and clerical jobs is no longer regarded as the basis of productivity it once was. Much is now known about the value of working in groups and on more interesting tasks as a potential boost to job satisfaction. If greater satisfaction can be provided through the restructuring of jobs in ways that link its achievement to the economic requirements of the organization, then the effort is well worth making.

What degree of definition?

A precise and clear definition of people's jobs in organizations was recommended by the pioneering writers on management. It remains a tenet of personnel management theory and practice that everyone's job should be clearly defined in a job description, which indicates what a person's responsibilities are in relation to the activity of the organization as a whole, to whom he reports, the resources and people he has authority over, the work he is expected to do including relevant programmes and deadlines, and the relationships he is expected to have with those in other jobs and departments. According to this traditional bureaucratic philosophy, the more specific and comprehensive the job description, the better. In practice one frequently finds employees who complain that they do not know the exact nature of their responsibilities or how their performance is being judged. They may suspect that management does not have a much clearer idea either, and this can easily lead to a feeling that the ship as a whole is drifting.

In addition to the use of job descriptions, jobs can also be defined through the institution of formal procedures, rules and systems which management insists shall govern the ways in which people carry out their work. The advantages of definition are very much those of the formalization of organization, of which it constitutes a major facet, and which will be discussed further in Chapter 6 on 'Control'. The process of defining jobs in a formal manner, as with the planning of a formal procedure, has the merit of forcing management to work out carefully just how the job is to contribute to the operations of the organization as a whole. What is the job holder to do? Why should he perform certain tasks and not others? If he is to be held responsible for achieving certain results, what information does he depend on, and with whom must he consult, liaise and so forth? The exercise of defining and re-defining jobs can therefore be salutory in encouraging a manager to review the logic of his staffing and organization.

A further argument for job definition is that it reduces the degree of ambiguity which people have about their jobs. It may well be necessary to have a reasonably clear job description in order to attract candidates to a post in the first place. If people are confident that they are acting within a sphere of authority and competence which has been clearly laid down for them, they may respond by taking more initiative than if they have constant anxieties about over-stepping the mark because their sphere of legitimate action has not been defined. In addition, the specification of what is expected of an employee and the work he is to do provides a basis upon which his performance can be assessed. If it is not clear what management expects of someone, neither he nor management can talk very sensibly about his performance.

There are various circumstances in which the traditional bureaucratic approach to job definition will not be appropriate. Take the small organization, for instance. Job descriptions and formal procedures require time to prepare and may need the assistance of a personnel specialist. This is an overhead which a small concern may hardly be able to afford. In any case, when one is managing, say, up to a hundred people, involving a relatively narrow range of not very specialized jobs, then it may be quite feasible to leave everybody clear as to the work they should do simply through a process of personal communication and discussion. The only exception would probably be if there were special legal provisions attaching to how a particular job was carried out. It is because the task of planning, controlling, and co-ordinating work is generally so much simpler in the smaller organization that it is typically less formalized and bureaucratic in the ways it operates.

A high level of bureaucratic job definition will also be inappropriate in circumstances where a considerable degree of flexibility is required. This might take the form of a requirement for people to perform different combinations of tasks at frequent intervals, as in a craft workshop or a laboratory, or the flexibility might have to be in response to the input of completely new problems and tasks, as with many research departments. Job descriptions which specify the details of work to be done can very rapidly become out of date in such circumstances, and they may even encourage employees to cling to previous activities when different ones have become appropriate. To try and keep the production of new job descriptions up to the pace of a rapidly changing situation is simply a waste of time.

The types of job definition which have been mentioned, job descriptions and formal procedures, are directed towards defining the scope of a job and the methods which its incumbents should follow in carrying it out. This kind of definition is usually hierarchical, being more or less imposed on an employee. But more and more, the question is raised as to how far the individual should be permitted to determine the shape of his own job. The two main developments in the area of specialization—a growing employment of 'professional' experts and moves towards job enrichment—both require managements to grant more autonomy to people in carrying out their jobs.

Along with the introduction of more complex technologies and specialist skills in the workplace, it is becoming necessary to employ an increasing number of people who are capable of exercising an expert judgement, and whose jobs do not have to be defined by management in regard to methods of work. The definition of appropriate working methods is instilled into technically qualified and professional people through their training, as is a powerful ethic of autonomy in the performance of their duties. It is precisely for such staff to use their initiative and expert judgement that organizations pay the high salaries they can often command. In a somewhat comparable way, present-day thinking is moving away from the kind of job specialization at operative level which leaves an employee with little control over the way he organizes and performs his work. If employees are beginning to react unfavourably to job specialization on the grounds that they wish to exercise more control over their immediate working environment, then they are likely to react in a similar manner against any attempt to define precisely how they should carry out their jobs. Although precise job definition does not necessarily run counter to the enrichment of individual jobs (their increased responsibilities can, for example, be defined), it is not compatible with any form of semi-autonomous group working in which group members themselves define their jobs on a potentially flexible basis.

Another approach to job definition is possible, which can be made equally formal but which is more compatible with the developments just described. This defines jobs in terms of performance standards expressed as output levels, quality standards, expenditure budgets and the like. These standards can be agreed mutually between manager and employee (or work group), leaving the latter relatively free to define detailed tasks and the methods of carrying these out. This, of course, is the principle behind 'management by objectives'.

A manager has therefore to think carefully about the job to be done, the way he wants it to be done and the kind of person he hopes to appoint to the job (or who is already in it), when deciding with what degree of detail and precision it should be defined. Is the person I have in mind capable of deciding how to set about meeting the needs of the job simply on the basis of agreed objectives? Will the absence of detailed job definition encourage him to make the best of his own initiative or merely frighten him into inaction? How will my policy on this job fit in with the ways in which related jobs have been treated? Will a low degree of job definition lead to unacceptable levels of ambiguity and conflict? Can the organization afford to spend a great deal of effort and time on preparing job descriptions, manuals of procedures, organization charts and such like? Is the context of the job changing so rapidly that a high level of definition would be counter-productive?

It is questions such as these which will help to adjust the decision about job definition to the prevailing situation. At a pragmatic level, one finds that most managers do go through this process of evaluation, though it is sometimes the result of trial and error. For example, when examining the amount of job definition in British companies through formal documents such as written job descriptions, I found that managers in service industries such as insurance and advertising—and in a quasi-service industry, newspapers—tended to have jobs which were less strictly defined than were the jobs of equivalent managers in manufacturing companies. Service industries tend to employ a high proportion of qualified semi-professional staff, and in many sectors of advertising and newspaper operations the work is far from routine. These factors help to explain their generally lower level of bureaucratic job definition. Equally, a comparison between different management functions indicated that certain of these, especially finance and accounting, were consistently less subject to formal definition than were others. In the case of accountants, a manager would normally expect their professional training to define the conventions to which they are to work.

A final point concerns the question of appraising performance. One argument for precise job descriptions is that these provide a framework for appraisal. This argument is misleading in that it rests upon a confusion between appraisal of the methods used in performing a job (the means) and the result that is achieved at the end of the day (the goal). If agreement is reached between a manager and an employee as to what objectives are to be met at the end of a given period or assignment, then the methods of work employed may not be particularly critical. If expenditure is involved, this can be controlled through a system such as budgeting. Progress can be evaluated at appropriate intervals. Freedom to tackle the task and to relate with others as they think is appropriate will tend to motivate capable employees. If a more organic pattern of communication results from defining jobs less strictly this may well produce more creative responses to problems, which are well worth the extra friction that such a system generates. This approach to jobs has to be adopted in certain areas of activity such as the management of new products. It does not imply an absence of control and performance appraisal, merely a different method for achieving both. When looking ahead to future developments in Chapter 9, I suggest that increasing use is likely to be made of management through objective-setting rather than through elaborate job definition.

A note on orgnizational implications

Changes in the shape of jobs are likely to have two effects on the rest of the organization—a 'shunt' effect upon the distribution of authority hierarchically and a 'ripple' effect laterally upon communications with other jobs and departments.

If the changed shape of jobs involves the granting of more discretion and the allocation of new tasks to specialists or to operatives, then there are clear implications for line managers' own jobs. With job enrichment, for example, the transfer of responsibility to operatives eats into the traditional role of the first-line supervisor. Indeed, some experts have envisaged that the supervisor would become redundant as operatives undertook his functions, especially if semi-autonomous work groups are established as in some Norwegian experiments. However, when supervisorless groups have been set up the result has often been serious disagreements within the group on questions of planning, methods or individual conduct, with no-one there to manage the conflict. Current opinion, including that of many Swedish employers, takes the view that job enrichment can relieve supervisors of the more trivial everyday pressures of 'firefighting', progressing work and materials, or reallocating people to machines and tasks. It should allow them instead to devote more time to major responsibilities such as co-ordinating work groups, developing their members' abilities, taking part in recruitment and dealing with important technical problems. In so far as supervisors can be relieved through job enrichment, and line managers through specialist support, it may prove possible to alter the shape of organization towards a more flat form by increasing line management and supervisory spans of control. The advantages of this policy will be discussed in the following chapter.

Another vertical implication of job changes in the directions discussed concerns the approach to control which is adopted. The point has been made that job enrichment can fail if there is no impetus from top management to modify bureaucratic controls or a centralized mode of decision-taking. Similarly, changes to payment systems (which are in part a control mechanism) are usually required. These are further illustrations of the general conclusion that developments in job structuring to be successful do require complementary changes in the overall approach to organization structure, and this in turn implies a high level of senior management understanding. Much the same considerations are valid if one has in mind the development of specialist expertise within an organization. The organization must allow for appropriate changes in delegation and strategies of control so that the value of expertise or of job enrichment is gained; at the same time it must carefully design the interface with other units so that conflicts and discontinuities between the jobs concerned and other parts of the organization do not become excessive.

This last remark points to the problem of integration, and the 'ripple' effect of changes in job design. The broadening in range of specialist employment poses growing integration problems, and has generated considerable interest in concepts of team management which break down departmental or group barriers based on specialist functional differentiation. At the level of operative jobs, many of the developments described improve integration either by incorporating certain tasks previously performed by specialists and/or by grouping employees into teams which are integrated around a product rather than functional logic (group technology). Under the traditional specialized system operating in the British motor industry, for example, it would not be unusual for twenty minutes to be required to rectify a machine going off setting. An operator, his foreman, an inspector and a setter might all have to be involved. But if that operator could be given a restructured 'enriched' job incorporating some inspection and setting responsibilities, this delay could be greatly reduced because all the previously specialized functions would now be incorporated into the one man's job. The 'ripple' effect of such a change concerns a re-drawing of boundaries between operative and other jobs, and this can be seriously impeded if traditionally specialized job boundaries are reinforced by established demarcation lines and collective bargaining units.

Other important ripples which can spread across the organization as a result of job restructuring concern the planning of workflow, the integration of work groups and comparability in payment levels. The planning of workflow is affected in so far as greater flexibility must be incorporated in the form of buffer stocks with many forms of operative job restructuring. If a group technology design is adopted then considerable attention has to be given to the identification of families of products to be worked on. Integration of specialist jobs within groups has also to be complemented by measures to integrate the workflows between groups, and the programming of activities such as maintenance in a way that is orderly over all the groups in a plant. Thirdly, if pay rises are a concomitant of a job restructuring which is confined to certain employees or sections only, this may generate friction because of the threat to long-established differentials or comparabilities. Indeed, any change in the shape of jobs may be interpreted as signifying a change in status and hence have wider political consequences within an organization.

The design of jobs, then, is intimately linked to the design of organization as a whole. Job restructuring, to be successful, requires changes in the wider organization. Equally, as the following chapters will indicate, organizational design has consequences for individual jobs and for the motivation and behaviour of people in those jobs.

Making a decision on jobs

The previous sections have reviewed some of the major decisions which managers have to make about the kind of jobs to have in their organizations. A number of considerations were brought to attention which are relevant to decisions about job specialization and definition. The most important of these are:-

1 The requirements which management places upon the job and the manner in which it is to contribute to the activities of the organization as a whole. Is the task concerned with purely routine, repetitive tasks? Does it require little imagination, flair and creativity? Can it be relatively self-contained from other tasks? Is it relatively unchanging over time? If the answers to these questions are affirmative, then a high level of specialization and definition may be appropriate.

2 The size of the organization and of its departments. The larger these are, the more possible specialization becomes from a purely economic viewpoint, and the more necessary a formal definition of duties may seem to be.

3 The ability of available personnel and their expectations. The greater their capacity and expertise, the less (other things being equal) need a manager restrict them to a limited range of responsibilities unless the field is so technically complex that it is necessarily highly specialized. The greater their ability, the less reliance need be placed on a precise definition of their jobs. In order to motivate people to commit themselves to jobs, the degree of specialization and definition should, as far as is possible, match employees' expectations as to what is appropriate. It has been suggested that these expectations are moving over time towards a desire for less specialization and less direct job definition.

4 A manager's approach towards the shaping of people's jobs should not only be consonant with his evaluation of these various considerations, but it should also be consistent with the overall philosophy of management being applied. The structuring of jobs

must be matched by an appropriate structuring of the organization as a whole and an appropriate management style. Organizations in which an ethos of personal initiative is enunciated in a context of continued restrictions imposed by specialization or formalization are inviting an unfavourable response to what employees will see as a credibility gap. Ultimately a management philosophy is governed by a view of man in organization: whether he should be constrained by restrictions on his activities or allowed to exercise his judgement subject to the reinforcement of feedback on the performance he has achieved.

There are a number of fairly common symptons which serve to warn managers that all is not well with jobs in their organization. Difficulties in achieving consensus between personnel who are contributing to a common process or project may mean that their jobs are over-specialized in the sense that their official frames of reference do not overlap sufficiently with those of their colleagues. On the other hand, a continuance of bickering and rivalry between employees or departments may result from too great a degree of overlap between the functions they have been given or from a lack of agreed policy as to their respective areas of authority and responsibility. This last problem is one which frequently arises in any organization where there are dual authority structures, such as a matrix or line and staff arrangement. In such situations subordinates may be subject to the competing pulls of loyalty to two managers. The arguments for an organization of this kind, despite such problems of job definition, are considered in Chapter 4.

Some of the behavioural manifestations of over-specialization in operative work take the form of withdrawal from jobs that are no longer tolerable—such as absenteeism and quitting. They can also take the form of active protest such as strikes and sabotage. Where employees can avoid the formal definition of jobs which they find unacceptable, by developing unofficial practices of their own, they will generally do so. Such practices will often point to an inadequate design of jobs and they may be extremely significant in keeping a work situation going. In any case, most employees, managers and workers alike will tend to redefine their jobs away from what is officially prescribed both in order to mould the job to suit their individual preferences and to adjust to changed circumstances affecting the conditions under which their work is done. The presence of unauthorized practices and the redefinition of roles have to be recognized for the functions they may perform, and not necessarily regarded as an aberration from the 'proper' way jobs should be carried out. Indeed, a high degree of conformity to the formal description of a job, or to managerial expectations, may signal a lack of initiative and an adherence to the status quo that could be a serious cost to an organization, the survival of which depends on its responsiveness to external changes.

Summary

In shaping the jobs people do, managers are faced with two important choices. How far should jobs be specialized, that is allocated a narrow range of duties? Second, how defined should these jobs be? Both these choices are also tied up with a third one, which is how much discretion should job holders be given.

Different considerations apply to the specialization of expertise and to the specialization of routine operative work. In the former case the issue is whether to appoint staff to take responsibility for the application of new expertise which is relevant for the functioning of the organization. Organizational growth makes it easier to support this kind of specialist overhead, although the organization's field of activity also has a bearing. The main problem arising with this form of specialization concerns the integration of specialists with the primary objectives of the organization, especially in view of the limited perspectives they often adopt.

Specialization of operative work has developed apace since the beginning of the twentieth century. In recent years it has attracted much criticism on the grounds of underutilizing human potential and alienating the mass of employees. There has been considerable interest in experiments to reverse this trend.

Specialization and definition of jobs are complimentary problems in so far as the former is concerned with the scope of responsibility and the latter with its depth. With definition, the issues are (a) how much of a job should be prescribed and how much left to the employee's discretion, and (b) should definition focus upon duties and methods (means) or upon performance standards (ends). In the past, the weight of argument has tended to favour a high degree of formal job definition focusing on duties and methods, although one can find considerable variation in practice. Much depends upon the type of work to be done and the people to do it. With professional work, for example, it is less appropriate to define methods than to reach agreement on objectives, and one can envisage this conclusion applying to an increasing number of jobs in the future. A highly formal approach to job definition will also probably be uncalled for in a small organization.

Suggested further reading

A book edited by Louis Davis and James Taylor, *The Design of Jobs* (Penguin 1972) contains most of the important articles which have been written on its subject, especially on designing operative level jobs. Ray Wild, *Work Organization: A Study of Manual Work and Mass Production* (Wiley 1975) provides a comprehensive introduction and describes many job restructuring experiments. *Job Reform in Sweden* published by the

Swedish Employers' Confederation (English version 1975) is a valuable account of Swedish experience. A summary of Norwegian developments is given by Einar Thorsrud's article 'Democratization of Work as a Process of Change Towards Non-Bureaucratic Types of Organization' in Geert Hofstede and M. Sami Kassem (editors), *European Contributions to Organization Theory*, (Van Gorcum, Assen 1976). Robert D. Caplan et al's *Job Demands and Worker Health* (U.S. Department of Health, Education and Welfare 1975) reports a detailed study into the medical evidence on stress and strain associated with different types of job. A worldwide survey of group technology experiments is the *Final Report on A Study of the Effects of Group Production Methods on the Humanization of Work* (International Labour Office 1975).

A number of writers strike a cautious note about experiments into operative job restructuring. Several of the papers in Lloyd Zimpel, *Man Against Work* (Eerdmans Pub. Co. 1974) are examples, especially those by William Gomberg and Thomas H. Fitzgerald. J. Richard Hackman, 'On the Coming Demise of Job Enrichment' in *Man and Work in Society* (Van Nostrand - Reinhold 1975) draws attention to the ways in which job enrichment is inadequately implemented. E. Lauck Parke and Curt Tausky, 'The Mythology of Job Enrichment', *Personnel*, September-October 1975 challenges the view that job enrichment schemes will work just on the basis of raised job satisfaction alone. 'Job Enrichment: No Real Future in Sight', *Vision*, November 1973, strikes a cautious note about the European scene.

Henry Mintzberg, *The Nature of Managerial Work* (Harper & Row 1973) provides a review of problems and research on management jobs. John Child, 'Parkinson's Progress: Accounting for the Number of Specialists in Organizations', *Administrative Science Quarterly*, September 1973, describes research on the trend of specialist employment within organizations, while John Child and Tony Ellis, 'Predictors of Variation in Managerial Roles', *Human Relations* 1973 (No. 2), analyses the trend of differences in the shape of managerial jobs.

CHAPTER 3

THE SHAPE OF ORGANIZATION—TALL OR FLAT ?

'I intend to study universal hierarchiology.'
Lawrence J. Peter, *The Peter Principle*.

A theme running through the previous chapter was that developments in job design could relieve the supervisory burden placed upon the line manager. The delegation of specialist activities to experts should relieve the operations manager. The delegation of extra responsibilities to operative employees should relieve the first-line supervisor. In principle an increase in delegation down the hierarchy as a whole will reduce the supervisory burden at each level of management. This means that managers and supervisors can increase the number of subordinates reporting formally to them—their spans of control.

Arguments coming from many motivational theories carry a similar implication. They point to the granting of increased discretion and scope for personal achievement as positive incentives for employees to become more committed to doing a good job of work, and this implies less direct managerial supervision. Modern thinking on job design therefore has a considerable bearing on the old debate over the pros and cons of tall versus

*I should like to make acknowledgement to the author of an anonymous civil service working paper, 'Survey of the Literature on Levels of Management', which I have found helpful in preparing this chapter.

flat shapes of organization. For it suggests that the trend in organizational development should be towards a broadening of managerial spans of control and a consequent flattening of organizational hierarchies.

Tall and flat organization structures are usually identified by the number of hierarchical levels there are in the organization relative to its total size. A tall structure is one that has many levels relative to total size, while a flat structure is one that has few levels relative to total size. On the basis of normal practice an organization employing, say, three thousand people and having nine hierarchical levels from chief executive to the lowest level inclusively would be somewhat 'taller' than the average. An organization of the same size having only four levels would be considerably 'flatter' than the average which available research suggests is about seven levels for an organization of three thousand people. Another way of making the same distinction is to say that a structure is tall when it has a low average span of control, and that it is flat when it has a high average span of control.

The problem of hierarchy

It has been found, among American, British and German organizations in the business, service and governmental fields, that the maximum length of the hierarchy varies in a very predictable manner with the total size of organizations. As organizations grow from small units up to about one

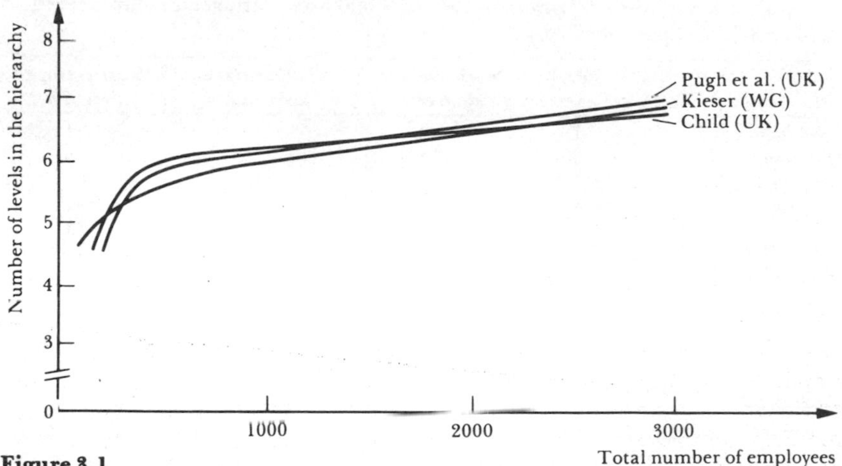

Figure 3.1
Variation in number of levels with size of organization—Results from three studies

Studies by: Professor D. S. Pugh and colleagues, 46 Midlands organizations of different types, data collected 1962-64; Professor Alfred Kieser, 51 West German manufacturing companies, data collected 1970-71; the author, 82 British manufacturing and service companies, data collected 1967-69.

thousand employees, their number of levels generally rises from the four levels of chief executive, department heads, supervisors and operatives which is typical of the organization employing one to two hundred persons, to about six levels at around the thousand mark. The rate of increase in levels which typically accompanies growth is, however, a decreasing one. Even at ten thousand employees the norm is only around seven to eight levels. Number of levels is calculated here in a way that counts chief executive and operative as a level each and counts deputy managers as extra levels but not personal assistants. The way in which the number of levels has been found to vary with size of organization is shown graphically in Figure 3.1, which draws upon three different surveys.

The shape of the graph suggests that on the whole managements attempt to hold down the increase in levels as their organizations grow. As we shall see, there are good reasons for doing this. Basically, there is a choice between increasing levels of management or increasing spans of control as the total size of an organization rises. For example, simple arithmetic shows that the difference between an average span of control of four and one of eight in an organization of four thousand non-managerial personnel can make a difference of two entire levels of management and nearly eight hundred managers. Barkdull has produced a table, shown in Table 3.1,

Table 3.1
The number of levels and managers required with varying average spans of control in a hypothetical organization of 3,600 non-managerial employees and 200 first-line supervisors.

	Level	With average span of 3	With average span of 4	With average span of 6
Number of	1	1	1	1
managers	2	3	4	6
required	3	8	13	none
at each	4	23	none	none
level	5	67	50	34
Total managers		102	68	41
First-line supervisors		200	200	200
Non-managerial employees		3,600	3,600	3,600

Adapted from: C. W. Barkdull, 'Span of Control: A Method of Evaluation', *Michigan Business Review,* 15, 1963, pp. 25-32

which illustrates the effect of varying the size of average spans of control on the number of levels. The figure shows how a hypothetical organization with 3,600 non-managerial employees, and 200 first-line supervisors, requires seven levels and 102 managers with an average span of three, six levels and 68 managers with an average span of four, and only five levels and 41 managers with an average span of six. Barkdull appreciates that in real life organizations do not build up their structures as evenly as the hypothetical organization in his table. Nevertheless, while the figures might be somewhat changed in reality, the overall effect would not be substantially altered.

The choice, then, facing managers in growing organizations is between extending the number of hierarchical levels or average spans of control. This trade-off is felt more acutely the larger the organization. It is pertinent therefore to examine the arguments that can be raised for and against tall and flat structures.

Arguments for and against tall and flat structures

If it were not for difficulties which can arise with wide spans of control, the case against relatively tall organization structures would be overwhelming. Tall structures involving many levels of management raise administrative overheads. They can lead to communication problems and a dilution of top management control. They can make it difficult to distinguish clearly between duties at different levels in the organization. They may reduce the scope for subordinates to exercise responsibility and hence have a deleterious effect on motivation.

The economy brought about by a reduction in the number of management levels has already been demonstrated by the preceding examples. In effect, the productivity required of each manager is increased through increasing his span of control. How far this policy can be taken will depend on factors such as the personal capacities of managers, the burden on management that is imposed on them by the nature of the organization's operations, and the opportunities there are for devising appropriate information processing, control and integrating systems which can relieve some of this burden.

Very often when managers complain that they have problems of communication with operative employees and first-line supervisors, one finds that they are operating with a tall structure. The ways in which communication can become distorted in passing up and down through hierarchical levels is well documented. Subordinates frequently interpret as merely advice or guidelines for action what their managers had intended to be firm instructions. These instructions consequently become diluted or re-interpreted, especially if the communication is purely verbal as a certain proportion must always be. In passing up information, there is also a well-known tendency for those at subordinate levels to present communication in terms that will least offend the recipient and indeed some communication may not be passed on at all.

The link between an over-extended hierarchy and communication problems was evident in a factory producing drinks with which I have some acquaintance. This factory employed about 1,200 employees and managers. It had nine levels in its main production hierarchy. The chief executive was keenly aware of what he called 'communication problems' between himself and the shop floor. He attempted to overcome these by somewhat unorthodox methods such as paying spot visits to the shop floor almost every day, working some days at operative jobs, and accompanying drivers unannounced on their runs to the company's distribution depot. In themselves these appeared to have generated a high regard among employees for their chief executive—but at a cost and without solving the real problem. Among production managers and supervisors there was considerable dislike of this approach, deriving primarily from apprehension at what this persistent 'by-passing' implied for their authority. It was in any case questionable whether so much top management activity aimed at improving communications was being judiciously balanced against the time required to develop longer term strategic policies for the business. It seemed to an observer that the net effect of the chief executive's methods was more to create a diffuse feeling that status barriers were being broken down than to create the conditions for precise information to be communicated effectively and on an everyday operational basis up and down the hierarchy. A reduction in the number of managerial levels would almost certainly have made a more significant contribution to that end.

A structure with many levels of management can make for difficulties in distinguishing sufficiently discrete levels of responsibility and authority between positions at adjacent points in the hierarchy. The Fulton Committee pointed to this as a problem in the British Civil Service. The Committee expressed the view that 'to function efficiently large organizations including government departments need a structure in which units and individual members have authority that is clearly defined and responsibilities for which they can be held accountable'. The Committee identified a number of typical features of civil service organization which were preventing the clear allocation of authority and responsibility. One of these was the large number of hierarchical levels and correspondingly narrow spans of control in most civil service departments. In these departments there were usually at least nine levels from Permanent Secretary down to Clerical Assistant, and spans of control averaged only between two and three.

This very narrow and tall structure meant that the same work was passing through too many hands. While this accorded with civil service traditions of multiple drafting and checking of work, it also severely restricted the scope for individual officers to exercise discretion in the pursuit of their duties. From the standpoint of administrative overheads the system was wasteful (as Parkinson had pointed out long before), and from the standpoint of managerial control it made an assessment of individual performance difficult in the extreme. Part of the problem in the civil service lay in a confusion of levels of management with grades in the salary structure. As the Fulton Committee put it, the salary grading structure with its twenty or so grades 'is essentially a pay structure: it is not designed to determine the actual organization of work. The precise organization of each block of work, and the number of working levels in it, should be determined solely by what is required for the most efficient achievement of its objectives.'

In the case of the pre-Fulton civil service, the personnel effects of too many levels amounted to the same as those of narrow spans of control. It is likely that within a managerial or executive structure most staff will prefer to have opportunities of exercising discretion and taking initiatives commensurate with their relatively high abilities and qualifications. In this situation, narrow differentials in the hierarchy and narrow spans of control are both likely to impair motivation. Unless the content of the work being performed is highly complex and/or innovative, as in a research team, this narrowness will almost certainly result in excessively close supervision or in much of the same work being gone over again by one's superordinate manager. Neither prospect can readily attract the enthusiastic commitment of able employees.

The weight of argument is therefore in favour of restraining the increase in numbers of management levels which is otherwise a typical concomitant of organizational growth. A policy of restraint on levels along with continued growth in the total size of an organization means a widening of average spans of control. What objections are there to wider spans of control, and are there any limits as to how far the widening can go?

It was a cornerstone of classical management theory that managerial spans of control should be limited. A figure of between three and six subordinates was usually recommended. Classical theorists such as Sir Ian Hamilton, Henri Fayol, Colonel Lyndall Urwick and V.A. Graicunas argued principally from the personal limitations of human beings—since a manager's span of attention, memory, energy and other capacities are limited, he will be unable successfully to supervise the work of more than a few subordinates. Graicunas in a famous paper of 1933 demonstrated how an arithmetic increase in the number of subordinates is accompanied by an exponential increase in the number of relationships the superior has to manage.

The classical theorists were primarily concerned with the maintenance of control from the top of an organization. They wrote at a time when relatively little was understood about the ways in which organizational design can affect human motivation or about the ways in which the demands made upon managers can vary according to the kind of work that is being undertaken. So they found themselves arguing for the general application of two principles—limited spans of control and a limited number of hierarchical levels—which were mutually inconsistent, above all in the larger organization. On the one hand, spans of control were to be limited so that it was possible to retain adequate supervisory control over subordinates, sufficient communication with them and adequate co-ordination between their activities. On the other hand, they advocated a restricted number of hierarchical levels so that loss of control down a hierarchy and the dilution of instructions before they reached the point of action should be kept to a minimum. In effect, these two principles were speaking strongly for the administrative advantages of small-scale organization, a point of view that carries great weight as I shall argue in concluding this book.

The principle of limited spans of control has percolated widely within managerial thinking, and it is probably a major factor in the development of excessive levels in organizations. There is a school of thought that seeks to reverse this trend by widening spans of control wherever possible. It is often said that the greatest scope for widening spans of control lies in the middle of hierarchies, and several studies have found that in practice there tend to be narrower spans of control in the middle levels of management than at the top, or for that matter at first-line supervisory level.

In a small non-ferrous metal manufacturing plant where I conducted a study of managerial organization there were five levels in the production hierarchy. The plant had only about two hundred and fifty employees. While the plant general manager had six subordinates reporting to him and there was an average production supervisory span of 20, there was a one-over-one relationship between a works manager and a production superintendent. There was relatively little difference between the work content of the superintendent and of the foremen who reported to him, and many of the latter were impatient at the lack of discretion this situation gave them over matters such as the planning of work. Their greatest complaint was, as you might guess by now, inadequate communications up and down the hierarchy. The over-manning within the management of this particular company had its roots partly in a policy of avoiding managerial redundancies when the owning group had in the past closed or rationalized other sites.

In an influential article published in 1950, James Worthy described how it was deliberate policy in the American Sears Roebuck company to break the span of control principle by having as many merchandising managers as possible reporting to each store manager. The conventional intervening level of management between merchandising and store managers was also abolished. Worthy's view was that 'flatter, less complex structures, with a maximum of administrative decentralization, tend to create a potential for improved attitudes, more effective supervision, and greater individual responsibility and initiative among employees'. Store managers had so many subordinates reporting to them that they were forced to delegate some decision-making authority. Giving more discretion to subordinate managers not only improved their morale, according to Worthy. It also put more pressure on them and consequently improved their performance—'they cannot be running constantly to their superiors for approval of their actions; they have to make their own decisions and stand or fall by the results.' By being forced to manage, these managers learned to manage. Store managers, knowing they had to delegate more authority, took greater care in selecting, training and briefing their subordinates. And despite the wider spans of control, the abolition of one hierarchical level improved communications between store managers and their subordinates.

Worthy, of course, was arguing merely from a single case and in fact he did not present any specific details or statistics to support his conclusions. Others have, however, argued in support of his view. Suojanen pointed out that the principle of a limited span of control was first developed in military organizations (both Sir Ian Hamilton and Urwick were military men), where the requirement of operating under emergency conditions leads to a greater reliance on the formal hierarchical command structure to achieve co-ordination. In large governmental and business organizations, operating conditions are different. Also, the principle was put forward before social science research had drawn attention to the ways in which informal and lateral relationships can assist co-ordination and reduce the need to effect integration through supervision by superordinate managers.

In response to these criticisms, Urwick reformulated the span of control principle, stating that no manager should supervise the work of more than six subordinates whose work *interlocks*. In the Sears Roebuck case, he argued, spans of control could be widened to advantage because the work of the merchandising managers did not interlock appreciably. Where there is a considerable degree of interdependence between the tasks of subordinates, the burden of supervision is increased, assuming as Urwick did that the subordinates cannot carry out the necessary degree of mutual integration themselves—an assumption that is today being challenged by experiments in teamwork as we shall see in Chapter 5. Urwick did appreciate that reducing the number of levels in an organization can improve communications and devolve more authority and responsibility onto junior managers. He took the view, however, that in industry there was too much emphasis on reducing the inefficiencies of excessive levels at the expense of ignoring the need to limit spans of control.

The problem of striking a balance between hierarchical levels and spans of control, particularly acute for the large organization, can be stated clearly enough; but the practical question is how to deal with it. The debate over span of control began to move out of the realms of the abstract in making reference to the extent of interlocking between subordinates' work. It is only by locating the problem in a realistic context that some useful guidelines can be formulated. First of all, what considerations should a manager bear in mind when thinking about the shape of his organization?

Deciding on hierarchy and spans of control

If an organization is small, its management can afford to opt for very few levels or for narrow spans of control without forcing the other dimension of shape into an unacceptable position. In the absence of strong constraints, the small organization would be advised to economize in its levels of management for the reasons given earlier. In a larger organization the trade-off becomes more acute. The question is now how far can the number of levels be limited by increasing the span of managerial supervision. Factors to take into account here are to do with technology, with the competence and training of staff, and with motivation.

Joan Woodward found in her research on 100 manufacturing firms in South-East Essex that the more successful ones adopted a shape of organization that varied according to their main production technology. Among firms engaged in one-off or small batch production, the appropriate shape was one with relatively few hierarchical levels and wide middle management spans of control. As one moved up the scale of complexity in production technology through mass production to process production so structures became taller and more narrowly based, with longer hierarchies and smaller middle management spans. Within each category of technology, the best performing companies were those closest to the median in the type of structure adopted. At first-line supervisory level the relationship between technology and span of control was curvilinear. That is, the largest spans tended to be found in mass production technologies.

Woodward's research was a pioneering effort and it has been qualified in important respects by later work. Certain of her findings have, however, been confirmed, such as the way in which first-line supervisory spans vary with technology. In general, her research serves to draw attention to the technology-related factors which managers have to think about when deciding on questions of shape, especially spans of control. These factors are :

1 The degree of interaction between the personnel, or units of personnel, being supervised,

2 The degree of dissimilarity of activities being supervised,

3 The incidence of new problems in the supervisor's unit,

4 The degree of physical dispersion of activities,

5 The extent to which the supervisor must carry out non-managerial duties, and the demands on his time from other people and units.

The greater the incidence of these factors, the heavier is likely to be the burden of supervision and hence the more severe the limit on the number of subordinates a person can manage without inefficiencies setting in. The ability to operate large supervisory spans of control in a mass production system (including mass production clerical work) can be appreciated in that the incidence of all the above factors is likely to be low. At the other extreme, in a unit developing prototype or one-off special order products the reverse is likely to be the case. There will be new problems to tackle, a range of specialized skills to draw upon and to co-ordinate, and probably a large call on the supervisor's or manager's time to advise on difficult technical and operational matters. Spans of control will have to be kept narrow. In process plants there may be a fairly frequent changeover of production requiring supervisory attention and, even if that is not the case, most companies prefer to retain a relatively high ratio of supervisors to employees because of the high cost of failure, damage or accident with high investment plant.

A characteristic of larger organizations, and of large mass production manufacturing units especially, is the employment of many specialist support staff. Some of these staff will be appointed to roles which are designed to relieve the supervisory burden of line managers, by taking over responsibilities for the planning of work, quality control, work study, personnel, training and other matters. The use of staff personnel should therefore allow for the widening of spans of control at the levels to which they are offering direct assistance, although their presence will necessitate a broadening in spans of control at a higher level of management. If staff personnel are also able to assist in the development of standard procedures, and if the tasks of the organization are sufficiently repetitive or familiar to permit the application of set procedures, than the burden of management can further be reduced with a consequent widening of spans of control.

The ability, competence and skills of managers and subordinates must also form part of the assessment. The ability of managers to take on a wide span of supervisory responsibility varies from individual to individual. The greater the competence of subordinates, the less closely do they need to be supervised and the less often does their work require review. Therefore as the competence of managers and subordinates rises, possibly over time through experience and training, so it becomes feasible to widen spans of control and to reduce levels of management. The ability to modify the shape of structure in this direction should be one of the benefits of a successful policy of management and manpower development. The chances are that it will also prove more satisfying to the people involved, since the degree of discretion being allowed to them will be tending to rise along with their competence (and in most cases their desire) to exercise it. If the situation involves the management of highly skilled or professional work then a balance will probably have to be struck between (a) the capability and wish of personnel to be left alone to carry out tasks as they see fit, applying their own judgement, and (b) the technical complexity of the overall operation itself which may require considerable consultation and integration of different specialist contributions. If the necessary degree of teamwork can be achieved without close managerial involvement (and this should be the aim) then supervisory spans can be broadened; otherwise the burden on managers is likely to be heavy and spans of control will have to be narrow.

In technically complex work, particularly that of an innovative or developmental kind where there is considerable new information to be processed and uncertainties to be coped with, a high degree of cohesion between a group of subordinates will normally be necessary. The employees concerned will have to work closely and constructively together in a problem-solving mode. Research which has been carried out into the conditions favourable to group cohesion draws attention to the desirability of keeping down the size of groups. As group size increases, particularly beyond seven or eight members, there is a tendency for factions and cliques to form, generating conflict; the participation of individual members falls off and the number of relationships to be managed increases sharply as the classical theorists pointed out. In effect, this research lends support to Urwick's view that whenever there is a requirement for subordinates' work to interlock—for them to work in cohesion as a team—then a significant constraint may be imposed on the size of an effective span of control. The constraint may, however, be relieved to some extent if subordinates can be organized into smaller separate groups rather than a single group.

The relevance of motivation has been touched on several times already. One argument for broadening spans of control and reducing levels is, as Worthy put it, that people respond positively to the chance of exercising more responsibility and having more scope to their job. This is the cornerstone of the theory which lies behind job enrichment in general. It should be borne in mind, nevertheless, that people cannot be looked upon merely as materials which respond automatically to a given change in their environment. Apart from the question of different innate capabilities, it is not certain that everyone will welcome, let alone seek, greater responsibility, especially if that carries the objective costs of a greater burden of worry, of time spent on work and so forth. It depends a great deal on the nature of people's attachment and commitment to their job and their organization—why they have entered that employment and what they most seek from it. If employees are both capable and committed, the motivational basis for keeping a small number of levels and using broad spans of control will be present. It will, however, be absent if employees cannot or will not willingly assume greater responsibility. In fact, if management is not successful in motivating employees its supervisory burden is *ipso facto* increased, and considerable judgement has always to be exercised in trying to discern whether the type of supervision is creating poor motivation by its inappropriateness or whether close supervision is a necessary response given the intrinsic qualities of the employees who are available on the labour market. A similar point has always applied, of course, to the choice of a payment system—if this is in tune with employee expectations and the task system then the burden of supervision is eased and spans of control can be wider to that extent.

I have reviewed the main considerations that a manager would be advised to take into account when assessing the shape of his organization or parts of it. The next step is to find a method for making this assessment as specific as possible and this entails the assignment of points in the form of a simple weighting system. In this way, one systematically makes explicit the judgements that are in any case made implicitly.

A useful method was developed by the Lockheed Missiles and Space Division, following top management's identification of an organizational problem arising from a proliferation of levels and narrow spans of control in middle management. Attention was therefore focused on the span of management control and seven factors were selected as the most critical ones for its evaluation. These factors were: similarity of functions managed, geographical contiguity of functions managed, the complexity of those functions, the direction and control required by the personnel being managed, the degree to which the manager had to provide co-ordination, the amount of planning he had to carry out, and the assistance received by the manager from staff and support personnel. When these seven factors had been isolated, a set of point values was established for the first six, which together represent the burden of supervision placed on a manager. Provisional point values were tested against actual cases and a final set was agreed upon on the basis of experiment, experience and common sense. The point values finally assigned are shown in Table 3.2.

The seventh factor, the amount of assistance given to the manager by the organization, was treated differently because it lightens rather than increases the supervisory burden. It was given a range of negative weightings reflecting the degree to which the burden of supervision on a manager was reduced.

In a manner similar to job evaulation, the points values for each managerial or supervisory job were then added together to produce an overall 'supervisory index'. Units which were thought to be effectively

Table 3.2
Elements in the supervisory burden of managers and their assessment

Element	Degree of supervisory burden, and points allocated				
Similarity of Functions	Identical 1	Essentially alike 2	Similar 3	Inherently different 4	Fundamentally distinct 5
Geographical contiguity	All together 1	All in one building 2	Separate buildings, one plant location 3	Separate locations, one geographic area 4	Dispersed geographic areas 5
Complexity of functions	Simple repetitive 2	Routine 4	Some complexity 6	Complex varied 8	Highly complex, varied 10
Direction and control required	Minimum supervision and training 3	Limited supervision 6	Moderate periodic supervision 9	Frequent continuing supervision 12	Constant close supervision 15
Co-ordination required	Minimum relationships with others 2	Relationships limited to defined courses 4	Moderate relationship easily controlled 6	Considerable close relationship 8	Extensive mutual non-recurring relationship 10
Planning required	Minimum scope and complexity 2	Limited scope and complexity 4	Moderate scope and complexity 6	Considerable effort required guided only by broad policies 8	Extensive effort required; areas and policies not charted 10

From: H. Stieglitz, 'Optimizing Span of Control', *Management Record*, 24, 1962, pp. 25-29.
For definitions and method of allocating point values see the Appendix to this Chapter.

organized and managed, and where managers had wide spans of control, had their readings on the supervisory index taken as standards. These standards were then used to assess an appropriate span of control for other managerial positions. Table 3.3 shows how the supervisory index was in this way utilized to suggest appropriate spans of control for middle management positions. Different conversion standards (rates of supervisory index to span of control) were used for first-line supervisors. The Figure also shows the distribution of actual spans found for 150 middle managers who were surveyed in the first stage of the programme.

The dotted line on Table 3.3 indicates the shift of the suggested standard span of control along with changes in the index of supervisory burden. Nearly all the jobs surveyed lie to the left of the line; in other words they had narrower spans of control than the standard. The company therefore went ahead with a reorganization to increase average spans and to reduce the number of hierarchical levels. The results are impressive. For example, in one unit the average span was increased from 3.8 to 4.2 subordinates and levels reduced from five to four; in another average span was widened from 3.0 to 4.2 and levels reduced from six to five. A more dramatic change occured in another unit where two levels of management were eliminated (reduced from seven to five), the average span of middle management increased from 3.9 to 5.9, management personnel were reduced by seven (mostly in transfers) and management payroll cut by an annual rate of over $70,000 (at 1960 prices).

The Lockheed method cannot be applied in a purely mechanical way, and in practice considerable judgement is needed in assessing the extent that each factor is present in each manager's job, whether other factors should enter into the calculation, and in deciding whether the suggested standard span is appropriate in any given case. Here, the other considerations I have mentioned must enter into the assessment, including the individual capabilities and motivations of both managers and subordinates. It is also possible that one or more of the six supervisory burden factors, such as the need for planning, may be of sufficient importance to warrant giving them much higher point values than was the case at Lockheed.

I have spent some time describing the Lockheed approach because it has been applied in practice with encouraging results. The same type of approach could be applied within virtually any kind of organization. Managements would, however, need to decide what were the most relevant factors to include in the supervisory index and what were appropriate weightings to attach to them. Stieglitz, writing on the Lockheed method, cautioned that anyone who attempts to use it should first recognize that 'there is no really neat, packaged formula that anyone can use to determine the proper span of control for a particular supervisor. Nor is there anything close to a foolproof device for determining the proper number of levels that should exist in an organization.' Nonetheless, given

Table 3.3
Conversion of supervisory index into suggested spans of control

Supervisory Index	Range of actual spans (150 middle managers) 2	3	4	5	6	7	8	9	10	11	Suggested standard spans of control
40-42		1	1	1							4-5
37-39	1	1	4	5	4						4-6
34-36	10	9	13		3						4-7
31-33	10	6	12	7	3	1	1				5-8
28-30	12	17	7	3	2	1					6-9
25-27	3	3					1	1			7-10
22-24	1	1	1			1		1	1	1	8-11
Total number of managers	37	38	38	16	12	3	2	2	1	1	

From: C. W. Barkdull, op. cit.

that we now have some appreciation of the considerations relevant to these decisions, a method that leads us to make a systematic evaluation of them is a definite advance on ad hoc implicit judgements.

Summary

Managers face the problem of maintaining a balance between the number of hierarchical levels in an organization and the spans of control of managerial and supervisory staffs. This trade-off between tallness and flatness in the shape of the formal authority structure becomes a particularly acute problem for the large organization in which both hierarchies and spans of control may become extended beyond the optimum. Growing organizations often find themselves multiplying hierarchical levels in an attempt to avoid increasing the burden of supervision faced by individual managers.

An extended hierarchy brings considerable disadvantages of administrative overheads, communication failure and low motivation among those removed from sources of major decisions. Long hierarchies based on very narrow spans of control may offer people little opportunity for personal discretion and initiative in their jobs. The question therefore arises as to whether spans of control can be widened.

In examining this possibility, some way has to be found of taking relevant circumstances into account, which together contribute to the burden of supervision borne by a manager. Judgements are constantly being made on this matter, and a method used in the Lockheed Corporation is of interest since it demonstrates the possibility of making a systematic evaluation of supervisory burdens which can then point up any potential for widening spans of control, reducing management levels and economizing on managerial overheads.

Suggested further reading

The issues covered in this chapter have been rather neglected by writers in recent years. Elliot Jaques, 'Grading and Management Organization in the Civil Service ', *O & M Bulletin* August 1972, examines the question of management levels in the British civil service. Worthy's seminal paper on widening spans of control, 'Organization Structure and Employee Morale' appeared in the April 1950 *American Sociological Review*, and a review of relevant research is provided by Lyman W. Porter and Edward E. Lawler III in 'Properties of Organization Structure in Relation to Job Attitudes and Job Behavior', *Psychological Bulletin*, July 1965. A more recent review of discussion and research is provided by Alan C. Filley, Robert J. House and Steven Kerr, *Managerial Process and Organizational Behavior* (Scott Foresman, 2nd edition 1976), Chapter 18.

Two papers on the Lockheed approach are C. W. Barkdull, 'Span of Control: A Method of Evaluation' *Michigan Business Review*, 1963, and H. Stieglitz, 'Optimizing Span of Control', *Management Record,* 1962.

Appendix to Chapter 3 The Lockheed approach to evaluating span of control

From:
1 C. W. Barkdull, 'Span of Control: A Method of Evaluation', *Michigan Business Review,* 15 , 1963, pp.25-32.

2 H. Stieglitz, 'Optimizing Span of Control', *Management Record*, 24, 1962, pp. 25-29.

Definitions of Factors

The definitions of the seven factors were established as follows:

Similarity of Functions. This refers to the degree to which functions performed by the various components of personnel reporting to a supervisor are alike or different—whether they are the same functions, (perhaps organized on a geographic basis) or whether they differ in nature (perhaps grouped because of their relation to one another). Its importance is that as the functions increase in their degree of variability, the more interrelations have to be kept in mind and the fewer number of persons the supervisor can effectively handle.

Geographic contiguity. This factor refers to the physical locations of the components and personnel reporting to a supervisor. Geographic separation of functions makes for greater difficulty in supervision because of the necessity for more formal means of communication, time to get together for necessary discussions, and time to personally visit the separated activities.

Complexity of functions. This factor refers to the nature of the duties being performed by the majority of non-supervisory personnel, and involves a determination of the degree of difficulty in performing satisfactorily. It is generally considered that salary and hourly ratings are a reasonably fair reflection of complexity. Hence this factor was related to the job classifications of the more important of the non-supervisory positions in the component. Generally the greater the complexity of the function supervised the smaller the number of persons a supervisor should be expected to handle.

Direction and control. This factor refers to the nature of the personnel reporting directly to the supervisor and reflects the degree of attention which they require for proper supervision of their actions. High level competent managers with years of background and experience, or highly qualified scientists with Ph.D's, will require minimum attention except for general administrative and planning matters; while other personnel might require closer supervision, direction, guidance, and training. This also reflects the extent to which responsibility can be delegated to subordinates; the extent to which problems and decisions can be resolved at subordinate levels; the amount of training they require; and the degree to which objective standards can be applied. The greater the degree to which subordinates require direction and control the smaller the span should be of the subject supervisor. (This factor may appear to measure the same thing as complexity, and to some extent they are counteracting. However, while complexity measures the *work* of the non-supervisory personnel, direction and control measures the degree to which subordinates *require supervision*.)

Co-ordination. As opposed to the previous factors which mainly relate to the duties and personnel supervised, the factor of co-ordination (and the next one—planning) reflect the nature of the supervisory position itself. It measures the extent to which the supervisor must exert time and effort (a) in keeping the functions, actions and output of his components properly balanced, correlated and going in the same direction to accomplish the goals of the activity, and (b) in keeping his components keyed in with other activities of the division to accomplish divisional plans and programs. Again, the greater the complexity of the co-ordination functions and the greater the amount of time required to perform them, the fewer number of people who should report to him.

Planning. This factor refers to the importance, complexity, and time requirements of one of the primary functions of a manager or supervisor — that of reviewing the objectives and the output requirements in the future, and programming the actions, organization, staff, and budgets necessary to accomplish them. Some distinction must be made in the evaluation of a given position as to how much of these functions is actually performed by others for him, and where planning must be done on a continuing basis or might essentially be accomplished once a year when budgets and programmes are proposed and approved. As the importance, complexity, and time required of the supervisor increase, the more prudent it will be to reduce the number of persons reporting to him.

Organizational assistance. This factor considers the assistance received within the organizational component from direct line assistants, assistants to, staff activities or personnel having administrative, planning and control responsibilities, and (at the first-line supervisory level) leading hands or their equivalent.

Points values assigned to factors

Similarity of functions

One point — identical. Employees would be of the same occupation doing the same type of work. In a typical situation, a particular function (such as assembly) would be organized by teams or groups working on identical units or giving identical service.

Two points — essentially alike but having distinguishing characteristics in the nature of the functions. This rating would be applied to those components which perform similar work or work of the same nature at different geographic locations.

Three points — similar but with distinct differences in approach or skills required. Typically, each employee or component would be doing work in a general classification (e.g. general accounting, physics, manufacturing engineering) but in different segments of that field (nuclear physics vs ionic physics, or payroll accounting vs property accounting etc).

Four points — inherently different but with common purpose. This rating, would apply, for example, to those components (such as development manufacturing) which are closely tied to a single end product or result but where each component performs different phases of the total process (such as development assembly, electronic assembly, final assembly and production control within a development manufacturing activity).

Five points — fundamentally distinct, with different areas of responsibility and requiring entirely different types of personnel skills. The scope of responsibility is fairly broad and the components are organized on a functional basis, each function requiring specialized skills and knowledge.

Geographic contiguity. Location of personnel or subsidiary components are:

One point — in one contiguous area in one building;

Two points — in separate locations within one building;

Three points — in separate buildings within a plant location;

Four points — in separate buildings in a geographic area (in different parts of one city);

Five points — in widely dispersed geographic areas (in several separate parts of the state or country).

Complexity of functions

Two points — simple, repetitive duties which require little training (less than six months) and which follow simple and well-defined rules and procedures. Examples would include typing, stock handling, mail handling, simple assembly.

Four points — routine duties of little complexity requiring individuals to exercise some but not a great amount of skill and/or judgement in following rules and procedures. Examples would include production machine operations, reproduction operations, receiving and shipping.

Six points — duties of some complexity requiring two to three years' experience and training and which require the application of reasonable judgement and/or skills. Examples would include production planning and scheduling, equipment maintenance, accounts payable etc.

Eight points — complex duties involving a variety of differing tasks, requiring four-six years' experience and training and which require the application of considerable creativity, judgement and skills. Examples would include personnel administration, management planning, industrial engineering, buying, financial planning, test mechanics, special tool builders.

Ten points—extremely complex duties which might involve a wide variety of tasks which require long training and experience (eight-ten years). Abstract or creative thinking and/or the necessity for consideration of many factors in arriving at courses of action. Examples: research scientists, engineering development.

Direction and control

One to three points—minimum supervision, direction and control. Subordinate positions would be filled by highly qualified, trained and experienced individuals who perform within general assignments and with limited direction by the supervisor. Subordinates would not be expected to secure detailed approvals from their supervisors. Subordinates would be top-level professional, technical and scientific personnel.

Four to six points—limited supervision, direction and control. Subordinate positions need only occasional contact with the supervisor. Such contact would be necessary, for example, to obtain over-all counselling on a project, to assure that actions are in keeping with company directives and the objectives of the supervisor. Relations with other activities in most cases would be resolved by the subordinates. Internal problems would generally be worked out by the subordinate. Typical subordinate positions would include senior engineers or supervisory personnel in technical and professional areas.

Seven to nine points—moderate periodic supervision, direction and control. Subordinates would be working to a set of fairly well-defined rules of conduct either by professional practices or by company policy and procedure. Exceptions requiring supervisor action and unusual circumstances could be expected to occur with moderate frequency.

Ten to twelve points—frequent supervision, training, and control. Subordinates require continuous regular checking and instruction. The supervisor would be expected to check frequently to assure that subordinates do not make errors in their work.

Thirteen to fifteen points—constant and close supervision, instruction and control. The closeness of supervision could result from the type of work (very important and costly experiments); or from the type of employees (knowledge and skills are such that continual, careful instruction and discretion are required). Unusual occurrences would be referred to the principal for decision. Regular rules, guides or procedures would be very difficult or impossible to prepare.

Co-ordination

Two points—a minimum amount of co-ordination. The functions of the components are such that their work or output does not have a significant effect on other activities. This situation might occur in a pure research activity the output of which is not required to meet any precise objectives.

Four points—a limited amount of co-ordination. The principal should meet occasionally with his subordinates and/or other components to make sure that their functions and/or output are properly conforming to quantity, timing, or procedure requirements. The resolution of problems would be readily determined from well-defined courses of conduct. Co-ordination might be substantially performed by other departments, such as a scheduling department.

Six points—a moderate amount of co-ordination. Supervisors would be required to integrate output, timing, and procedures. Functions of subordinates might be so closely related as to require the principal to keep them co-ordinated.

Eight points—a considerable amount of co-ordination. A significant amount of the principal's efforts would be required in discussing and resolving mutual problems of timing and quality of output and matters of procedure. The functions of his component would be rather closely tied in with other activities so that mutual and complementary action would be desirable. Some of these relationships could be defined, but others could not.

Ten points—extensive co-ordination. A great amount of the principal's time would be spent with subordinates and with others in keeping activities in balance. This would apply to certain staff who work closely with others in developing programmes or resolving mutual problems of a non-recurring nature. This might also occur with a responsibility cutting across several organizational lines. In applying the point values to the supervisory job, a distinction must be made between those situations which require the principal to perform these duties and those where subordinates can accomplish the desired co-ordination without the principal's assistance.

Planning

Two points — of minor importance and complexity, requiring a minimum of time and effort. Functions which are routine in nature where the plans are simple and easily determined based on very precise criteria or where plans are prepared by some external organization.

Four points — of limited importance and complexity requiring some measurable time and effort. Activities which do not require a great amount of planning. The criteria for plans and the boundaries within which plans are to be prepared are broadly defined.

Six points — of moderate importance and complexity requiring a moderate amount of time. Planning would be necessary to accomplish objectives and programmes, and there would be some criteria to follow.

Eight points — of considerable importance and complexity requiring a large amount of time. Some guidance on planning is available but there would be a number of variables without clear guideposts.

Ten points — of great importance and complexity requiring a considerable amount of time and effort. Planning is largely uncharted and deals with many variables, requiring abstract thinking.

Organization

Direct line assistance and staff activities or personnel which have administrative, planning and control responsibilities: multiplier factor: .60.

Direct line assistant only: multiplier factor: 70.

Staff activities or personnel which have administrative, planning *and* control responsibilities: multiplier factor: .75.

Staff activities or personnel which have administrative planning *or* control responsibilites: multiplier factor: .85.

An assistant to, performing limited planning and control functions: multiplier factor: .95.

Leading hands or equivalent (applicable to first-line supervisors only). The number of leading hands (and the accompanying multiplier factors) in the organization are: one leading hand .85; two leading hands .70; three leading hands .55; four leading hands .40; five leading hands .25.

(This assumes that a leading hand will give guidance to eight-twelve employees and spend some 20%—30% of his time in duties of guidance, job assignment and training.)

CHAPTER 4

THE SHAPE OF ORGANIZATION—GROUPING ACTIVITIES

'Put a miller, a weaver and a tailor in a bag, and shake them.' Part of an old proverb.

The preceding chapter was concerned with the vertical configuration of people and jobs — how much vertical differentiation should there be within an organization. This chapter considers the problem of selecting a pattern of horizontal differentiation between groups, departments and divisions. Given the total range of jobs in the organization, the question arises as to how they should be grouped together in the most suitable manner. Another way of putting this is to ask on what basis the people in an organization should be specialized. There are several models to choose from here. Each has its own logic which management has to assess in terms of its appropriateness to the situation at hand.

The logic of task systems.

When designing an organization, it is clearly a fundamental requirement that people be allocated responsibilities which accord with identifiable parts of the total task to be undertaken. The nature of this task, whether it is to cure illness or to produce motor cars, determines the operational decisions that have to be taken and the relationships in which members of the organization must engage. Typical operating decisions are about the methods and resources used in carrying out the work, the sequence of activities to be performed and how to deal with exceptional contingencies (such as faulty material or a power failure) when these arise. Effective relationships have to be maintained between people who need to exchange information about the planning and progress of the organization's work, and between people who contribute directly to linked stages of the basic process itself.

The system of tasks within an organization as a whole is therefore the point of reference when considering how to group people together in a formal structure. The practical difficulty here lies in the fact that tasks can be seen to fall together on several quite different logical grounds. They may be linked by virtue of shared expertise or function, process, product, time horizon or geographical location. The choice of how to group people and their activities depends on which of these task system logics are felt to be most significant.

Members of an organization may share a common expertise and draw upon the same set of resources in their activities, even though they are applying their efforts to different products or services. Such people belong to the same *functional* area, of which the training function provides an example. The training of operatives within a company could be serving a number of different production lines, and the training of salesmen may similarly be directed towards strengthening several different sales teams. Many of the methods of instruction and some of the same instructional equipment will, however, be used across all these areas of training, as might the same training staff. In other words, there is within the training field a body of shared expertise, experience and resources which can be applied to more than one operational area. This degree of commonality provides a logical link between training activities, and the same logic can be found connecting tasks in other functional areas such as accounting, research or production.

Closely related to the logic which links together tasks falling within the same functional area is the relationship between tasks that share a common *process*. For example, a range of different products can often be processed through the same plant as is the case with some chemicals such as acids. Different engineering goods can be manufactured by passing through the same configuration of machine tools. In these examples, the same plant is used for similar manufacturing processes. A company can often achieve considerable economies by employing a common production facility for a range of products if this is technically feasible. A common plant facility would normally be administered by one production function, grouping all the production activities involved into a single department.

The activities of people located in various functional areas will collectively contribute to the tasks of developing, making and distributing a given product or service. Such tasks within an engineering company would include market research, design, development, production engineering, production planning, costing, training of operatives, and sales promotion. A company may be producing several products which are sufficiently similar in terms of markets and technical know-how to draw largely upon the same configuration of specialist contributions. The inter-connecting logic here is that different specialist tasks contribute to the same *product* or family of products. An example of this logic applied to the public field can be seen in hospitals where medical and other staff are grouped into different sections dealing with maternity, paediatric, accident and other particular services.

The product-based logic of tasks recognizes how the contributions of different specialists need to be integrated within one complete cycle of work. In contrast, functional and process task systems recognize the qualitatively different intrinsic nature of the specialized resources which are applied to all of an organization's product or service technologies. The product logic is primarily technological, envisaging a flow of work laterally across functional areas. The functional logic is primarily hierarchical, drawing attention to the vertical grouping of people in depth within the boundaries of separate specialized sections of the company.

A further logic linking different tasks is present when they share approximately the same *time horizon*. The fact that some decisions are long term, in the sense of committing resources for some years ahead usually with a correspondingly long period before the pay-off can be assessed, while others are short term, has been advanced as the main justification for a hierarchical division of tasks and of the people responsible for them. This is the argument for, as it were, a vertical specialization of jobs, with time horizon and discretion being progressively restricted as one passes down through the levels of the hierarchy. (The previous chapter raised the question of whether an extended hierarchy is desirable.) Another aspect of the time horizon logic can be seen in tasks concerned with forecasting future conditions facing the organization. Such forecasts of trends in future demand, technical developments, social changes and the like are brought together as a common foundation for forward planning. For this reason, and because conclusions about the future may have to rely upon shared assumptions about trends in the various sectors, there will be a powerful logic for recognizing the inter-connections between forecasting tasks when deciding on where organizationally to locate the people who have responsibility for undertaking those tasks. Some of the contrast between the work of different functions derives from their time horizons. Those for a research and development function, for example, normally reach much further ahead than those of a production operations function.

Finally, different tasks may be carried out in the same *geographical location*. This geographical connection could coincide with the other task system logics, if for example one plant specializes in the production of a single family of products or if a particular function such as research and development is located completely on one site. Whether or not tasks are located together on one site or in the same region can be extremely significant. For, as Robert Townsend has put it, the potential for disastrous internal breakdown in a company is equal to the square of the distance — measured in hours — between the home base and outlying sites. The other side to this coin is that tasks carried out in the same physical area do for that reason alone share some commonality from the point of view of their management.

These distinctions between different task system logics are important since they provide the principles by which the activities of an institution can be grouped. These principles constitute important guidelines for management. They can in practice be combined in various forms, and it is also possible to follow one principle for grouping some activities and another for grouping other activities. Some of the structures for grouping activities which follow from these task system logics are very familiar, such as the functional structure, the product structure, the divisional structure based on products or geographical areas, or the forward planning group within an organization. One basic choice, to start with, is that between the functional and product models.

Alternative models for grouping activities: functional and product

When an organization is extremely small, consisting of a handful of people, any formal arrangement for defining and grouping their activities is unnecessary. If the members of the organization are contributing specialized skills and knowledge, the allocation of tasks to them can be quite adequately managed within the confines of face-to-face relationships in what is essentially a primary group. Problems of designing formal organizational structures arise with growing size and complexity.

The functional form of structure is normally adopted once an organization grows beyond the primary group stage. It is particularly appropriate if the organization is basing its growth upon a single range of products or services which is sold or dispensed almost exclusively within the one domestic market. The functional form groups activities into separate departments which provide specialist contributions to the common product and its market. The co-ordination of these departments is achieved formally by the chief executive perhaps backed by an executive committee or board. In practice, however, a great deal of co-ordination is often achieved informally via everyday meetings over lunch, and so forth. Figure 4.1 depicts a simple functional structure in a small engineering firm. Within the production area activities are shown to be grouped by process into machining and assembly. The arguments which can be advanced for and against the functional model apply to the process model as well.

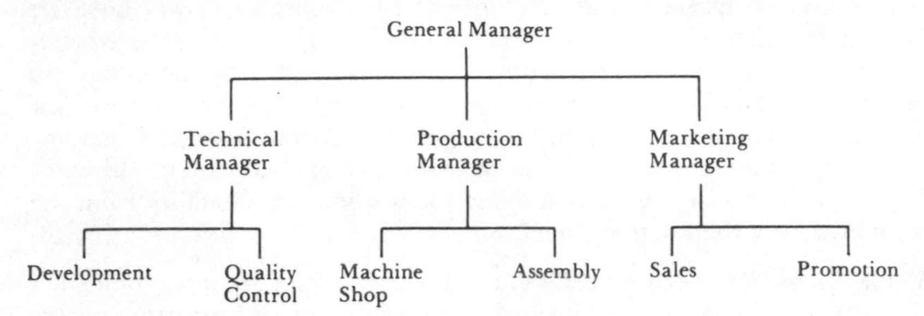

Figure 4.1
A functional structure

The grouping of activities by function offers a number of advantages, which are particularly relevant for the smaller organization confined to one field of activity. It is economical on managerial manpower because it is a simple structure, co-ordination being left to top management rather than to several divisional general managers or to integrating personnel such as product managers. When specialist technical expertise, in say research or marketing, is critical, costly and scarce – and that is especially so for the smaller unit – then it is appropriate to pool available experts together within a single relevant functional department. This helps to maximize their potential level of utilization on a time-sharing basis across the whole organization. It also makes it easier to co-ordinate the specialists concerned. Similarly, when there are economies of scale or of concentrating resources in production (plant); in engineering (e.g. test or laboratory facilities); in distribution (e.g. warehousing) and so forth, it is beneficial to group such facilities and the people operating them together into single functional departments. Finally, a functional structure provides clearly marked career paths for specialists, and so makes it easier to hire and retain their services. They also have the satisfaction of working with colleagues who share similar interests.

Difficulties start to arise with the functional model once an organization diversifies its products, markets or services. Diversification is very often a necessary condition for its continued growth. If an institution is becoming larger, more diversified and subject to tight time constraints in adopting new products and services, then it is more than likely that a purely functional form will begin to break down under strain.

Some of these problems were experienced by a producer of speciality ferrous metals when it decided to diversify into a technically more difficult type of steel production, mainly for the aircraft industry. This new sector was seen to offer particularly favourable prospects for the company's future growth. Products for the aircraft industry required different research skills and a more refined manufacturing process than was true of the firm's traditional outputs. They were also marketed differently, not to a large number of manufacturers (some very small) but to a few aircraft sub-contractors producing to strict government-controlled specifications. Some aircraft sales were also to customers overseas, another new departure for the firm.

The company right from the outset established a separate section to handle sales of the new steels. It proposed, however, to retain responsibility for their production, specification and quality with the functional departments which were already well established. Very soon, troubles began to emerge. Deliveries of the aircraft steels began to fall behind the fairly demanding schedules normal for that market, and it was extremely difficult to get reliable information from either the technical or production departments on the status of work in progress. Existing rules on economical batch sizes had not been amended to take account of the new products with their greater value added and shorter delivery times, and work was thus being held up in the factory. Unexpected technical problems also emerged because the new steels required more delicate handling in process. It was not long before competitors in this field brought out technical modifications superior to the company's own specialized steels, modifications which its technical staff had not anticipated. It was said that the aircraft sales staff should have alerted the company of these developments, but the sales personnel in turn complained that there was little real interest among other departments in the company's new products. The company managing director and the general manager found themselves increasingly drawn into having to sort out operational crises of this kind which they felt should be resolved at a much lower level.

It was decided after a while to set up a separate technical department and a physically separate production facility for the new steels. These were grouped together with the sales team into a separate division under a product manager solely concerned with aircraft steels. This step was felt to be justified for a sector which was growing at twice the rate of the firm's traditional markets, and where it looked as though an opportunity was being lost because of internal problems. Responsibility for the other products was given to a second product manager. Despite the initially higher costs involved in duplicating certain facilities and offices, much of the uncertainty, poor co-ordination and misuse of top management time disappeared with the new arrangements. The company in fact continued to develop its competitive strength in aircraft work and to take advantage of the growth opportunities it offered.

This company had moved from a grouping of activities by function to a grouping by product. The core of its new structure is presented by Figure 4.2

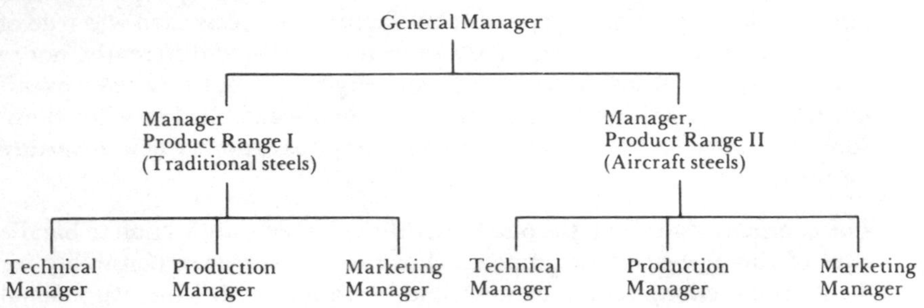

Figure 4.2
A product structure

A product structure becomes a more appropriate way to group activities when an organization produces two or more ranges of products, or types of service, which are different in their technical make-up, production requirements or types of outlet. An extreme case is to be found in the conglomerate corporation, engaged in a range of totally different areas of business, where its subsidiary divisions are sensibly left to operate in effect as separate product units. So far as any particular product is concerned, the more rapid is the change in its competitive conditions, the higher the rate of new technical developments, and in general the greater the pressures for rapid response to external changes, then the more advantage the product structure will enjoy over the functional form. For it has the virtue of directing specialized contributions to a common product focus. This is particularly appropriate when there are many urgent joint decisions to be taken between specialists, and when it is necessary to utilize positions such as the product manager in order to co-ordinate and establish deadlines for product developments. A complete move over to a product structure will, however, mean forgoing the advantages of functional forms which I mentioned earlier, and which may be especially significant in a smaller organization.

In practice, the exact balance between adopting functional and product groupings of activities must be assessed in the light of symptoms which signal the need for a shift in emphasis. For example, communication overload may emerge. Top executives become drawn too frequently into day-to-day co-ordinating decisions to the detriment of the attention they give to strategic issues. Perhaps it is taking too long to get the go-ahead from top management to continue work on new projects, and this is building up a sense of frustration and low morale. If these problems arise, some movement from a relatively centralized functional organization to a product form where co-ordination is lodged within a product group or division will probably be appropriate.

Within the specific field of production, we have seen how group technology represents a move towards a product logic of organization in which machines are grouped according to product families or in which groups of people assemble complete units rather than specialize on short cycle operations. The problem which initially stimulated experiments in group technology was the growing complexity of workflow routing with consequent planning, co-ordinating and lead-time difficulties. The opposite case is illustrated by a situation in which a company's products are losing their competitive appeal because of poor design and quality. The solution to this problem could require some strengthening of functional organization, at least in the technical area, and a greater resistance to pressures for short design-to-production lead times.

Some contrasting effects of organizing on a functional as opposed to a product basis are illustrated by Walker and Lorsch, writing in the *Harvard Business Review* for November-December 1968. They studied two manufacturing plants making the same product for the same markets and using the same materials and technology. Their parent companies were also similar. They had very similar management styles and objectives, and employed the same range of functional specialists. But in the functionally organized plant only the manufacturing departments and the planning and scheduling function reported to the plant manager, while the other plant had a partly product basis of organization in that all its specialists with the exception of plant engineering reported to the plant manager. (This plant did not, however, have a fully fledged product structure incorporating functions such as marketing.)

Walker and Lorsch found that in the functional structure specialists focused sharply on their specialized functional goals and objectives. They identified closely with their counterparts in other plants and at divisional headquarters rather than with the members of other functions in the plant, or with common plant objectives. Their outlook was generally a short-term one, and the plant had a high degree of formality (job definitions, clear distinctions between jobs) across all functions. In the other plant with more of a product structure linking functions together, the functional specialists seemed more aware of common product goals. There was more variation in the time horizons adopted; for example, production managers concentrated on routine matters while quality control specialists were more concerned with longer-term problems. This differentiation in time horizon was encouraged by the way the product form of structure brought specialists together in problem-solving and this led to a sensible specialization of effort. In the functional plant, each department tended to worry more about its own daily progress. In the product organized plant, similarly, there were greater differences between functions in the extent to which organization was formalized.

The net effect of these contrasts was that communications were more effective in the product structure plant, and conflicts appeared to be resolved more openly. Managers there were more involved in their work but also experienced more stress partly as a consequence. The functionally organized plant was actually more efficient and less costly in operation, but it was also improving its productivity at a much lower rate than the product organized plant. The product organization appeared to enhance the plant's adaptive capability largely through improving the integration between functions. In stable conditions when there is time enough to achieve co-ordination through paper systems and other formalized methods, the functional structure may be advantageous. In conditions demanding some change and active problem-solving, a product form may prove superior because it encourages more intensive communication, confrontation of issues and integration of effort.

A method for deciding on the grouping of activities

Underlying the discussion so far has been the theme that people should be grouped together in a way which accords with particularly intense communication and information sharing needs. There are several dimensions to this notion of intensity. Communications between different positions or sections may have to be particularly frequent; they may involve the discussion of complex information requiring shared judgements as to how to proceed; they may concern matters that are particularly vital to the successful performance of an institution's overall task. It is quite feasible to approach the analysis of these requirements in a systematic manner.

A judgement first of all has to be made as to how well an existing structure is functioning. If a re-examination is thought to be required, then a basic discipline consists of systematically listing the various workflows in the organization, the points at which decisions have to be made, the sources of information (files) which are assessed and updated, the personnel involved and the frequency with which communication is required between them in the light of workflows, decisions and information needs, the reasons why particular personnel must inter-relate, and so forth. These data can readily be summarized in flow charts, of the kind frequently used for purposes of system analysis.

Data from flow charts provide the basic information for making a judgement about the intensity of relationships required in the organization. The next stage consists of evaluating the links between jobs and activities which have been identified. One method for doing this is to draw up a list of major jobs and/or functional categories. These are then

Activity ↓	1 Market research	2 Order handling	3 Marketing programming	4 Sales installation	5 Engineering specification	Etc
2 Order handling	3					
	3 / C					
3 Marketing programming	3	1				
	4 / C + D	5 / B or C				
4 Sales installation	3	1, 2 + 3	3			
	2 / C	3 / B or C	2 / C			
5 Engineering specifications	3	3	3	1 + 3		
	1 / -	1 / -	1 / -	6 / A or B		
6 Factory programming						
7 Stock control						
Etc						

Within each box

Reasons for Linkage	
Required Closeness	Type of communication

Reasons for linkage key:
1. Co-ordination required
2. Sharing of data
3. Transfer of data
4. Economy of effort
5. Use of same equipment
6. Effective control
   etc

Required closeness key:
6. Absolutely necessary
5. Especially important
4. Important
3. Ordinary closeness
2. Unimportant
1. Not desirable

Type of communication key:
A Face-to-face
B Telephone
C Written
D Formal meetings
etc

Figure 4.3
Matrix of relationships between activities (part of)

related to each other in the form of a matrix. Each pair of jobs or functions can now be assessed by reference to various criteria which govern their relationship. These include the basic reasons why the activities are linked (if at all), how close the relationship between them needs to be, and what kind of communication is required. These criteria are themselves interdependent. The reason for linking functions will determine their appropriate mode of communication and closeness. The closeness of relationship will depend on how frequently decisions need to be taken, which depends on the processing and passing of information between the functions, on the complexity of the information and so forth.

Part of such a matrix is shown in Figure 4.3, which is based on a purely hypothetical small batch engineering company. This particular matrix is concerned with the links between certain marketing functions and engineering specifications, factory programming and stock control. The data incorporated are a categorization of the main reasons for a linkage between the functions, a simple scale of how close the relationship needs to be (including the possibility that no formal link at all is desirable), and a classification of what mode of communication should be the norm. On the whole, one would expect two closely related functions to communicate on a direct basis, face-to-face or by telephone, but there will be cases where documents are necessarily the mode of communication even in a frequently activated relationship. It is important to stress that the way the matrix is drawn and the categories of information incorporated into it depend on what best suits a particular organization.

Following on from this stage, a diagram can be drawn of the different functions, starting with those which it has been concluded should be most intensively related to each other. It may be felt appropriate to modify scores on closeness of relationship by incorporating notes to identify instances where a close relationship does not *a priori* make it desirable to group functions together, perhaps for professional reasons or because an electronic data processing system can provide the link instead. The closely related activities which it is felt should work together can be linked together on the diagram. Other functions can then be progressively incorporated into the diagram. One way of representing the gradation in desired intensity of relations between functions is by drawing different thicknesses or sets of lines connecting the activities. Once this diagram is completed, it becomes feasible to delineate clusters of activities which fit together logically. These clusters can then form the basis for a grouping of activities. Part of such a diagram, following on from the matrix in Figure 4.3, is shown in Figure 4.4.

An exercise of the kind described can provide a useful aid for making decisions on the grouping of activities. It is based purely upon the logic of task systems and as such is neutral to considerations which derive from traditional boundaries drawn between functions and the politics which attach to these. In the hypothetical example, a task analysis actually implies that certain 'marketing' functions should operationally be grouped together with 'production' programming and that a technical 'sales' function should go together with 'engineering' ones. Politics and professional differentiations are, however, part of the real organizational world. A purely task based analysis of the kind described would have to be subject to thorough discussion, not only to test its apparent logic against the criterion of political acceptability, but also to provide an opportunity for identifying any relationships which have been wrongly evaluated.

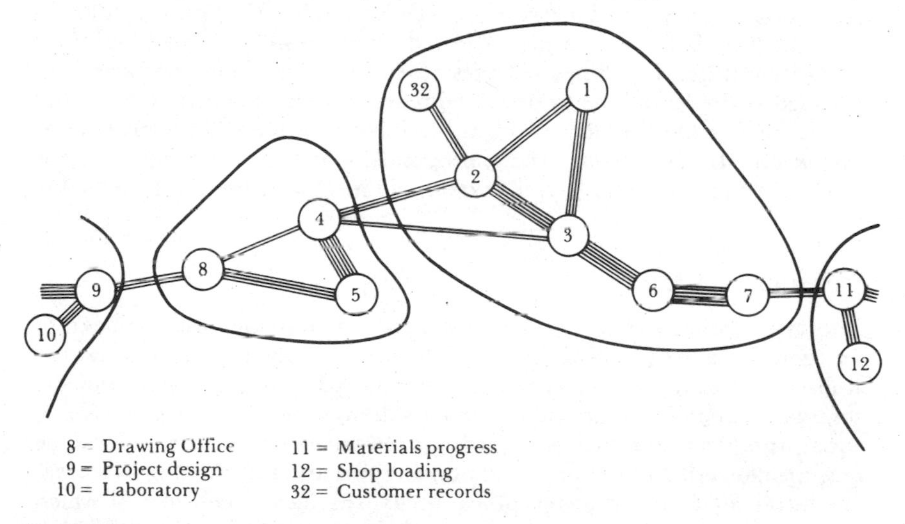

Figure 4.4
Clustering of related activities previously identified by means of the matrix of relationships

It is important at every stage to take account of the personal element. The people who occupy jobs and who are in charge of activities can do a great deal to condition the effectiveness of communication and working relationships. This factor is relevant to assessments of the potential for making structural changes. Opinion on the personal aspect of relationships as well as on task aspects can be secured through a process of extensive discussions among managers and staff. Indeed, in the absence of such consultation, people are unlikely to appreciate the arguments for structural changes, or feel committed to them. Personal and political considerations are always involved in the design of organization structure.

Some years ago, when a member of the Rolls-Royce Oil Engine Division, I helped to carry out an organization design survey similar to that described.

This identified a set of relationships between personnel who were concerned with different aspects of customer contact. Their effective co-ordination was being seriously reduced by their membership of separate sales, financial and engineering functions. Following many discussions with all the staff in these areas, they were subsequently regrouped for operational purposes into one marketing function concerned with the major product — diesel engines. This made for a significant improvement in information sharing, relations with customers and general effectiveness. The most important lesson to be drawn from this experience was not so much that the technique of task analysis was useful for assessing the appropriate grouping of activities (which it was) but that participation in the process by the people affected was vital for its successful implementation. For other changes in systems and structure were also planned at the same time by people who were technically more expert, but whose very expertise led them to dismiss the need for much prior discussion. In the event, their proposals generally met with serious resistance from departmental managers and most were not implemented.

Divisionalization

The systematic analysis of relations between activities may appear to recommend a re-grouping into a different functional cluster as in the Rolls-Royce example just cited. If the required clustering is around the common demands of particular products then, other considerations being equal, the pendulum swings towards a product structure. It could also be that the clustering of required communications and information sharing is delineated by different geographical areas, the local conditions of which vary considerably. One organization may choose to expand by diversifying into new product ranges and hence be inclined to adopt a product structure, while another may expand by diversifying its original product range into new geographical areas and hence be inclined to group its activities into area units. Major product or area based organizational units within a company are normally designated as divisions.

The divisional form of structure, as it developed in the United States, had three prime characteristics. First, profit responsibility was assigned to general managers of divisions which became essentially self-contained business units. Second, the corporate headquarters had a general office which was mainly concerned with strategic planning, appraisal of policies and projects and overall financial control, including the allocation of resources between the divisions. Third, corporate managers were committed to the performance of the organization as a whole rather than to that of any individual division. During the 1960s, large European organizations have been adopting the essentials of this type of overall structure at an increasing rate, though many have not gone so far as their

American counterparts in creating a central HQ office in its own right as opposed simply to building up certain central staff groups. Franko describes these developments at length in his book *The European Multinationals* (1976).

If a divisional structure is adopted by an organization, it is important to note that within each division the problem of how best to group activities still arises. This could be done according to a functional mode, or there could be a grouping around specific products within the general divisional field, or some mixture of the two. In large organizations, the decision of how to group activities has to be taken for whole unit and for sub-unit levels, once these are clearly differentiated as in a multi-divisional structure.

Both product and area divisions are found among multinational corporations, with the product division form predominating. The sequence of structural changes typically found in these organizations, which are mostly American, shifts from one dominant pattern of grouping activities to another. In many cases, the first major change came when a diversification of products within the domestic market encouraged corporations to move from a functional to a product division structure, and sometimes to a regional division structure.

The entry into overseas activities was often through the purchase of a foreign subsidiary. This might be left to operate largely on its own for a while. Then, as overseas business expanded, it became worthwhile to group activities concerned with foreign operations into a separate international division typically managing both foreign subsidiaries and exports from domestic production. If home activities became diversified into different product groups and if this range of products were then shipped abroad as well, the point would be reached where economies of co-ordination could be achieved through amalgamating home and overseas activities into global product divisions. Even if this product diversification did not take place, as more parts of the world were covered, and possibly local manufacturing sites set up, so again it became increasingly logical to group the whole organization's activities into global area divisions. Finally, the diversity of both products offered throughout the world and geographical regions covered has today led some multinationals, Unilever for example, to experiment with mixed forms of structure in which several principles of grouping activities are found together. The sequence of structural development which has been most commonly followed is shown diagrammatically in Figure 4.5.

The ways in which organization structures have developed along with growth and diversification will be discussed further in Chapter 7.

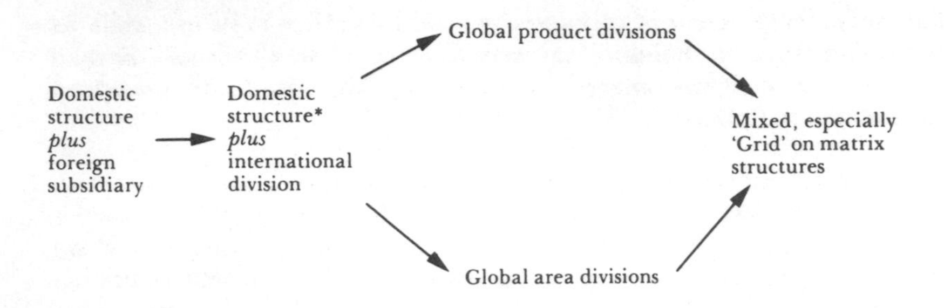

Figure 4.5
The most common path of structural evolution among multinational corporations

*Among American-owned multinationals it has been more common for the domestic structure to be divisionalized before adding an international division.

Mixed structures

The divisionalized structure is the form of grouping activities which most larger and diversified British companies are now following, commonly with divisions based on different product ranges, and sometimes based on geographical location of customers. Compared to the traditional functional form, divisionalization offers several advantages. Major decisions are taken nearer the point of action so relieving top management time for more strategic matters. Profit responsibility is delegated to divisions and this permits the organization's main activities to be evaluated separately. This ability to assess the return achieved by different sectors of activity is an important aid to making decisions on how to allocate investment within the organization. Decentralization of decisions and responsibility is likely to motivate middle managers and provide them with an earlier training in general management.

Yet problems have emerged with divisional forms. One problem is that there may not always be a clearly superior basis on which to create divisions in the first place. Divisionalization by product may, for instance, lead to poor co-ordination and even open competition between separate divisions which are dealing with the same customer or client. This is a difficulty facing one large British food company at the time of writing, which has several divisions supplying the same retailing organizations with consequent diseconomies of distribution, of selling effort and problems of inconsistencies between the trading arrangements offered. A geographical area divisionalization which might help to avoid these kinds of problems can, on the other hand, lead to a duplication of production facilities, technical effort and so forth because the logic of common product technologies is not recognized.

The very act of creating divisions, which become the main points of identity for their members, is of course literally divisive. There are quite likely to be conflicts between divisions over the allocation of new investment, and over matters such as the use and funding of shared central services. The interests of a particular division might conflict with those of the organization as a whole if the role of that division is seen to be only a short-term cash generator,while other divisions are seen to have greater potential as areas for development. As a result the high profit earning division would perceive corporate investment to be going elsewhere to lower profit earners.

Another difficulty, which some of our largest organizations are now facing, is that divisions themselves may grow too large and become too diversified with the result that they no longer represent an appropriate grouping of activities around a single business area which is clearly defined in market and/or technological terms. One response to this is to divisionalize the divisions, which threatens to bring management to a point of horrendous complexity. This is part of the problem of managing ever-growing giant organizations. It could lead eventually either to the running of divisions as independent units or to a more frequent use of the holding-company structure in which subsidiaries of a manageable size organize homogeneous business units that are linked to a small central unit only on the basis of performance accountability.

Should divisionalization based on products or areas run into difficulties, the functional form is not normally an appropriate structure for a diversified organization to return to. Because so many organizations in all kinds of fields have today become diversified in their activities, there is a growing interest in various types of mixed structure which may offer some of the advantages associated with more than one logic of grouping activities.

One form of mixed structure incorporates different logics of grouping activities side by side, as it were. For example, divisions may be retained as operational profit centres, but advisory services, planning functions and the control of shared resources such as mobile plant and stock are centralized on a functional basis. This structure has sometimes been called a 'systems' model, and it has been used in the airline, construction, petroleum and pharmaceutical industries. It has the virtue of economizing on investment in shared resources as well as helping to maintain consistency in corporate policies. Another mixed structure emerges when the need for economies in, say, production or research, dictates the grouping of all these activities into one function, but where diversity in markets served argues for a splitting of marketing into area or product divisions.

A different type of mixed structure is the 'matrix', in which one logic of grouping activities is superimposed totally on another. This may just take a temporary form as in the case with what is usually called a project team. Here, a project team or task force is superimposed on a permanent structure, usually of a functional or departmental kind, in order to draw together resources from different functions, or even divisions, for a special purpose. The time period of the project is limited, and it will normally be of strategic importance to the organization in order to warrant such a radical departure from the normal disposition of responsibilities. The establishment of special project teams can be quite effective in getting major changes or new developments accomplished, but if team members remain responsible for their normal work as well they can become seriously overloaded and also experience divided loyalties.

The project team illustrates the principle of the matrix structure, which is that formalized lines of lateral communication are superimposed upon the separate vertical hierarchies of departments. Matrix structures in this respect formalize the informal lateral communication which would normally exist between departments and upon which many organizations rely heavily to keep themselves running smoothly. In its more permanent form, this structure is often known as a 'grid' structure when it applies to a whole organization and as a 'matrix' when it is used within a sub-unit of the organization. In a generic sense we are talking of 'multidimensional' structures, but in practice the term matrix is most commonly employed. Within a fairly small and self-contained engineering company, the matrix would mean that an individual like a quality inspector is a member of several activity groupings. He would belong to a functional quality control department, but at the same time he is called upon to respond to the requirements set out by two or more product managers in terms of operational priorities. Figure 4.6 illustrates in simple form how such a structure might appear. A grid structure in a large multinational food corporation could mean that a local manager in charge of selling breakfast cereals in Australia will report both to a worldwide breakfast cereal division and at the same time to an area division co-ordinating all of the corporation's activities in Australasia.

Although there is considerable agreement on the principle of matrix structure, this is accompanied by a wide variation in practical application. The first main phase of matrix structure development came when the American government made it a condition for research and development projects in the 1960s that contractors should have a project management system. This had the advantage of allowing the representatives of government agencies to deal with one individual — the project manager — who had full responsibility for meeting costs and deadlines, rather than having to negotiate with a number of functional heads each only having partial responsibility. The government was in effect insisting that contracting firms made provision for their own effective co-ordination. The firms could either have adopted a fully fledged product-cum-project organization, or they could adopt the matrix by superimposing project management on top of the existing functional structure. Those which chose the matrix structure did so in the belief that it was essential for the technical quality of their work and for the longer-term development of their resources not to break up established functional departments such as research and development.

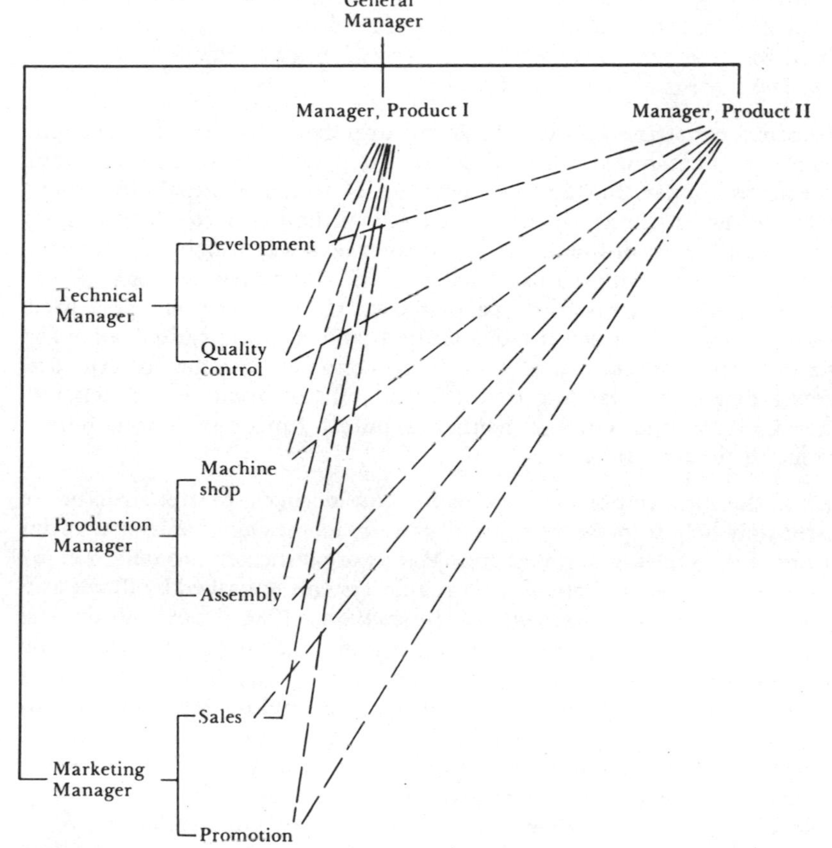

Figure 4.6

A matrix structure combining functional and product forms. Example of an engineering company

Today, matrix structures are found in institutions as diverse as ITT, Monsanto Chemical, National Cash Register, Texas Instruments (and other large American companies), insurance companies such as Skandia Insurance in Sweden, and management schools such as my own University of Aston Management Centre. In some organizations, the matrix structure has been extended to the whole company as in Dow-Corning, Lockheed Aircraft and the British Aircraft Corporation, or to major divisions as in ICI.

Despite applications such as these and many more, little guidance has been made available for managers on the operation of matrix structures. This is partly due to the fact that the experience available suggests that there is a three to five-year period of settling down while people adjust to what is a complex system with dual (or even more) reporting relationships. During this period, the performance of an organization may show little improvement and there can even be set-backs.

The case for matrix structures lies in the argument that they are trying to optimize two potentially conflicting benefits. First, they attempt to retain the economic operation and development of technical capability associated with the functional grouping of common human resources. Second, they attempt to co-ordinate those resources in a way which applies them effectively to different organizational outputs – products or programmes. In the smaller organization particularly, the number of specialized personnel who can be employed is limited, and the duplication called for by a product structure could be quite uneconomic. The matrix structure offers a means of balancing the different pulls of resource and demand criteria in conditions where neither a purely functional nor a purely product structure is suitable.

One of the most important reasons for considering a matrix structure is that it may help to preserve flexibility in the increasingly more structured setting of the growing organization. Matrix organizations are said to enjoy similar advantages to those of the 'organic' systems described by Burns and Stalker in *The Management of Innovation* (1961), particularly the capacity to respond quickly and creatively to changes in a dynamic environment. Because people are not wholly members either of a functional department or a product group, it should be easier for them to accept movement between teams and even departments as the need arises. Another encouragement to flexibility is that the presence of formally designated multiple reporting relationships and groupings of people is likely to encourage open lines of communication within the organization as a whole. So if an organization is operating in several different areas and experiencing rapid change in some of them, the adoption of a matrix structure may help to match its degree of internal flexibility to that required by the complexity, change and consequent uncertainty of its operating context.

Some of the other advantages claimed for matrix structures are not unique to that particular organizational model. For example, it is claimed that matrix structures release a great deal of top management time from problems of operational co-ordination. While this may be true, so long as the conflicts which can arise in a matrix structure do not absorb top management energies instead, it is a benefit also potentially offered by the divisional type of structure.

Other advantages are shared by divisional and matrix structures. Both in principle involve some delegation of authority which can motivate and help develop managers below the senior level. The matrix structure may in fact offer the additional motivation which stems from working participatively in teams, and this may be especially important for more junior personnel who now find that they have a say in significant decisions. Matrix structures expose specialists to situations where they have to take account of a wider range of considerations than those arising within their specialist area. This should broaden their outlook and involve them in challenges of a more general management nature without the anxiety of being cut loose entirely from their functional mooring as can happen in a purely product based structure. Finally, a matrix structure like a divisional one should encourage competition within the organization. This can be a valuable spur to innovation and achievement, so long as its potentially destructive aspects are kept under restraint.

There is not as yet very good evidence to substantiate these claims for the matrix structure, and there are known problems which have to be set against them. These centre on the conflict which often arises, and which can lead to individual stress and administrative costs.

The matrix structure attempts to formalize an already existing conflict between functional and product programme criteria. A third dimension of conflict may be formalized as in Dow Corning where an area-reporting relationship is added to functional and product ones. This formalized conflict tends to generate conflicting objectives and accountabilities at a personal level, creating a highly charged political atmosphere with disputes about credit and blame and attempts to manipulate the balance of power. One advocate of matrix structures attempted to minimize the difficulties imposed by this radical departure from the classical management principle of preserving a unity of command by saying that most of us were quite used to coping with this type of situation, as we had done in childhood with dual parental authority. One knows, however, just how devastating for the individual this situation can be when the two authority figures are in conflict, and when loyalties are torn apart.

Some degree of conflict between functional managers and product managers is endemic in a matrix structure. They will not always agree over priorities of resource allocation or over the time and cost allowed to functional activities. The balance of power between the multiple authority structures is critical but delicate. It must be maintained if the full benefits of the matrix are to be gained. In the move from a functional to a matrix structure, functional executives will experience a dilution of their power and of the initiatives open to them, particularly in regard to making innovations and dealing directly with professional contacts outside the organization. Their role may appear to have become purely supportive and reactive. Professional and expert staff working together within functional areas as well-established groups may find these disrupted with the change in structure. They are likely to express considerable anxiety at the weakening of what they see as their specialist identity and clear line of career progression. They may also feel that the quality of their work will now be sacrificed to pressures for speed and cost-cutting coming from product or programme managers.

The threat to occupational identity is one source of stress which employees can experience in a matrix structure. Other sources of anxiety derive from the conflict which reporting to more than one superior can engender, and from the ambiguity as to expectations which the fluidity of the matrix form tends to promote. It has been suggested in the light of these problems that roles and project objectives should be precisely defined in a matrix structure. While objectives and performance parameters can be defined, it is not clear how roles can be further specified without threatening the flexibility which is one of the advantages of the system. To a large extent conflict and stress is the price that has to be paid for adaptability and change.

A further problem which arises with matrix structures is that they generally incur greater administrative costs than a more conventional structure. The multiplication of hierarchies means an increase in managerial overhead. The presence of conflict means that managerial time has to be devoted to its resolution, while the taking of positions can engender excessive paperwork to justify a case and a rigidity of behaviour more usually associated with bureaucracies. Indeed, senior management may find itself becoming excessively engaged in resolving these operational difficulties if the threshold of trust and understanding among functional and product managers is not reached.

These problems may be well worth facing up to if a move to a matrix structure is felt to reflect the cross pressures and complexity of information processing which an organization has to face. If an organization is diversified in its activities and is in a field where technical complexity requires that it utilize the services of multiple specialities, and if it is facing competitive time and cost pressures, then a matrix structure with all its cross-cutting strains and stresses is simply reflecting a situation which objectively exists in any case. Many organizations are not in this position, but an increasing number are coming to be.

The matrix structure is the most far-reaching of a number of mechanisms which management can employ in an attempt to enhance the co-ordination of different functions or organizational sub-units. The behavioural problems which can arise in a matrix structure serve to remind one that a purely structural design will not of itself guarantee any desired pattern of behaviour. The structural and behavioural approaches which may be adopted in an attempt to enhance organizational integration are considered further in the following chapter.

Summary

The activities of people within an organization can be grouped together according to a number of different principles. A functional grouping comprises people employing a similar expertise. A grouping by process recognizes commonalities in plant and technology employed. A product grouping brings together people who are contributing to a common product or service. Other bases for organizationally grouping activities together are their sharing of a similar time horizon or their location on the same physical site.

These principles of specialization are useful in delineating the choices available to organizational designers. Considerations which enter into the choice between, say, a functional or a product structure, or a mixed form, centre very much upon contingencies such as the size of the organization, the diversity of its activities, and the speed at which it must adapt to its environment. The two most common models for grouping activities are the functional and product division types. The virtues of low overhead and simplicity characterizing the functional model are balanced by the co-ordinative, motivational and adaptive advantages of the product model. The matrix structure has been developed as an attempt to secure the best of both models, but the abandonment of unity of command which is entailed can produce conflicts and personal ambiguities especially while the system is settling down.

When examining in detail ways in which activities are, or might be, grouped together, a systematic evaluation of required relationships is called for. The outline of a method for carrying out this evaluation was described in the chapter.

Suggested further reading

An excellent concise discussion of the issues covered in this chapter is provided by Jay Galbraith, *Designing Complex Organizations* (Addison-Wesley 1973). A chapter by Michael Davis, 'Current Experiments and Trends in Management Structure' in *Renewing the Management Structure* (British Institute of Management 1972) describes alternative models for grouping activities in a clear and straightforward way. Part 1 of John M. Stopford and Louis T. Wells, Jr. *Managing the Multinational*

Enterprise (Longman 1972) analyses the development of organizational forms among multinational companies with special reference to diversification. Lawrence G. Franko analyses European multinationals from a similar perspective in *The European Multinationals* (Harper and Row 1976).

One of the most comprehensive analyses of matrix organization is provided by Donald Ralph Kingdon, *Matrix Organization* (Tavistock 1973). A good concise introduction is Kenneth Knight, 'Matrix Organization — A Review', *Journal of Management Studies,* May 1976.

Also referred to were Arthur H. Walker and Jay W. Lorsch, 'Organizational Choice: Product vs. Function', *Harvard Business Review,* November-December 1968; and Tom Burns and G. M. Stalker, *The Management of Innovation* (Tavistock 1961).

CHAPTER 5

INTEGRATION

'If a house be divided against itself, that house cannot stand.' Mark iii, 25.

Lack of co-ordination is one of the charges most frequently levelled against large organizations. 'The right hand doesn't know what the left hand is doing' is an often-heard reaction among clients and customers. There are indeed cases where the system virtually breaks down when subjected to any pressure of urgency. The result is delay, frustration and waste. One example, recently brought to light by a special report of the Carnegie Endowment, concerns the maladministration by two of the world's largest famine relief organizations of aid for 22 million people affected by the West African drought since 1968.

The American Agency for International Development (AID) and the United Nations Food and Agriculture Organization (FAO) are the two agencies in question. The aid donated by countries was generous in itself — up to October 1973 over twenty countries had provided £60 million. Yet sickness and malnutrition continued at an alarming level, considerably worse than that recorded in Bangladesh. The report identifies inadequate bureaucratic organization as the culprit, with several instances of poor integration. For instance, warning telegrams from the drought-stricken area were not sufficiently collated or acted upon — they were instead tucked away in filing cabinets scattered around the world. Even when the rescue operation got under way, plans proved to be unco-ordinated. Grain piled up in Dakar, Senegal, because there was insufficient transport to move it inland. An observer said that the only plump animals he saw in the area were the rats of Dakar port. The report alleges that these failures were due in part to a lack of co-operation between different groups: 'Over the entire episode, in spite of the dedication of many officials at all levels, there was the shadow of bureaucratic factors in the US or UN scarcely related to human suffering in Africa – programmes continued or initiatives neglected out of institutional inertia, rivalries between offices and agencies, and unwillingness to acknowledge failures to the public.'

This may be an extreme case, but shades of the same problem affect most organizations. One organization with different divisions operating on the same site has just discovered as I write that one division has been making employees redundant while another has been recruiting similar labour from the market. This expensive and image damaging process carried on despite the presence of a central personnel department! Why should managers experience such difficulty in co-ordinating and integrating the efforts of the groups and departments in their organizations?

Why is integration a problem?

Any organization has centrifugal tendencies, with individuals and departments straining to pursue their own chosen paths. It is in fact something of a wonder that organizations hold together at all. Within a small primary group of up to, say, twelve persons considerable pressure can come from other members of that group for an individual to fit in with group norms or else run the risk of complete rejection. With larger organizational units this system of informal integration and control tends to break down, and rival groups can form. There is a natural tendency for a collectivity of some size to break down into smaller, often competing units. In an organization, this differentiation is usually formalized. People are grouped into separate departments and those departments are allocated different tasks. One department is charged with producing the goods and services, another with selling and distributing them, and so on. This process of internal specialization develops hand in hand with growth in the overall size of the total organization – various research studies have found a high and remarkably consistent correlation between the size of organizations and their degree of internal specialization.

When an organization becomes larger and more differentiated, communication links become more tenuous. The natural tendency is to communicate with others within the same department, and with whom one shares common problems and experiences. These common problems and experiences reinforce people's identity with their own specialized department at the expense of integrating with other departments in pursuit of an overriding objective. Departments undertake work of a quite different kind requiring different methods; they operate to different time horizons and at a different pace. They have their own objectives to follow which can conflict with those of other departments when it comes to the practical level of everyday operations.

Industrial managers are familiar with conflicting requirements such as the maintenance of high quality and the maximization of production at a low cost, the mixing of orders for different models so as to maximize incoming sales revenue and the minimization of costs through preserving economic batch sizes, or the need to avoid stockouts while keeping capital tied up in inventory to the lowest possible level. In organizations where it is necessary to develop a steady stream of new services or products, it can be difficult to maintain agreement between research departments and other departments over the money to be invested in development, the control of its expenditure and the deadlines to be worked to.

Problems of integration generated by the allocation of different objectives and targets to departments are reinforced by differences in outlook among personnel themselves. Specialist personnel, qualified in different areas of expertise, are recruited to man the various departments. These people will usually have developed an identification with the norms and criteria of their occupational specialism and they may well have pursued a career in that specialism by moving between several organizations. So a personnel officer may regard himself as much as a 'personnel man' as a member of Organization X; so might an accountant, a scientist and other specialists. This identification with a particular occupational role will often be sustained by the fact that specialists have to have contact with others in the same special field outside the organization, and indeed many will belong to their own professional associations. I have found in my own studies of over eighty British companies that the attitudes even of quite senior managers differed sharply according to the functional area in which they were working. It also became apparent from this research that the more departments an organization was broken down into, the more difficult it was for those managers to reach agreement on how to handle problems that came up for decision.

These contrasts between the various parts of an organization, deriving from differences in their targets, ways of working, contacts outside the organization, training and so on can easily become crystallized in the form of stereotypes. How often the sales department of an industrial firm is caustically referred to as the 'gin and tonic brigade', a comment deriving to a degree from the life-style salesmen have to pursue as part of their job. Equally, production personnel have been called unhelpful reactionaries more than once, perhaps when opposing a marketing request which threatens their plans and schedules. Other departments (not least the accountants) come in for their share of abuse too. These apparently harmless labels can signify a quite deep-seated antipathy between different parts of an organization based upon considerable misunderstanding of other groups' objectives, methods of work, and problems. Where such stereotypes are entrenched they have to be dispelled before an adequate level of integration can be achieved. The requirement, then, in the words of one thoughtful supervisor is that 'activities should be divided, not people'.

Centrifugal 'strains toward functional autonomy', as one writer has called them, can be regulated without very much difficulty if an organization is carrying out its work under fairly stable conditions without too many unplanned developments forcing it to come to rapid decisions and make frequent adaptations. In circumstances like these, different departments can be integrated by their following certain standard procedures or plans which are laid down by top management or by mutual agreement. The necessary exchange of information and views between departments can be effected through the programming of regular meetings. Any differences of opinion can be resolved through their referral up the hierarchy to the point where both parties share a superior in common — right up to the chief executive if necessary.

The resolution of conflict and integration of specialist contributions through this kind of system clearly takes time. Time becomes a particularly scarce resource when there are pressures on the organization to act quickly. A firm may be under severe pressure from its competitors; a local authority may face a public impatient to hear the results of its planning decisions; a relief agency will be placed under strain by a natural disaster. If the problem in question is a complex one, perhaps involving many technical, legal or environmental issues, then the difficulties of bringing together all the necessary specialist evaluations in a limited period of time become even more acute.

Over the last few decades, both the rate of change and the complexity of problems faced by most organizations have been steadily increasing. The amount of information they have to process in a given time period is therefore significantly greater than before. In addition, their margins of profit or of tolerable expenditure have on the whole been falling, and this reduces the 'slack' which is available to delay a decision or to commit errors because of inadequate information. The more that information processing requirements increase and the less tolerance there is for sub-optimal performance, the greater is the necessity for managements to secure an intense degree of integration between all the parts of the organization.

Some common integration problems

One of the most common problems of integration appears in the relationship between, on the one hand, functions such as sales (or client contact) and purchasing which have to accommodate themselves to the world outside the organization, and on the other hand functions such as production or engineering which are responsible for generating products or services. This is the problem of integrating the 'peripheries' of an organization with its 'core', and without this integration an organization will not remain viable.

One example of a problem concerning integration between sales and production has been related by A. J. M. Sykes and J. Bates. They studied a British company with six sales departments and eighteen different plants. In this company there was constant conflict between the production side which wanted to limit the range of products in order to increase the volume of output for each one and reduce unit costs, and the sales departments which attempted to force production to comply with the customer's exact specifications regardless of the case for standardization. Conflict also arose between the different departments on the sales side, because each department tried to secure the earliest possible delivery date for its customers without regard to the system of priorities which the company had laid down. These priorities were intended to give preference to certain types of order (e.g. export) and to certain large and important customers. The sales clerks had been recruited from production clerks and they were able to organize preferential treatment for their 'own' customers through informal deals with the production clerks.

The company overcame these difficulties by setting up a Sales Organization Liaison Department (SOLD) between sales and production. This is shown in Figure 5.1. SOLD's main functions were to secure information on production capacity and sales requirements, to co-ordinate these in terms of delivery schedules for customers, to act as a liaison between sales and production by keeping each informed of the others' requirements, to formulate a comprehensive pricing policy, and to maintain statistics, producing reports for the Chairman and Board. Detailed instructions were drawn up as to how SOLD was to operate. It was, for example, required to allocate orders to plants having the capacity to deal with them and which were convenient for customer delivery; it was to give delivery dates to sales departments in accordance with the company's system of priorities, and to progress orders.

In this example, integration was significantly improved by the establishment of a new co-ordinating department and by setting up new procedures. Another case, from the United States, has been related by George Strauss, and it concerns problems of integration between purchasing staff and other departments inside the organization, including engineering and production. The buyer's basic responsibilities were:

1 To negotiate and place orders for materials with outside suppliers on the best possible terms but only in accordance with specifications set by others; and

2 To expedite orders, that is, to check with suppliers to make sure that deliveries are made on time.

The communication system before SOLD

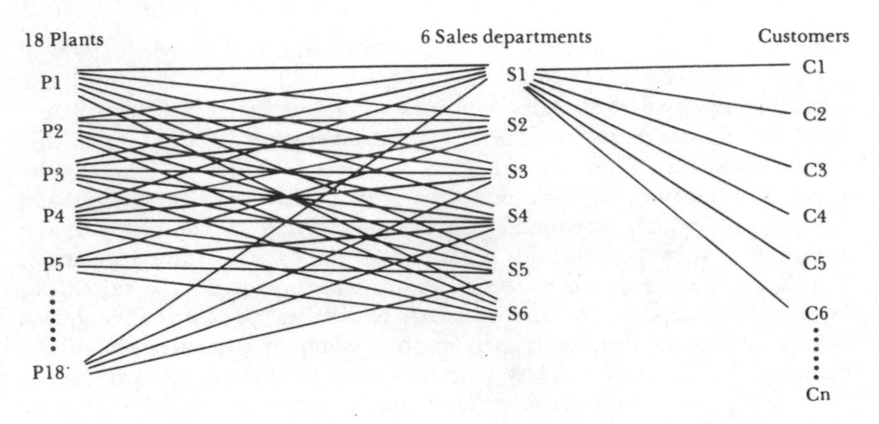

The communication system after SOLD

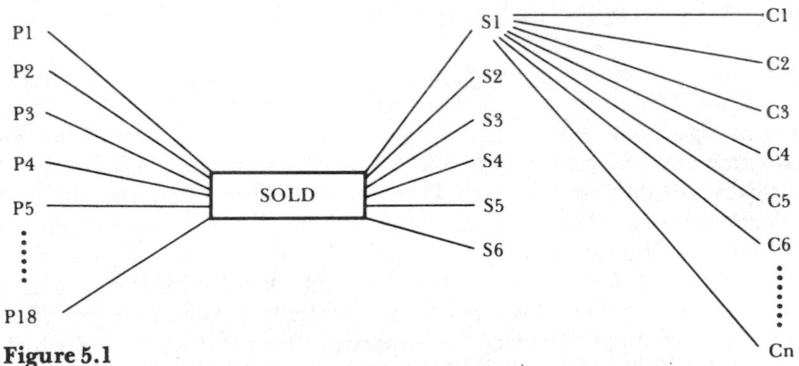

Figure 5.1
An example of integration between sales and production departments

From: A. J. M. Sykes and J. Bates, 'Study of Conflict between Formal Company Policy and the Interests of Informal Groups', *Sociological Review,* November 1962, pp. 313-327.

Conflicts with engineering arose because engineers preferred to specify exactly what they wanted without leaving any discretion to the buyer; also because by training and functional responsibility engineers look first for quality and reliability, while buyers were required to take low cost and quick delivery into account as well. Conflicts with production scheduling arose because schedulers would often seek extremely short delivery times (under pressure themselves from sales) or require materials in uneconomic order sizes.

In an attempt to ease these problems in dealing with other departments, the buyers had adopted various devices; some mainly to protect themselves, others in a more constructive attempt to improve integration. Among the latter were the use of direct contact to persuade other departments to take purchasing criteria into account, and an attempt to modify the workflow pattern in order to stabilize the situation. For example, some buyers got the production schedulers to check with the purchasing department about the possibilities of getting quick delivery before they made out a requisition.

Other areas in which problems of integration commonly occur are: (1) the securing and evaluation of information from outside the organization for planning purposes, especially in a divisional organization; (2) the promotion of innovation and the integration of the specialists concerned into the mainstream of the organization; (3) the creation of effective production management teams; and (4) the co-ordination of complementary services offered by members of different professions. These four areas will be considered briefly, because they help to illustrate the dimensions of the problem as well as some of the solutions which have been tried.

1 Scanning and planning

Aguilar in his studies of how companies scanned their environments (*Scanning the Business Environment* 1967), found one multidivisional firm where integration was seriously deficient. In this firm there was a headquarters group planning function which saw its role as gathering information that would assist the company in finding completely new areas of business into which to diversify. Each division also had a planning department, securing and evaluating information from outside which could indicate desirable modifications to existing products. These two levels of scanning and planning activity were unco-ordinated with the result that no effort was being put into possibly the most fruitful area for expansion, namely the development of new products within the company's present area of business. Planners at each level, group and division, assumed that the other level was covering this gap.

Many organizations are in fact feeling their way towards a more effective way of integrating the various activities which feed into the planning of corporate strategy. There is some debate as to whether the formulation of strategies should remain a purely general or line management function or whether it should use the expertise of specialist staff such as corporate planners and marketing specialists. The arguments for involving specialists are several: (a) unless a good part of the groundwork in strategy planning is given over to specialists, it may end up by not being done at all due to the operation of Gresham's Law ('routine drives out forward planning'); (b) through establishing a specialized planning group, relevant expertise can be utilized and this may lend a certain objectivity to an area of decision-making where line managers tend to argue from their limited departmental or divisional viewpoints; and (c) a specialist corporate planning group can provide a means for providing synergy (constructive integration) between the forward plans of the sub-units in a complex diversified organization.

One of the biggest problems, however, in utilizing specialists is that it is not easy to ensure that a specialist planning group remains effectively integrated with line management. One difficulty is that when an activity such as planning is delegated, its value in top management eyes may become reduced. It is easy for the legitimacy of a staff group to be called into question, for its supposed 'lack of realism' and 'academic' attitudes, and this is particularly likely when the group is submitting proposals for change which are perceived to threaten established ways of working or the political balance within the organization.

2 Innovation and change

In the field of developing new products and services, a great deal of attention has been given to the problem of integrating scientists and other research specialists. There are two aspects to this problem: first, the integration of the specialists themselves into effective work teams, and second, their integration with the main line activities of the organization.

A solution favoured by many managements is to draw together all the staff contributing to a new project into a project team. This is set up for the life of the project to see it through. In order to meet both the integration problems just mentioned, it is important to include as members of the project team not only appropriate technical staff but also representatives of the marketing or customer contact function, people from costing and from production engineering or its equivalent function. Studies of innovation indicate that one of the main reasons for commercial failure in new products is a lack of understanding of customer needs, pointing to a serious absence of integration between research and marketing personnel.

A paradox in the organization of innovation derives from the need for the innovators to form a self-contained group of their own with considerable autonomy and the requirement that this very same group be not cut off politically and in terms of shared understanding from the main sections of the organization upon which the refinement, production and launching of the innovation depends. The autonomy helps to provide the group with an identity and freedom from interference that should motivate creative processes; yet at the same time a bridge must be maintained to the rest of the organization.

When a project team organization is used to try and achieve these requirements, it is commonly managed on the following lines. The team accepts targets agreed with management for accomplishing the various stages of the new development and it is normally subject to budgetary constraints. It is usually left to decide on its own pattern of working. If the project team is acting solely as a co-ordinating mechanism, then it would be allowed to decide how to integrate the work going on within the specialized functions it represents. Membership of the team may vary according to the stage of development which has been reached, although it is generally considered important for certain key personnel to remain team members for the total development process. In an industrial development, for instance, one would expect to find research and marketing personnel, at least, involved from start to finish.

This method of integration comes close to the 'organic' system of management which is well-known nowadays to readers of management literature, and which was first described by Tom Burns and G. M. Stalker in their *Management of Innovation* (1961). A similar approach is often employed in creative service activities such as advertising, university teaching and the social services.

Other specialist groups can be involved in the attempt to foster innovations and changes, as well as research scientists. Operational researchers and systems analysts, organizational development specialists, and internal consultancy groups are examples of other specialists whose role is to promote effective change. These specialists often experience considerable insecurity because, far more than is usually true of research scientists, the employing organization is capable of continuing to operate without them. They may well face considerable line management criticism that they simply represent an additional overhead cost. As a result, the members of these specialist groups often feel considerable self-doubt and behave in a manner which makes co-operation with central established departments all the more difficult. Maladaptive responses to their uncertainty on the part of specialist groups include a turning inward and withdrawal from the pressures experienced as coming from other parts of the organization and an inflexibility in the plans presented to line management, including a refusal to accept criticism. Given that established departments will be predisposed to regard any proposed changes which affect them with reserve if not hostility, this kind of behaviour on the part of specialists can readily lead to a complete breakdown in their integration with the organization as a whole.

An adaptive approach to managing this kind of situation breaks into two aspects: (a) the internal management of the specialist team so that its portfolio of projects, its staffing and its awareness of present and future client needs are adequate; and (b) the management of the team's external links with its client departments in the organization, so that the language it uses and the relationships it develops are those which will enable it to make an effective contribution. The two planks upon which the integration of specialist groups to client departments can be built are mechanisms to link them into such departments and the securing of senior management backing for their activities which gives them organizational legitimation. Linking mechanisms are discussed later in this chapter. The value of political sponsorship for specialist innovative activities is indicated by the research of the Science Policy Research Unit at the University of Sussex into successful industrial product innovation, which found support from a powerful senior manager to be one of the main predictors of a project's completion and successful commercialization.

3 Production management teams

The backbone of the traditional line and staff relationship is to be found in the area of an organization's core operations — the production area in a manufacturing firm. Here the integration problem is not that of bringing together specialist and other departments to deal with a specific issue or project. It is, rather, a problem of making available to production a range of services on a continuing and reliable basis. These services are in nature technological (such as industrial engineering, production engineering and quality control); financial (budgetary control, cost reduction and management control information); personnel (such as recruitment and training) and planning (production control). In a large and complex multi-product, multi-line facility, the integration of these services to production management is a formidable task. In Britain, a common criticism of manufacturing industry is that it has been failing to achieve this task adequately both at senior and junior levels of production management.

One attempt to achieve more adequate integration in this area has been underway in a British confectionery factory. The concept employed has been that of a factory director's team, which is progressively being reflected at lower levels in the production hierarchy as time goes on. Previously, production, quality control, industrial engineering, management accounting, industrial relations, employment and other functions were organized in a strictly functional manner. This was not conducive to an effective working relationship between production and the service-providing functions. For example, departmental production managers found that the information on costs and variances being provided by management accountants was not presented in a breakdown suited to their needs but in a form dictated by conventions emanating from the Financial Director's office. This structure has now been replaced by the creation of a 'Factory Director's Team' comprising the Factory Director and his immediate production subordinates, the senior management accountant, the manager in charge of production services (primarily factory and employment services), the industrial relations and quality control managers. At the next level down in the production hierarchy, senior production managers are in turn supported by their own teams comprising management accountants, production services and quality control specialists. The management accounting function has been broadened into a 'financial performance' function oriented to assisting in performance improvement as well as financial control.

This method of integrating production and ancilliary services appears to be improving the quality of information available to production and raising standards of production performance, although at the time of writing the new arrangements have only been operating for just over a year. There is always room for debate as to which functions should be integrated with production in the formal reporting sense. In the case described, quality control and personnel have not been placed under direct production authority — in the former case so as to preserve an independent view on quality standards which are particularly critical in a food company, and in the case of personnel to preserve what are seen to be economies of scale and functional rationalization given that the personnel function also services all the office areas on the site (including several divisional and head office departments) as well. Another feature worth noting in this case is that in addition to lateral integration via the creation of production management teams, vertical integration has been fostered by the overlapping hierarchical membership of those teams. Following the principle of 'linking-pins' first advocated by Rensis Likert, production managers are members of their hierarchical superior's team.

At the junior level of production management, first-line supervision often poses problems of integration. One frequently finds in industry that the members of several specialist departments contribute to the organization or manning of production on the shop floor. Departments such as production planning, stock control and quality control impinge directly upon the organization of production, while others such as work study, industrial relations and the employment office have an indirect effect. In studies which we are carrying out at Aston University of first-line supervision, many cases have arisen where production foremen are uncertain of their authority in relation to these 'staff' functions. Given this uncertainty, the supervisor is not placed in a sufficiently authoritative position to act as an effective integrator of specialist activities. One approach to this problem could be the creation of supervisory 'teams' to reflect the more senior production teams which have been described. These teams would perhaps only meet periodically, and they would have to be led by supervisors of sufficient calibre. Such an arrangement might help to create conditions in which specialists are co-ordinated by the supervisor, rather than by-passing him and failing to integrate with each other. This kind of problem seems to be less severe in most areas of office supervision, but where it arises, a similar approach could be worth considering.

4 Integration of professional services

One field where poor integration has had tragic consequences is the social services in Britain. There have been several cases in recent years of children's deaths which might have been avoided had there been closer working relationships between specialist groups into whose purview the cases fell. The Seebohm Report on the development of the social services in England and Wales published in 1968 in fact specifically called for the improved integration of specialist contributions through a move away from existing divisions between health, children, welfare, psychiatric and other fields and towards the creation of a 'generic' approach. Too often it had been the case that, say, a problem of family breakdown had been treated separately by different professional specialists, at the expense of co-ordination between them and to the bewilderment of the clients. Following the Seebohm Report, Social Services Departments have tackled this problem in several ways – normally either by creating generic social work teams in which specialists work together or by giving individual social workers sole responsibility for cases.

Many of these common problems of integration have concerned 'lateral' relationships across the organization between groups or departments at roughly the same hierarchical level. Sometimes the problem concerns poor 'vertical' integration between levels, as in the example given of a gap between HQ and divisions in scanning and planning. In describing the problems, I have touched upon some possible improvements including direct contact between members of different departments, the establishment of liasion units and the establishment of project teams. I shall shortly set out these structural mechanisms for improving integration more systematically, but first it is appropriate to refer to some research evidence that demonstrates how effective integration can contribute to the overall performance of an organization.

Integration and performance

In a study of ten American companies (*Organization and Environment* 1967), Lawrence and Lorsch found that the most successful firms had adapted their internal structures to suit the demands for information processing imposed by the kind of environments in which they were operating. Six of the companies were in the plastics industry, characterized by considerable market and technological change and by much uncertainty about future developments. In this kind of environment it was necessary for research departments to work to long time horizons and to operate in a way that allowed adaptation to new developments. Marketing departments had to work against shorter time horizons than did research, but still faced somewhat more uncertainty than the production function. In the more stable industries studied, containers and food manufacturing, the required degree of difference between functional departments in their patterns of operation was less.

The more that the outlook and behaviour of managers in different departments had to differ, the more difficult it was for them to achieve integrated effort. A condition for good performance was found to lie in the achievement of an adequate level of integration, and it was more difficult to reach this in a more differentiated organization. In the high performing companies, this tension between a requisite degree of differentiation and a requisite degree of integration was managed through effective mechanisms and procedures for resolving conflicts between departments. While in all the successful companies these procedures tended to involve the open confrontation and working through of differences, the type of mechanisms used and the location of points of integration within the organization varied according to the contingencies faced by firms in the different industries.

In the high performing plastics organizations, with a large degree of internal differentiation, the combination of integrative mechanisms used included a special co-ordinating department, plus permanent integrating teams each made up of members from the various functional units and from the co-ordinating department. A great deal of reliance was also placed on direct contact between managers at all levels. In a high performing food organization, which was less internally differentiated, less complex formal integrative devices were employed. Managers within functional departments were given co-ordinative or liaision roles. If a special issue arose which presented a more urgent need for collaboration, temporary teams would be set up comprising specialists from the various units involved. There was also a heavy reliance on direct contact between managers. Finally, in a high performing standardized container manufacturer with a relatively low level of internal differentiation, integration was achieved primarily through the managerial hierarchy. There was some reliance on direct contact between functional managers, and also on paperwork systems which helped to resolve more routine scheduling requirements.

The conclusion that an achievement of effective integration can contribute substantially to high organizational performance is supported by the work of some other researchers, though I should add that much of this work is very preliminary in nature. A study of British building and printing firms carried out by members of Ashridge Management College concluded that the level of integration secured by management is at least as important a factor in designing organizations as is the maintenance of control. Historically, managements appear to have concentrated more effort on attempts to achieve tight control, and relatively little attention has been given to integration. This is reflected in the conventional organization chart which normally just illustrates the authority channels through which control is achieved. In the research mentioned, integration appeared particularly important in the printing firms where a low degree of integration between departments was associated both with poor profitability and low job satisfaction among managers.

The choice of integrative mechanism

In deciding on methods to achieve better integration between parts of an organization a choice has to be made with regard to (a) the degree of integration required, (b) the difficulties of achieving this that are inherent in the situation, and (c) the costs of alternative integrating mechanisms. There is, on the whole, an inverse relationship between the sophistication of an integrative device and its overhead cost to the organization. Let us examine some of the alternatives.

The late James Thompson in his seminal book *Organizations in Action* (1967) identified three main categories of integrative mechanism, into which the examples so far mentioned will be seen to fall. The first category is integration via standardization. This involves the establishment of rules or procedures which channel the actions of each job holder or department into a direction consistent with the actions of others. Secondly, plans and schedules can be established so as to integrate the actions of separate units. Integration via planning is somewhat more flexible than standardization in that plans can usually be modified fairly quickly. Thirdly, there is what Thompson called integration via 'mutual adjustment'. This refers to integration via the transmission of information directly between people and the mutual adjustment of their actions in the light of that information. A wide range of integrative mechanisms would fall into this category, including those aimed at increasing direct co-ordination laterally across the vertical divisions of an organization structure.

The traditional bureaucratic form of organization, which is still the normal model for most of our large organizations, generally relies heavily on the first two of these categories for integrating the activities of its departments. An elaborate system of rules and procedures is worked out, improved and extended over time. These procedures can be designed to formalize what experience has shown to be the best practice in handling a set of recurrent problems. By formulating a body of procedure and operating plans the contributions of separate departments can be clearly specified and so integrated into the task as a whole. If exceptions occur, and these are really seen to be aberrations from a routine, then these can be referred up the hierarchy to a point where the various departments concerned share a common boss. Integration, in other words, is also maintained by hierarchical referral when something out of the ordinary crops up. If matters of procedure and operating policy require some discussion from time to time, a third bureaucratic mechanism for integration can be actuated, namely the committee meeting. Although committee meetings fall into the category of mutual adjustment, they are usually highly formal and pre-arranged. In stable conditions, a programme of such meetings is often arranged for twelve months ahead.

There are several merits to this system of integration, which can operate quite adequately when conditions are stable and predictable. Many people like to know where they stand, and bureaucratic integration is based on a system of clearly defined rules and procedures which are there for all to see. It is also a relatively cheap approach to integration, once its procedures and systems have been well tried and tested. It does not call for any overhead of special co-ordinating staff, nor does it necessarily require a great deal of manpower to be locked up in 'endless meetings'. Nevertheless, once an organization moves into less stable conditions and the requirement for information processing increases, the traditional bureaucratic approach to integration begins to creak in its joints.

This has been the experience of a major British company. During the last ten years or so, this company has experienced a decline in the market share of its main products, generally keener competition, a falling rate of profit, more volatile commodity markets and a distinct worsening in its climate of employee relations. It has recently been operating under conditions of government imposed price restraint. At the operating level a policy has been followed of rapid expansion in the number of different lines produced and a reduction in inventory levels. The company has been subject to greater external change and competitive pressure. In order to cope, it has adopted product and inventory policies that call for much more processing and exchange of information between departments, to improve scheduling, avoid stockouts and so forth.

In thinking about adjusting to this greater information processing load, the company has been working on a number of fronts. It is reorganizing many of its production facilities around product groups and setting up teams of specialists to work closely within new 'divisions' with the division manager. This does mean a duplication of certain resources, but at the same time it integrates staff more effectively around the production of particular classes of products. In addition various investigations are underway with a view to improving systems of information handling.

These entail the use of more planning and clerical staff and also the eventual extension of computerization.

The improvement of information processing systems, often through a better definition of inputs and electronic data processing, can assist the problem of inadequate integration between the different levels of an organization. As well as providing better feedback of information to operating units, it can provide managers at a higher level with a better picture of what is going on over a range of units. This may help them to balance and integrate these units as a whole.

Other devices are available for improving the quality of lateral integration, between groups and departments at approximately the same level. In the absence of any formal provision for lateral integration, informal contact will often arise. One often hears people say that 'If we had to go through the official channels, we would never get anything done on time'. The problem is that one cannot necessarily rely on effective informal arrangements emerging, and those that do, as in the case of the SOLD company with its sales-production liasion problems, may not reflect the policy priorities set down for the organization as a whole. In any case, formal integrative arrangements can be designed in a way that facilitates rather than prevents the development of informal relations.

Jay Galbraith in his *Designing Complex Organizations* (1973) discusses each of these integrative mechanisms in detail. He makes the point that as information processing requirements in an organization rise in conditions of greater change and complexity, so the bureaucratic approach is able to cope with decreasing effectiveness. The alternatives are then fourfold. First, the organization can increase its resources of manpower or accept lower standards of decision-making efficiency — this is clearly a path leading to the lowering of performance. Second, the organization can be divided up so as to group people around the clusters of most intensive communication need — this is the divisionalization approach and will tend to incur additional costs of resource duplication. Third, the organization can improve its vertical information systems so as to relieve the load on the hierarchy. Such improvement will, however, normally require additional investment in clerical staff, computer time and so forth. Finally, the organization can attempt another way of increasing its capacity to process information. This is via the development of lateral relationships at appropriate points down the hierarchy, along with a complementary delegation of discretion to the people concerned. While, as we see shortly, the creation of lateral relationships can also entail overhead costs, Galbraith believes that they offer the greatest potential for improving integration.

The following passage, taken from an internal consultative document issued in 1973 by the British company just mentioned, illustrates the way in which managements are coming to appreciate the value in moving beyond traditional formal hierarchical structures by incorporating lateral integrative mechanisms:

> In organization terms we appear to have learned a healthy disrespect for formal structures and relationships and functional boundaries. In a number of areas task-oriented arrangements have been developed which transcend the traditional structures in the interests of overall effectiveness. In an organization of our size and complexity we need a formal structure and clear definition of accountability, but it is a promising sign that we appear to be capable of adapting and evolving appropriate structures to meet changing requirements. Examples of developments in this area include the increasing use of the project team approach (notably in the new product development and engineering areas) and the evolution of our whole long range planning process. Elsewhere there has been an acceptance of the viability of matrix structures (working for more than one boss), and the need for more emphasis on team building, with an acceptance of team objectives.

The various forms of lateral integration are listed below, in order of increasing sophistication, difficulty in design and overhead cost. By and large, the heavier the information processing load, deriving from pressures and complexity in the tasks to be done, the further down the list will a management have to go in order to secure an adequate level of integration. As one goes down the list, the more sophisticated approaches tend to subsume those higher up the list:

1 Bring about direct contact between managers or employees who share a problem.

2 If departments are required to have a substantial amount of contact, one or more of their staff can be given special responsibility to act as a liaison officer with counterparts in other departments.

3 If a development or problem arises which calls for the contribution of several departments until its completion or solution, then it would probably be appropriate to set up a temporary task force to deal with it, with members drawn from those departments.

4 If such inter-departmental problems constantly recur, then permanently established groups or teams provide a method of integration.

5 If the management of lateral relationships becomes a problem, perhaps because of their complexity, then a special integrating role can be set up – that of a 'co-ordinator' or similar title. It may be necessary to endow the co-ordinator with a department of staff as was done in the case of SOLD.

6 A further development of the separate integrating role is to decide that it should have a definite claim upon the resources of functional departments. Indeed these may disappear as separate departments. In industry such integrator-managers are often product managers in charge of the total operations required to market, develop, produce and service a product.

7 The most elaborate and sophisticated method of ensuring lateral integration is to establish a matrix system. Here, an attempt is made to combine integration of personnel within functionally specialized departments with their integration around a common contribution to products or programmes.

The research conducted by Lawrence and Lorsch, referred to in the previous section, concluded that organizations operating in more dynamic environments with greater differentiation between their major functions needed to invest in more powerful integrating mechanisms. The thrust of this conclusion is supported by Van de Ven and his colleagues who examined 'co-ordination modes' used in 197 units of a large American state government employment security agency. They distinguished between three such modes: (a) co-ordination through setting programmes of work and establishing procedures – an 'impersonal mode'; (b) co-ordination through feedback in a 'personal mode', whereby individuals such as managers, co-ordinators and liaision officers are the means for two or more groups making mutual adjustments; and (c) a 'group mode' whereby planned or unscheduled meetings serve as the mechanism for mutual adjustment.

It was found that three conditions were associated with the different usage of integrating mechanisms. These were how difficult and variable was the work to be done (conditions which create uncertainty), how dependent employees had to be upon each other in order to get work done, and how large each work unit was in terms of people employed. As uncertainty in the work increased, so lateral communications and group meetings tended to be used instead of integration via programming. As interdependence between employees increased, there was a greater use of all integrating mechanisms except for programmes and procedures. As size of work unit increased, so there was more use of impersonal modes of integration based on formalized planning and programming. This last relationship appears to be one more facet of the general association between increasing scale of organization and the formalization of structure.

Although the design of organization structures can influence the patterns of behaviour and relationships in an institution, it is always difficult to predict just what its effect will be because so much depends on the predispositions of the people concerned, how they perceive the structure in question and how they react to it. This is as true of structural mechanisms designed to improve integration as it is of any others. Structural mechanisms may be established in a way which is quite appropriate for achieving integration, but these can have a limited impact if there is interpersonal conflict or animosity between different groups. A certain threshold of trust and willingness to work together is required, and managements may have to devote considerable efforts towards building this up – towards 'teambuilding' as it is often called. The reverse is also true: teambuilding is less likely to produce integration if the structural design is deficient. What can be done, then, to complement improvements in structural integrative mechanisms with improvements in personal relationships between groups?

Teambuilding, an aid to integration

Many problems of integration are caused by the hostile feelings that one group, or department, may have for another. We have seen that departments will have different goals and criteria of performance, and that it is very easy for them to form unfavourable stereotypes of one another. It is natural for individuals to identify with their own department rather than with other departments or with the organization as a whole. It is also quite understandable that people tend to vent their feelings of frustration or aggression on 'outsiders'. The heads of some departments may feel personal antipathy towards each other, and this in turn is likely to reflect upon the attitudes of their respective staffs.

For reasons such as these it is quite likely that certain feelings of hostility will manifest themselves between different departments which have to work together, and this will make it more difficult to achieve an adequate degree of integration. Once conflict arises, then its effects will often become cumulative. Within a department, these effects typically include more conformity, 'pulling together' and defensiveness. As groups, the departments 'close-up', seeing only the best in themselves and the worst in others. As between the departments communication tends to decrease, their members do not listen to the 'adversary', personal relations deteriorate, and scoring political points becomes more important than solving common problems on their merits. In fact, the more that relations between departments are defined in terms of 'if they win, we lose', the more likely is a breakdown in integration. The more that relations are linked in people's minds to joint problem-solving, the less likely is such breakdown.

Lawrence and Lorsch found that successful integration in the companies they studied was characterized by a great deal of open confrontation of issues by the members of different departments. This openness can only be based on a genuine understanding of other departments' outlooks, ways of working and problems. Stereotypes are destructive of this understanding, and much of the task of teambuilding amounts to the dispelling of stereotypes.

There are various methods of accomplishing this task, though it is not easy to break into a situation of deteriorating relationships and start a reversal of the trend. Very often the intervention of a third party, a superior in the hierarchy or even a consultant, is required in order to start off a frank mutual discussion of the stereotypes that each department has of the other. Understanding and integration can subsequently be built up between the departments by reformulating their objectives or targets in terms of an overriding goal which both accept as essential and also attainable. If joint projects are called for, then task forces drawing on members of two or more departments can often provide a positive experience of working together. This can create mutual trust and confidence, as can other ways of bringing members of different departments to work together, such as nominating joint representatives to committees. If a lack of co-operation between departments stems from personal antipathy between their heads then changing one or both is probably required before teambuilding can meet with success.

In the past few years, much work on so-called 'organizational development' has concentrated almost exclusively on developing teamwork. This effort has not always been successful, because teamwork cannot be expected to thrive when the structural and environmental conditions are wrong. If departments are put under pressure to pursue mutually conflicting objectives and if the formal structure makes no allowance for their need to work together, then the methods I have described for developing teamwork are less likely to bear fruit. Equally, the appropriate structural arrangements have to be operated on a basis of goodwill between people and they cannot guarantee effective integration on their own account. The right integrative mechanisms and interpersonal climate are both required for conflicts of opinion to be handled in a constructive manner.

Summary

Inadequate co-ordination between the different departments and specialist staff of an organization is often a source of frustration to its clientele and a cause of poor performance. Integration is a problem that develops with the growth of organizations and their subdivision into separate sub-units. It is exacerbated by the variation in outlook between people trained in different functional disciplines and by the conflict between specific criteria of performance which are attached to separate departments. Points at which poor co-ordination is commonly found in an industrial organization include the relations between sales and production, between research and other functions, and between personnel and technical officers over shopfloor priorities. In the social services there has been a problem over the co-ordination of different specialists dealing with the same problem case.

There are a range of structural devices which can be employed to promote better integration in an organization — from arranging face-to-face meetings right up to the use of a full-blown matrix system. Which provision or combination of provisions is appropriate depends upon the degree of integration that is required, the difficulties of achieving this that are inherent in the situation and the cost of investing time and staff in co-ordinative activities. Structural adjustments can, however, only go part of the way towards enhancing integration. If conflicts between units derive from hostility or entrenched stereotypes then a teambuilding approach aimed at confronting these issues directly will also be required.

Suggested further reading

James D. Thompson provided an important early analysis of integration requirements and mechanisms in his *Organizations in Action* (McGraw-Hill 1967). Jay Galbraith, *Designing Complex Organizations* (Addison-Wesley 1973), examines in some detail the ways in which integration can be improved across the departments of an organization. Paul R. Lawrence and J. W. Lorsch, *Organization and Environment* (Harvard Business School 1967), describe research into American firms which indicates how inadequate integration is associated with poor performance. The same writiers in *Developing Organizations: Diagnosis and Action* (Addison-Wesley 1969) describe a practical approach to making decisions on how much specialization and co-ordination between organizational units is required in the light of environmental and other contingencies.

Two studies which describe how integration problems were resolved through the application of new structural forms are A. J. M. Sykes and J. Bates, 'Study of Conflict Between Formal Company Policy and the Interests of Informal Groups', *Sociological Review*, November 1962, and Tom Burns and G. M. Stalker, *The Management of Innovation* (Tavistock 1961). A perceptive analysis of the problems which can arise in the integration of specialist groups with the departments they are intended to service is given by Andrew M. Pettigrew in 'Strategic Aspects of the Management of Specialist Activity', *Personnel Review*, volume 4, 1975. Alan C. Filley, *Interpersonal Conflict Resolution* (Scott, Foresman 1975), provides a review of methods to resolve the human problems that stand in the way of effective integration.

In this chapter reference was also made to F. J. Aguilar, *Scanning the Business Environment* (Macmillan 1967), and to Philip Sadler, Terry Webb and Peter Lansley, *Management Style and Organization Structure in the Smaller Enterprise* (Ashridge College, Management Research Unit 1974). Three other studies cited were Andrew H. Van de Ven, Andre L.

Delbecq and Richard Koenig, Jr., 'Determinants of Coordination Modes within Organizations', *American Sociological Review,* April 1976, C. Freeman, A. Robertson and colleagues in the University of Sussex Science Policy Research Unit, *Success and Failure in Industrial Innovation* (February 1972), and George Strauss, 'Tactics of Lateral Relationship: The Purchasing Agent', *Administrative Science Quarterly,* September 1962.

CHAPTER 6

CONTROL

'Order is Heaven's first law.' Alexander Pope, *Essay on Man*, Epistle iv.

'Everything is under control.' Managers say this with thinly disguised desperation as often as they say it with conviction. Control was only one of the five basic managerial functions which Henri Fayol identified back in 1916. Yet it has generally received a lion's share of attention in discussions on organization structure. Many writers have seen the main contribution of organization structure to lie in the means it provides for controlling behaviour. In fact, organization is often taken to be synonomous with the organization chart, which in its conventional form lays down official channels of control.

Control is essentially concerned with regulating the activities within an organization so that they are in accord with the expectations established in policies, plans and targets. While control implies the presence of integration, integration *per se* is concerned specifically with the extent to which differentiated activities are mutually supportive and synchronized — do they work for or against each other? Managers have tended to pay considerable attention to the achievement of control in the hierarchical sense of ensuring that instructions are carried out, and this may be at the expense of giving attention to the lateral dimension of integration across the organization. Heads of departments often feel that they are expected to demonstrate that they have 'authority' over their employees as a basic criterion of their competence rather than, for example, that they have co-ordinated adequately with managers in other areas. Many management techniques have also been developed to assist in the achievement of control, such as budgetary and other cost control systems, management by objectives, O & M, work study, manuals of procedures, exception reporting and so forth.

In the past, many managers have been inclined to equate control with close direction. That is to say, they have delegated with reluctance and have only felt secure in doing so once they had limited the effective discretion of subordinates through formalized job descriptions, rules and procedures, and standard operating systems. In so doing they have sought to ensure 'orderly administration' and to avoid the danger of chaos – different individuals going their own ways, costs running away, and other incipient signs of breakdown. This policy has, however, generated its own costs of low motivation on the part of people subjected to tight and rigid controls, especially highly trained specialists and staff. Often a passive resistance develops – 'treat me like a moron, or someone who can't be trusted, and I'll behave like one' – and this inhibits initiative and creativity because people become unwilling to pass ideas and information back up the line. The recognition of this problem has qualified the traditional approach to control. In addition, the growing internal complexity of organizations consequent upon the diversification of their activities and the employment of specialists has today brought co-ordination to the fore as a management problem and this has placed the problem of control in a broader perspective.

The traditional view of control, essentially imposed from above rather than stemming from each individual's sense of personal responsibility in his job, gave attention only to one side of the control problem. For it ignored the need to secure motivation and feedback from the people at whom control is directed. It is well recognized that even the most precisely defined controls relating to budgeted expenditure, or to the performance of operatives, can result in distorted feedback if those controls are regarded as illegitimate or threatening by the people to whom they are applied. For example, one of the problems some firms have faced when contemplating the installation of one-line computer recording of shop-floor production so as to improve production control is the likelihood the operatives would, for their own reasons, choose to record false information or give false information for their supervisors to record.

A centralized 'top down' approach to control has become increasingly difficult to sustain in the conditions confronting many large organizations today. The sheer size and diversification of such organizations, and their consequently attenuated lines of communication, enforce a degree of decentralization in which control parameters are established with some reference to objectives and proposals generated in sub-units such as divisions. A great deal of information relevant to the control process is generated via operating units, some of it technically complex and specific to the nature of their activities, and this is a further factor in the move away from a totally top down approach.

Control involves the definition of what people and units are to do, the establishment of criteria against which the performance of their activities is to be assessed, and a feedback of information as to what has in the event taken place. There should also be provision for 'feedforward' control in which predictive forecasting information is used as a basis for assessing whether adjustments to plans are necessary. Expressed in this way, a management's choice of control methods should be compatible with the needs of the operating situation and what will motivate people to carry out their tasks in the manner desired. If, for example, a firm has to innovate and adapt in order to compete in a rapidly changing environment, then its management should not seek to encourage rigid and conformist behaviour. An attempt to control the organization which encourages, even enforces, behaviour of this kind will not enhance the overall performance of the firm. Seen from the dispassionate perspective of overall performance, rather than the sometimes more limited view of those who happen to be directing an organization at a given point in time, control is simply a means of securing an objective like all the other functions of management. Running a tight ship is no good if it is heading for the rocks and none of the crew dares, or is motivated, to do anything about it.

The balance between orderly administration and unity of action, on the one hand, and the encouragement of initiative and a full contribution from the employees of an organization, on the other, is a difficult one to strike. This becomes a matter for judgement when choosing between structural approaches to control. Three basic choices are involved here: (a) between centralization and delegation, (b) between formalization and informality, and (c) between a heavy supervisory emphasis, reflected in narrow spans of control and a high proportion of managers to total employees, and a light supervisory emphasis.

Centralization or delegation?

I have expressed the choice in these terms because a great deal of confusion has surrounded the term 'decentralization'. For some people, decentralization implies participation or devolution; that is, an extension of control from the top of a hierarchical system to lower levels. For others, the term suggests divisionalization, which in fact normally involves delegation but not necessarily any significant transfer of control. The definitions I shall follow, are, first that centralization is a condition where the upper levels of an organization's hierarchy retain the authority to take most decisions. Second, delegation is a particular meaning of the term 'decentralization' and describes a condition when the authority to make specified decisions is passed down to units and people at lower levels in the organization's hierarchy.

Centralization and delegation are not simple dichotomies. There is a considerable choice of possibilities and variations in between. For example it will probably be sensible to delegate routine operational decisions, while it is unlikely that non-routine and strategic decisions will be delegated to any marked degree. Also a divisionalized organization which has operational decisions delegated to divisional heads may at the same time have highly centralized divisions — this has sometimes been a source of considerable complaint among divisional departmental managers. Another point is that centralization and delegation as discussed here refer to the taking of decisions rather than to the involvement of people in preparing the ground or in implementing them. These other aspects involve questions of participation and integration which were discussed in the previous chapter.

Both centralization and delegation are strategies for maintaining control, and each has certain advantages which have to be traded-off in the light of the needs a given organization has to cope with in its particular circumstances. Centralization is an approach where control is exercised by confining decision-making to a small group of senior people or even one man. In other words, no-one else has the right to act on his own account and discretion. Delegation is an approach where decision-making is passed downwards and outwards within the formal structure, but where there are strict limits imposed on the scope and type of decisions that can be made without referral upwards. For example, a formal rule which states that 'You, as manager of X department can spend up to £500 on consumable items without having to obtain the signature of the manager above you so long as that expenditure falls within the limits of your monthly budget.' One can see that, although the decision has been passed down the hierarchy, the attempt to maintain overall control is very clearly incorporated into the arrangement.

What are the main trade-offs between centralization and delegation? These have been reviewed in a very useful article by an American professor, Howard Carlisle in the *Advanced Management Journal* for July 1974, and I shall draw upon his work. The arguments for centralization are:

1 If decisions are made at one point or among a small group of managers it is easier to co-ordinate the activities of the sub-units or individuals who report up to senior management. If, for example, a company is promoting several different product lines to the same

consumer market, centralization will make it easier to establish a co-ordinated programme.

2 From their position in the organization, senior managers have a broad organization-wide perspective on what is going on and how far this conforms to policies which have been agreed and established. They are therefore in a better position to make decisions which will accord with these policies and be consistent with the interests of the entire organization. This will avoid a loss of control due to people at lower levels making decisions which are optimal for their department or sub-unit but sub-optimal for the organization as a whole.

3 Closely related to the previous argument is the fact that centralized control provides a way of keeping the various functional areas of an organization—marketing, production, research and development, finance—in an appropriate balance one with the other. This can be done by centralizing decisions on resource allocation, on functional policies, targets, and so forth.

4 Centralization can economize on managerial overheads. It can avoid the duplication of activities or resources if similar activities are carried on independently by, say, different divisions within the same organization. Also, the centralization of management may allow for certain staff or specialist support personnel to be justified in desirable areas, whereas if management were more dispersed among segments of the organization it might be difficult for any one segment to justify employing its own staff or specialist personnel. This is one reason why functions such as planning, purchasing, legal and personnel are often centralized, feeding in to a senior management level where the major decisions on such matters are taken. This argument is, of course, part of the case for a functional grouping of activities discussed in Chapter 4.

5 Top managers are generally proven by the time they reach senior positions, and they normally have more experience than other employees. It is arguable, therefore, that they should be particularly capable of making good decisions and exercising appropriate judgement—this speaks for centralized control.

6 Finally, when strong leadership is required as in times of crisis and keen external pressures, centralization encourages this by focusing power, authority and prestige onto a central key position or senior group. It affords an opportunity for speedy decision-making in reaction to unexpected crises because of the advantages of centralized communication and co-ordination already mentioned.

To set against these factors which speak in favour of centralization, ther are other considerations in support of the opposite policy, one of delegation. These may be summarized as follows:

1 One of the complaints of senior managers is that they become over-burdened and cannot cope with all the matters that require their attention. In a comparison of average working hours among British and American managers which I published with Brenda Macmillan in the *Journal of Management Studies* for May 1972, this problem appeared to be most acute for top American executives some of whom were clocking up 80 to 90 hours per week in the office plus undertaking business-related social engagements. The problem was less marked among British managers, but in both countries it was senior people who worked longer hours on the job. If top executives are overloaded then the effective control they can exercise will be diminished and/or they will tend to sit on decisions which may require speedy attention. This is one of the most powerful arguments in favour of a delegated system and it obviously carries most weight in conditions of large-scale operations, complexity, rapid change and other features which add to the decision-making load of executives. Delegation can relieve some of this burden and make an organization function more effectively by leaving senior managers with more time for policy matters of longer-term consequence.

2 There are motivational considerations which speak in favour of delegation. Behavioural scientists have long argued that most people are willing to give more to their jobs when they have a high degree of individual freedom, discretion and control over their work. This assumes that their own personal goals are broadly in line with those contained in corporate policies, though many psychologists would argue that commitment to corporate goals is most likely to be generated when the individual feels he is obtaining something personally worthwhile from his job. The opportunity to make decisions and be involved can help to provide such personal satisfaction and commitment. This case for delegation is put to a particularly severe test in situations where people's tasks are closely interdependent with those of others. The question then arises whether all concerned will be sufficiently motivated and committed to integrate their activities without centralized direction.

3 Management involves judgement, the ability to cope with uncertainty and other attributes which are developed through having appropriate experience. Delegation of responsibility, as in the divisional structure where profit responsibility is attached to divisional managers, has proved valuable to many organizations in helping them to develop their stock of managers capable of assuming

'general management' positions. Delegation, then, can be a powerful aid to management development.

4 Delegation generally permits greater flexibility—more rapid response to change—at operating levels in organizations because decisions do not have to be referred up the hierarchy unless they are exceptional in nature. This advantage becomes particularly marked in the larger organization where hierarchies are likely to be more extended (and communication up and down will be slower) and where a greater number of matters are likely to crop up for decision over a given period of time.

5 There is a further consideration, related to the point just made. The person immediately involved with the problem will usually be more aware of local conditions or other relevant circumstances than will a senior man, sometimes several levels removed, who sits at headquarters and is naturally more remote. So long as he is aware of, understands and accepts corporate policies, the man on the spot is likely to make better decisions. A problem sometimes arising here is that the matter requiring attention has longer-term policy implications. In this case, delegated decision-making could lead to inconsistencies in actions taken on behalf of the organization, and these might clearly have serious consequences.

6 Finally, by establishing relatively independent sub-units within an organization where middle managers and even supervisors are responsible for their own operations, delegation can result in more effective controls and performance measurement. This is because separate spheres of responsibility can be identified and control systems applied to these units in order to provide more adequate feedback to higher management. For example, costs can be identified with, and allocated to, particular operations and responsibility is then rendered much more specific. Much the same control advantage was seen to accompany job enrichment schemes which gave employees the responsibility for producing distinguishable units of work rather than for minute partial tasks only. In the divisionalized form of organization discussed in Chapter 4, semi-autonomous units are normally established with profit responsibility, and local management is given a high degree of operational independence so long as its division meets profit targets. Sometimes divisions will be set up in parallel on a competitive basis as a stimulus to performance, and corporate management then in effect acts as a capital market in terms of allocating finance and controlling its use through an assessment of rates of return. This may serve to restore some characteristics of the free competitive market where these have otherwise been severely weakened by oligopoly.

It has become apparent, even from this brief review, that much of the choice between centralization and delegation has to be made in the light of specific conditions and situations. In a military situation where surprise and an immediate response to surprise are usually vital, the flexibility offered by delegated control is in most cases more effective. While a small army can sometimes operate effectively under the centralized control of a dynamic and tireless leader (and here one is thinking of ancient rather than modern times), modern large armies cannot proceed in this manner without serious liability. A good example emerges from the Middle East War of 1973 in the comparison between the remarkable adaptiveness of the small collection of a few brigades which under General Arik Sharon crossed over to the west bank of the Suez Canal working out their own tactics as they advanced day by day, and the paralysis which affected the centralized Egyptian Army. A considerable time elapsed before the Egyptian Commander-in-Chief, General Ismail, knew what was happening and by then it was too late. The following remarks by the *Sunday Times* Insight Team provide an interesting commentary on the relative virtues of centralized and decentralized control under conditions of the extremely variable environment of open war about which Rommel said 'Speed of reaction in command decides the battle':

> There was no Egyptian equivalent to the incessant Israeli patrol and reconnaissance activity. Junior commanders simply fought the Israelis as and when they presented themselves, and gave no priority at all to making combat reports (feedback). And even divisional commanders—men on the equivalent level to Arik Sharon—had little independence of action. The effect was that there were no real command centres closer to the fighting than Ismail's war room. An Egyptian officer, when asked, after the war, who had been the overall *field* commander, replied that it was Ismail, sitting in front of his multi-coloured maps. (*Sunday Times*, 30th December 1973, p.30)

The choice between centralized and delegated control must be made, first, in respect of different types of decisions which will vary in their strategic importance, and secondly, for the whole range of organizational decisions in the light of contingencies and capabilities which apply to the organization and its context *in toto*.

In studies I have carried out within British companies, and in investigations of a similar nature carried out by Professor Alfred Kieser in West Germany, the degree of centralization or delegation was assessed comparatively for a range of separate decisions. Strategic decisions, such as determining a new product or service, spending unallocated sums on capital items, and creating new sub-units within the organization tended to be taken at board and/or chief executive levels. In contrast, operational decisions to do with matters such as the methods of work to be used or when overtime was to be worked were considerably more delegated, usually to a supervisory or superintendent level in British firms and to a superintendent or production manager level in German firms. These differences in the degree of centralization as between different types of decisions are clearly sensible and reflect the intrinsic weight and long-term effects of the decision. However, this need to differentiate between decisions is a point which not all writers on the subject have taken into account. It is once again part of management's need to strike a balance.

Professor Carlisle, in the article cited, distinguishes thirteen variables which are of primary importance in 'determining the need for a centralized or decentralized structure'—that is, whether the approach to control should veer towards centralization or delegation over the whole range of decisions to be taken. Certain of these thirteen variables are more pervasive contingencies than others and I shall single out a few—size of organization, geographical dispersion of operations, technology and type of operating environment. The full list presented and discussed by Carlisle is:

1 The basic purpose and goals of the organization.

2 The knowledge and experience of top level managers.

3 The skill, knowledge, and attitudes of subordinates.

4 The scale or size of the organization.

5 The geographical dispersion of the organization.

6 The scientific content or the technology of the tasks being performed.

7 The time frame of the decisions to be made.

8 The significance of the decisions to be made.

9 The degree to which subordinates will accept and are motivated by the decisions to be made.

10 The status of the organization's planning and control systems.

11 The status of the organization's information systems.

12 The degree of conformity and co-ordination required in the tasks and operations of the organization.

13 The status of external environmental factors such as governments, trade unions, etc. (Carlisle, op.cit., p. 15)

Centralization, delegation and contingencies

The larger an organization, the more likely it is that a centralized approach to control will generate top management overload. One of the most difficult transitions for the young firm that is growing up comes when the chief executive, who may be the founder, has to hand over some of the reins to his subordinates. Many are reluctant to do so, out of a fear of losing control, insufficient confidence in the ability of others, or just sheer stubborn pride. But unless some adjustment in the system of control is made, it is almost certain that the continued growth and development of the organization will be held back. As an organization grows, the more difficult it becomes for any one executive or top management team to have the time or knowledge to make all major decisions. These decisions will become more frequent and demanding, since not only will the scale of operations be so much greater but they are quite likely to be more diversified and complex as well (more products, more geographical markets, and so on). So, large organizations are forced to move towards delegation in order to keep their wheels turning and it is quite clear from the results of comparative research studies that this connection between size and delegation is generally found to operate in practice.

Geographical dispersion is another contingent factor which sets up pressures for delegation. The more scattered an organization's operating sites, the more difficult it is for any one individual to keep an eye on the details of what is going on elsewhere. The costs of communicating such details and referring decisions to the centre rise as the number of locations increases, and the delays which would ensue become intolerable. A further consideration is that junior managers in scattered or more remote locations are in a better position to make decisions relating to their activities, because they know local conditions well and are therefore able to assess the circumstances of any issue that arises.

Large size and geographical dispersion, which in practice generally go together as attributes of organizational development, can be seen in these ways to generate greater structural complexity which sets up pressures for delegation. Complexity in its various forms is quite significant for the decision on how far to delegate. To take another aspect of complexity, technical complexity, it has been found that companies in science-based industries such as electronics and pharmaceuticals tend to have a greater overall degree of delegation than is found in other companies not handling advanced product technologies and not employing such a high proportion of experts capable of making operational decisions.

The technology employed and type of environment being served are relevant to decisions on control because of the requirements for information processing they impose. Where an organization is providing products or services under relatively stable conditions, it may (other factors being equal) be in a favourable position to operate a centralized system of control since its information processing requirements are relatively routine and probably not too intensive. In that case, decisions can be referred up the hierarchy and any delay this entails may be tolerable. For this reason, I have found in the studies just mentioned that organizations operating a more integrated type of production technology producing standardized products tend to be more centralized (allowing for variations in their size and other factors), while organizations having to utilize a more flexible, less integrated technology under conditions of some change (such as one-off production) tended to be more decentralized.

Other investigators have found a similar connection in practice between the degree of delegation and information processing requirements, whether such requirements are assessed by reference to their source in the environment (stable or dynamic market, technical and social conditions) or by reference to the way they affect how the work is done (technology). Although the size of the organization we are talking about makes a significant difference here, generally speaking it seems that stable conditions permit a higher degree of centralization and the delegation of less authority down the hierarchy than do rapidly changing and less predictable environments. It is only in the quite small organization that a concentration of decision-making in one man's hands makes for superior adaptation to external changes. As an example of the disasters it can perpetrate in a large organization witness the incapable German military response to pressures in the latter half of the last world war.

Formalization or informality?

Another means of controlling the behaviour of an organization's employees — that is, rendering their activities more predictable in a desired direction — is to establish written policies, procedures, rules, job definitions, and standing orders which prescribe correct or expected action, and then to back these up with systems for the documented recording of what has taken place in the way of communication and performance. These devices are all marks of formalization, known less affectionately as 'red tape'.

Formalization is not so much an alternative to moves along the centralization dimension as a complement in conditions where it becomes desirable to delegate. Given the investment in time required to establish a highly formalized system of administration and the fact that rules and procedures once established tend to take on a life of their own, formalization is clearly an approach best suited to conditions of relative stability. While all organizations require both some stability and some change, the question is in what proportion? Formalization can be relatively advantageous or disadvantageous depending on what balance between change and stability needs to be struck. While conformity to the demands of the job and predictability are essential in any organization, such conformity should not be blind since the consequent loss of initiative is a serious cost to the organization.

One of the facts of life for organizations is that as they grow they become more formalized. Research studies which have measured the degree of formalization in organizations have shown that a knowledge of their total employees alone permits one to predict their level of formalization with a reasonable degree of accuracy (over 50% of the variation in formalization is predicted by size alone in manufacturing concerns). Just as growth sets up pressures for delegation, so it is also accompanied by formalization. Ross Webber, writing in *Business Horizons*, April 1969, on 'Red Tape Versus Chaos' describes how this process took place in the Xerox Company:

> From 1958 to the present, the old family-dominated Haloid Company, manufacturing specialized photographic products, was transformed into the modern Xerox Company, which jumped from $27 million to over $700 million a year in revenue.
>
> In the late 1950's, the company was in a chaotic state. . . . Job descriptions were few, policies broad, procedures ignored, and controls weak. Yet the company was successful; it was successful because of top management's ability to define direction. Joseph Wilson, the president, spent much of his time selling the Xerox Company to his own managers, describing the revolutionary and beneficial impact of its information technology on society, and also pointing out how each manager's own interest would be served if the company advanced. (pp 47-48).

At this stage in the company's development, a lack of formalization encouraged its management to take initiatives — a premature introduction of procedures would have interfered with the spontaneous, innovative organic type of approach that was being followed successfully. The company began to grow rapidly and formalization began to develop accordingly. Once the market for its new technology had been opened up and expansion got underway, Xerox management's main concern turned to internal costs and efficiency. Decisions became more complex and more people had to be involved; procedures were set up to make sure that information reached everyone concerned, that contributions were co-ordinated and that the best methods (once established) were recorded. Webber gives an example of this rationale and what it entails:

> A Xerox research and development engineer has indicated how elaboration of procedures has affected him. In 1959 when he had an idea that required funds, he would walk into the office of the vice-president with a scratch pad and pencil, sit down, and sketch out the

> idea. A decision would be made quickly, and the researcher would begin working. Today, the same researcher must complete in multiple copies a regulation project form indicating potential equipment cost, material requirements, potential return, cash flow, and on and on. This is not simple red tape; multiple forms are not prescribed just to complicate the lives of people in the organization. Decisions about fund allocation are much more complex than in an earlier and simpler day. More and different projects are involved — they must be compared with one another on some consistent basis; and priority decisions must be reached with regard to organization objectives. Standard procedures for capital fund applications facilitate comparison, prediction, and control, essential functions of management in any organization. (pp 48-49).

Formalization assists control, and co-ordination, in the ways just described, in circumstances where there can be a substantial area of stability in an organization's activities. When an organization grows and centralized control becomes less and less effective, formalization serves to establish a framework of rules and systems within which decision-making can be delegated with reasonably predictable results. In fact, it has been found that large business organizations which combine delegation and formalization as their strategy of control tend to perform better on financial criteria than do equally large companies which are more centralized and less formalized. Environment and the nature of the business are, of course, relevant too, and a large firm operating in a dynamic environment can find itself in special difficulties since its size speaks for high formalization while its need to remain innovative and adaptive speaks for low formalization. Many have commented on the lack of innovativeness among large firms, and this structural dilemma has a lot to do with it.

When formalization is newly introduced into an organization, or increased, it is apt to be met with resistance. Not only are people's established informal ways of doing things threatened but also they are likely to view the intervention of formal systems as an attempt to reduce their discretion, even if the intention is only to improve co-ordination or information retrieval. If formalized controls are resented for this reason, or because they are overtight and misdirected, then the people affected will probably respond by rejecting the controls and their avowed purpose in ways that could range from paying lip-service to active sabotage, supplying false data and so forth. There are plenty of examples in industry and public life of how procedures when followed to the letter become self-defeating — 'working to rule'. 'Making out with the pencil' is also familiar enough, where achievement of expected standards is recorded on paper but the reality falls far short. An interesting case study of the problems that can arise with the introduction of formalization has been written by my colleagues John Berridge and Peter Tebbit on the basis of their experience in the hospital service — this is attached as an appendix to this chapter.

In the case study, which is based upon a real life situation, a Medical Records Filing Department in an urban hospital is faced with a substantially increased load of work when the hospital takes over additional outpatient duties. The department functioned in an informal and relatively autonomous manner, with considerable flexibility in manning. It enjoyed high morale and gave good performance. The department was in effect operating as a semi-autonomous work group. Nevertheless, the view adopted by the hospital authorities was that because of an increasing scale of work the department would benefit from the introduction of more formalization, in terms of formal procedures, working instructions and systems. The intention was also to increase managerial control — to 'get a grip' on matters as the man introducing formalization put it. The consequences of increasing formalization, and of the way this was done, were far from those anticipated, as can be read in the case. This case also serves to illustrate some of the problems of introducing change, which are discussed in Chapter 8.

Formalization may become necessary, but it carries dangers with it such as the type of non-acceptance by staff that I have just described. There are other points to guard against as well. If formal procedures, routines and plans are followed blindly, then an organization will lose direction. This is the much discussed 'displacement of goals by means' which critics hold out to be the hallmark of a bureaucracy (itself the epitome of the formalized organization). For example, the German war machine in 1914 felt committed to follow the Schlieffen Plan which had been meticulously drawn up years before, even when it became clear that the price of this rigidity was Britain's involvement in the war. The staff of some social welfare agencies investigated by American researchers have been found to adhere to procedures and formal performance criteria even when this was clearly contrary to the best interests of individual clients.

The problem is that once they become established and accepted, standing plans and procedures work to close out alternative perspectives and options — 'the matter is settled; it cannot be re-opened'. The advantages of control which are gained when plans and procedures are newly formulated, and hence particularly relevant to the situation, may be lost if the appropriateness of these provisions in changed circumstances is not reviewed at frequent intervals. The more change that the organization is experiencing the more frequent this review should be.

A note on supervisory emphasis

Another method of control in an organization is to supervise activities closely at each level. This is not the same as centralization, for close supervision does not necessarily mean that decisions are taken only at the upper levels of the hierarchy. The purpose of close supervision, from the perspective of control, is akin to that of formalization in that limits are set to the legitimate discretion of subordinates. Yet, again, close supervision is not the same as formalization even in principle. It can be used as a substitute for formalization or as a complement to it in situations where it is felt necessary to check that employees are keeping to formally laid down rules or job specifications.

The notion of 'supervisory emphasis' makes reference to the narrowness of managerial spans of control and to the proportion of managers and supervisors in the overall employment of an organization. These two features are inversely related in an organization of constant size. As was seen in Chapter 3, a high supervisory emphasis might be required for reasons other than that of maintaining control, if, for example, a manager had to co-ordinate widely disparate types of activity. As a means of control, though, supervisory emphasis incurs the significant disadvantages of overhead cost, loss of employee motivation and attenuation of organizational hierarchy with concurrent communication problems. Modern thinking on organization therefore tends to favour moves towards a reduction of supervisory emphasis and the encouragement where possible of 'self-control' by those doing the work.

Strategies of control compared

Centralization-delegation, formalization-informality and the degree of supervisory emphasis are three major structural dimensions of control. The appropriate position for an organization to adopt on each dimension will vary according to its circumstances. These dimensions are not, however, independent of each other, but in fact serve complementary functions for management. In particular, the use of formalization as a means to 'structure' the activities of people within an organization may facilitate both an increase in delegation and a reduction of close supervision.

In an interesting study of five Canadian post-secondary community colleges, Heron and Friesen examined the relative use of these three control dimensions over the period of college growth and development. This is practically the only study so far to have recorded such data over time on a comparative basis. What it showed was that as the colleges grew larger:

1 Their degree of formalization increased fairly steadily;

2 Their degree of delegation increased overall, but was reduced for a while during growth;

3 Their 'supervisory emphasis' (low first-line supervisory span of

control and higher percentage of managers to total employees) at first rose in step with delegation and subsequently tended to fall.

These relationships point to a number of tentative conclusions. First, the difference between small, young and larger, older organizations was marked. The small, young organization tended to be highly centralized, to have little formalization, and not a great amount of close supervision. As growth proceeded, delegation increased, but this was accompanied by a rise in close supervision and, after a while, by a rise in formalization. Then a crisis of control appears to have been reached in which formalization was increased sharply, delegation decreased, but supervisory emphasis declined. At this point, it seems that formalization was rapidly being instituted as a control strategy in place of reliance on direct supervision and that while formal procedures and job definition were being implemented some degree of re-centralized decision-taking had to compensate for the relative reduction in direct supervision. In later stages of development, formalization tended to increase fairly steadily, delegation was re-instituted and extended, and the degree of supervisory emphasis grew once more before stabilizing.

These interpretations are extremely tentative and go beyond those which Heron and Friesen have felt it appropriate to offer. They serve to make the point, however, that management is faced with some choice in its structural approach to control, in that different configurations are possible along the three dimensions identified. This choice will probably be constrained by the situation prevailing, but may nonetheless allow for some expression of what is felt to be a desirable managerial philosophy. Both from the point of view of meeting new employee expectations and of allowing sufficient flexibility to cope with contemporary rates of change, there is in fact today a growing interest in finding ways of promoting self-control and relaxing all three structural control mechanisms.

From overcontrol to self-control

The Egyptian Army was almost paralyzed in its response to Arik Sharon's thrust across the Suez Canal because it was overcontrolled for the fast moving situation it faced. Not only was its command structure highly centralized, but it relied on too much formalization as well. In peacetime, for example, communication followed elaborate formal procedures, involving large amounts of paperwork. Rather than being modified to accommodate the stresses of war, the system just broke down. In order to mount a combined reactive operation between two Egyptian army groups, it was necessary first to circulate orders bearing signatures from four different staff officers.

A high degree of centralization can be just as inimical to initiative among those excluded from decision-making as can excessive formalization. In research I conducted among some eighty British companies which also involved about 800 of their senior managers at the first two levels below chief executive, it became clear that retaining decision-making on policy matters above their heads had these effects. In centralized organizations, these managers perceived themselves (probably quite accurately) as having relatively little authority and a high degree of routine in their jobs. Their attitudes towards the system of authority characterizing their company, and towards innovation, were significantly more cautious, conformist and allied to the *status quo* than was the case with managers in companies practising greater delegation. As individuals, they appeared to have adjusted to the situation in which they found themselves (those with more initiative may, of course, have left long before), since they were far less inclined to express a willingness to take risks or to feel capable of handling variety and uncertainty in their work than was true of managers in less centralized companies. It appears, then, that centralized control runs the risk of generating a body of 'yes men' who would not have the capacity or the personality to step up into the hot seat themselves if something went wrong.

Formalization has also attracted misgivings: those of behavioural scientists who point to a fundamental conflict between formal organizational controls and the desire that many people have to express themselves and use their full capacities at work. The growing strength of that desire among the better educated younger employees of today is taken to be a powerful argument for job enrichment, whereby they are given work which is not only more interesting intrinsically but which also affords opportunities to make decisions, take initiatives and assume responsibility for these. Earlier assumptions about human motivation which underline many currently practised varieties of formalization may well have to be revised if managements are to retain the commitment of employees. While it was always true that formalized controls enforced unthinkingly for their own sake are counterproductive, a new factor is that more people today are willing and able to exercise self-control rather than having to accept externally enforced control.

Self-control, the following of strongly internalized norms of competence and conduct, has long been the mark of the professional. Professional people, more than any other group, resent having administrative controls imposed on them when they become employees of large institutions, as many now have. The proportion of professional and trained manpower in the working population of most societies is steadily increasing, and this in itself is establishing the requirement for a new approach to control. The question which faces management today is whether it is not timely to encourage their other employees to develop a similar mode of self-control within parameters worked out through discussion and negotiation. Experiments in 'autonomous group working' are a move in this direction.

In the context of increased industrial democracy and participation, it is likely that we shall see further moves away from centralization and towards a framework of mutually agreed methods of working rather than managerially imposed formalization. The nature of acceptable control will have to change along with changes in what people will accept as legitimate. It is likely that in the future we shall see more attempts to develop self-control on the basis of setting agreed objectives. This approach to control will involve responsibility on the part of self-managing units or teams for meeting agreed targets and completing projects. The teams' self-management will be assisted by a more frequent feedback to them of information on their progress as against targets, budgets and so forth. At longer intervals, they will evaluate their progress with higher management. The principle here is rather similar to the relations between head office and divisions in a large decentralized multidivisional enterprise.

This approach to control can only work with agreement on operating objectives. It therefore depends upon the presence of some shared culture among the members of an organization, and it is interesting to note the great effort which many large divisionalized companies are investing in building a common culture among their managers as a means to ensuring some predictability of behaviour and commitment to central corporate goals. If the approach is successful, however, it may sustain a common outlook among people far more effectively than more traditional centralized or formalized systems of control. For it offers what is probably the only way of reconciling the underlying need for the management process with the desire for more participation and self-fulfilment on the part of employees. It is also the type of control that seems best suited to handle the increasing rate of industrial change and uncertainty, where new markets, projects, processes, techniques and other developments become a way of life. In such conditions, specialist employees rather than higher management become the font of required knowledge and information, and traditional bureaucratic formalization with its built-in delayed action cannot cope with the speed of information processing and response that is required.

Summary

Control is an element of management which has received considerable attention in writing and debate. On the whole, control has been regarded as a process flowing down from the apex of hierarchies, and it is the directive element concerned with the giving of instructions which has been singled out. Today, there is somewhat more appreciation that effective control requires a positive commitment from employees if instructions are to be followed and accurate feedback secured on results.

The main organizational design decisions concerned with control are, first, how far to delegate decision-making, second, how much to formalize procedures and working practices and third, how much emphasis to place on direct supervision. The usual approach to delegation involves a formal specification of the limits to decision-making in order to preserve some consistency for predictability in behaviour. Formalization may also be a substitute for direct supervision. With changes in occupational structure and educational levels, however, the attitudes of employees towards managerial control are changing, and many spokesmen are calling for a more substantial devolution of decision-making within organizations. This development, together with the findings of research into motivation, is creating interest in methods of achieving self-control among employees on the basis of agreements with management to meet certain objectives or performance standards.

Suggested further reading

Two useful articles referred to in this chapter are Howard M. Carlisle, 'A Contingency Approach to Decentralization', *Advanced Management Journal*, July 1974, and Ross A. Webber, 'Red Tape versus Chaos', *Business Horizons*, April 1969. Chris Argyris, *Personality and Organization* (Harper and Row 1957), analyses the areas of conflict between management control and employee motivation. The author's paper 'Strategies of Control and Organizational Behaviour', *Administrative Science Quarterly*, March 1973, explores the association between centralization and formalization, on the one hand, and the behaviour of managers on the other.

Also mentioned was R. P. Heron and D. Friesen, 'Organizational Growth and Development' (University of Alberta, Edmonton, Canada, working paper March 1976). An informative history of a developing approach towards control in a large corporation, General Electric, is recorded in Ronald G. Greenwood, *Managerial Decentralization* (Lexington Books 1974).

Appendix to Chapter 6 Medical records at Anersley Hospital*

Anersley Hospital is a long-stay psychiatric and geriatric hospital of some 800 beds. It sprawls across an extensive site in a suburb of a large town; its many piecemeal additions over the past seventy years have no architectural distinction. Many of them are wood and metal huts and buildings erected during the 1939-45 war. During the last three years the hospital has

*This case was prepared by J. R. K. Berridge and P. R. Tebbit, University of Aston Management Centre.

become a centre for psychiatric treatment in the town and surrounding region, as small peripheral hospitals and wards are closed down in a rationalization programme. The number of beds in the hospital has declined as more patients are treated on an outpatient basis, and the concept of community care spreads. But outpatient clinics conversely have become a much more major part of Anersley Hospital's activities, and new facilities have been built to cater for the greatly increased number of outpatients.

The rather unplanned and erratic nature of Anersley Hospital's expansion was reflected in the haphazard siting of facilities and departments. Perhaps the Medical Records Filing Department was one of the worst examples of this. It was at the end of a long corridor on the extremity of the hospital buildings, right away from clinics, appointment clerks, or the rest of the Medical Records work. It was accommodated in a large wooden hut — one of a series leading off this corridor, and now mainly used as stores. The hut was dilapidated on the outside, but inside it had been made cheerful by the colourful posters and cartoons that the staff had pinned on the walls, and other touches of homeliness and individuality. An example of this was the hand-painted sign on the door above the official 'Medical Records Filing Department'. It simply read 'The Shack'. The desks and equipment in the Filing Department were equally worn and out of date, and the actual filing racks were a home-made selection of miscellaneous designs of varying ages that had just accumulated over the years. The physical layout is shown in Figure 6.1.

Working methods had also apparently evolved over time, and there were no procedures or systems. Patients' records were collected and returned quite informally by a variety of staff, nurses, clerks, orderlies and porters; the only security seemed to be whether they were known to the staff of the filing department. Sometimes clerks or porters who came regularly for records and knew the methods of filing would ask permission to help themselves to records if the filing clerks were particularly busy. Appointment clerks from the outpatient clinics would often come down casually to the filing department some two or three days before a clinic and jointly with the filing clerk search out the records needed, having a pleasant chat at the same time. Conversely, it was not unknown for a filing clerk to make a private arrangement with an appointments clerk to assist with the running of a clinic if things were busy at that end of the hospital. The surprising thing to a stranger was that the filing department worked markedly well. The success rate in finding records was very high, even those old, odd elusive ones. The degree of co-operation with consultant and nursing staff was high — there was never any quibbling about demands for records at awkward times, or at the last minute when extra patients attended a clinic. Undoubtedly the filing department worked on good memories and easy personal relationships, but it did work!

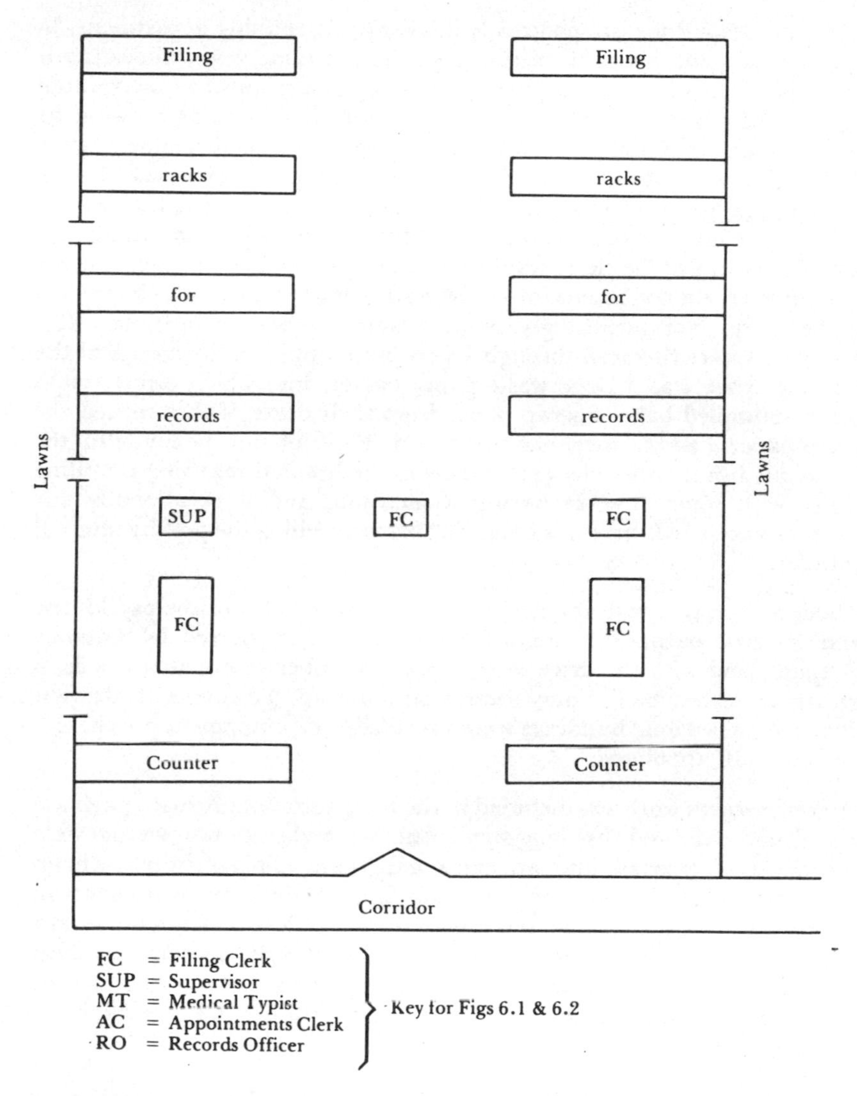

Figure 6.1

Mrs. Price is senior medical record clerk. She has been employed in medical records at the hospital for nearly thirty years, and has been in charge of the filing section for about eight years. Everybody in the hospital seems to know her, and she is liked for her equable temperament and pleasant disposition. Four female medical record clerks report to her, and she in turn reported to the Hospital Secretary under the previous structure, although this was changed about a year ago.

Although Mrs. Price was nominally in charge of the filing department, in practice, she and her four assistants all did the same work, allocating it amongst themselves in approximately equal proportions by mutual agreement. There never seemed to be any problem of keeping up with the constant stream of filing and requests, even with the added volume of work due to the new outpatient clinics. In a busy period, people would work through tea-breaks, and in slack spells they would liaise (that is, gossip) with their counterparts in other departments. At teatime, mornings and afternoons, one of the clerks would slip out down the road to a local bakery and bring cream doughnuts for all the staff plus any visitors who happened to be there. Not surprisingly, visitors were frequent happenings! The doughnuts were financed through a peculiar custom. In the corner of the working space was a large waste-paper basket, into which clerks would throw crumpled balls of scrap paper from their desks; if they missed the waste-paper basket, they had to pay a 'Fine' of one penny into the doughnut fund. Other clerical workers in the hospital regarded the filing clerks with some envy as having a nice job, and if occasionally any vacancies occurred there was never any problem filling the post by internal transfer.

About a year ago, with the decision to centralize many of the psychiatric and geriatric outpatient clinics for the conurbation served by Anersley Hospital, and with the drive to reduce the number of in-patient beds, a greatly increased load of outpatient work built up. To cope with the new demands, new clinic buildings were provided, new equipment purchased, and new staff appointed.

Medical records work was included in the reorganization. A spare pavillion was found (vacated by long-stay patients) and the two wards were expensively converted into an extra outpatient clinic facility with an integrated medical records department. The physical layout is shown in Figure 6.2. All the planning and design work was done at Regional Board level, with the liaison of the secretary in the Anersley Hospital at local level. The pavillion was completely rebuilt, tastefully decorated, carpeted, air-conditioned and equipped with the latest furniture, office equipment and filing racks.

An organization and methods study had confirmed the obvious inefficiencies of the old scattered medical records department. Medical records had been at one end of the hospital, and outpatient clinics and appointment clerks (effectively under the control of departmental sisters) at the other end. The medical secretaries had been located in several small offices around the hospital (for instance in small rooms attached to the wards where they could be at close hand for doctors) and frequently were unoccupied, due to lack of work in their sections. All three (records, appointments, and secretarial) were thus gathered together for reasons of economy and convenience in obtaining and processing documents.

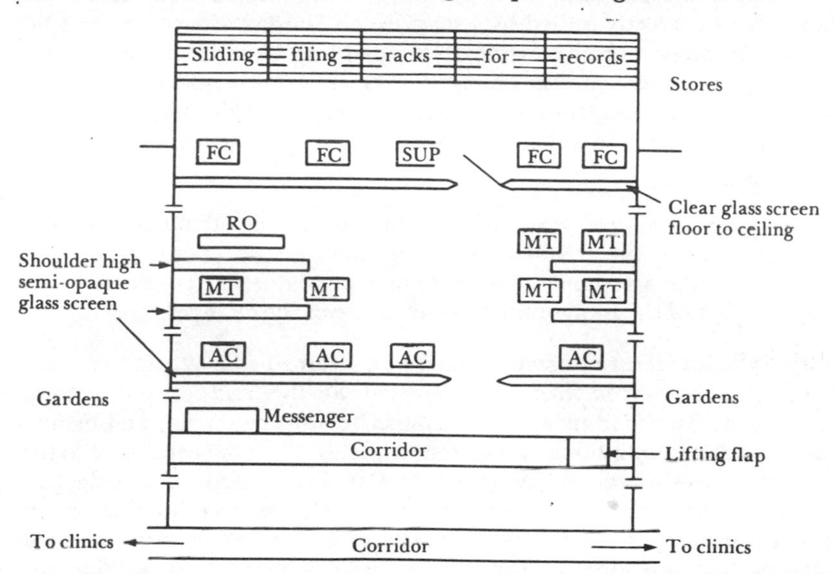

Figure 6.2

Just before all these alterations were completed, a group medical records officer was appointed to be in charge of the integrated department, and to supervise the changeover and start-up of the new system. The appointee was Mr. Fraser.

He is in his 40s and is an alert individual who is well informed about the technicalities of his job. He is keen to improve the medical records service. He earned a good reputation in his previous job as records officer in a smaller hospital. Mr. Fraser very quickly worked out master plans for the detailed operation of the new department, and for the transfer of equipment, records and personnel to the new office. He spent a considerable amount of time liaising with the regional design and organization and methods team so that he appreciated the finer points of their designs and recommendations and could use the equipment to the full. Then he converted this information into working instructions for the staff to follow in advance so that everyone should know her task as soon as she moved over. The actual movement of the records was his masterpiece of planning, and quite painless for the other staff — to such an extent that the Group Secretary congratulated Mr. Fraser on the continuation of the records service with scarcely any disruption. Friday clinics were cancelled that week; the records staff cleared up all outstanding documents on Friday morning — and then were given Friday afternoon off as a holiday. At 1.00 p.m. a veritable army of porters and helpers descended on the records office. With the hospital secretary and Mr. Fraser in charge following the master plan, every document was removed right across the hospital and correctly refiled by 4.00 p.m. on Sunday afternoon. At 8.00 a.m. on Monday morning medical records filing department started up again as if nothing had ever changed. The removal team knew the new locations and routines from the working instructions that Mr. Fraser had issued, and he was on hand all the time to issue supplementary instructions over any problems.

Working methods were very different in the new department, but Mr. Fraser had taken the trouble before the move to get people trained in advance through a series of instruction meetings which he conducted with every member of the filing staff. Here are some of the changes.

So that a real measure of security could be retained over records, a floor-to-ceiling glass screen had been erected at the end of the records department. All the filing clerks had desks behind the screen, and behind them were the sliding filing racks, shiny and new. The only entrance to the filing area was through one door next to Mrs. Price's desk – and she had precise orders from Mr. Fraser to admit only persons holding senior administrative positions in the hospital and whose names were on a list which he had provided for her. Reciprocally, it was laid down that the filing clerks were allowed to leave only at designated times, unless in exceptional circumstances. Anyone wanting records had to bring an authorization to a sliding window beside Mrs. Price's desk, hand the request over to her, and she would allocate it to one of the clerks. In practice, almost all requests were brought by the medical records messenger, a man who had been appointed when the new department was opened for duties of receiving demands from wards and departments, transmitting them to Mrs. Price, subsequently collecting them from her and taking them to the ward or department. Several of the filing clerks questioned the reason for this procedure when Mr. Fraser was instructing each of them at pre-move training sessions. He explained the need for professional standards of security with records – citing the unfortunate case that had befallen him some years earlier when a drunken porter had recited some rather explicit case notes to an enthralled audience in the 'spit and sawdust' bar of a local pub!

In many other ways, the new methods introduced by Mr. Fraser began (as he said) to 'get a grip' on the filing section. Gone were the piles of unfiled records that occasionally used to lie on desks overnight in times of rush – all work had to be cleared each evening. The use of tracer cards was made mandatory whenever records were removed, even for use within the medical records section. The master index was no longer treated in the 'cavalier fashion' (Mr. Fraser's expression for everyone working on it) that had prevailed – Mrs. Price alone was allowed to touch this, and all requests had to be made by the filing clerks to her. An attempt to paste cartoons and pictures onto the glass screen was quickly checked by Mr. Fraser (it was unsightly), and tea-break now consisted of a proper quarter-hour in the staff dining room where coffee and biscuits were provided for a small weekly sum.

Mrs. Price was instructed by Mr. Fraser how to keep a tally of the amount of work passing through the section (using controls devised by the O & M team) and to ensure that every clerk was doing her fair share of the volume of work each day. At the same time, Mr. Fraser kept a supervisory eye on the proceedings, and felt it his duty to squash some rather irresponsible behaviour involving trying to throw paper balls through the sliding glass door while it was open. In all (as he informed the hospital Secretary, Mr. Littlewood) he was instilling professional pride and values in the filing section. Mr. Fraser also made a point of building up Mrs. Price's supervisory position and skills by always ensuring that changes and instructions were made to her as his 'requests', to be passed on as instructions to the clerks.

During the six months that followed the move, the service provided by the medical records filing department began to run into difficulties. Records were obtainable far less reliably than previously — there were often delays, and the sudden requests at the last minute were often the subject of argument. Filing of records began to get behind, and so Mr. Fraser instituted a ruling that any records unfiled at the end of the day should be returned to Mrs. Price for safekeeping; the stock of such records grew alarmingly. Mrs. Price attempted to file them herself the following day (in addition to her normal work) but never seemed to catch up. It became understood that once records had been passed over to Mrs. Price, they ceased to be the responsibility of the clerk who had originally been assigned the task of filing them. The same sort of problems were experienced with the master index, as a pile of master index cards awaiting replacement grew higher on Mrs. Price's desk. Mrs. Price requested Mr. Fraser to let her staff do an hour's overtime each evening for a week to clear the back-log, but Mr. Fraser refused with the words 'If the clerks spent less time chatting, and got on with the job they're paid to do, there'd be no problem — the O & M team didn't recommend any overtime'. Although the clerks mentioned this solution to her, Mrs. Price never tried to raise the subject again with him. Due to inefficiencies caused by misplaced or missing records, the work was made slower, and the back-log became larger than ever. In an attempt to speed up the pace of work, the clerks began to omit the tracer card when records were removed (since they had managed alright without them before). When he discovered this practice was going on, Mr. Fraser used to have periodic surveys to check up; the arguments were bitter when he (inevitably) discovered missing cards, and the clerks used to refer to him as 'the bloodhound'. Clearly, Mr. Fraser did this because he was under pressure from nursing and medical staff, as well as departments, who complained to him about deteriorating service and incomplete records. Some complaints reached Mr. Littlewood, but being busy and also believing in delegation, he felt he should allow Mr. Fraser to have a full opportunity to sort out initial difficulties in the system without interference from above. After all, he was the group medical records officer.

The matter came to a head when, one evening at about 11.30 p.m., Mr. Littlewood was called from bed to the telephone by an icily-polite consultant who wished to inform him that he had been waiting for exactly three hours for the records of a patient who had just been admitted under a section of the Mental Health Act 1959. It was known that the man had been both an inpatient and an outpatient of the hospital before, but three hours' search by the night telephonist/records clerk had failed to reveal any reference or notes at all. Mr. Littlewood rang Mr. Fraser and tersely asked him to meet him at the hospital as soon as possible.

It took Mr. Fraser about twenty-five minutes to find the patient's records; they were in four different places, three wrongly filed and one unfiled. Mr. Littlewood searched also, and was dismayed with what he found. There were piles of notes stuffed into clerks' desk drawers, bundles of reports from departments weeks old lying in boxes in the innermost racks, there were missing or incomplete tracer cards, the master card index appeared very deficient, and beside Mrs. Price's desk was a new addition — a smallish wooden rack from the 'shack', with three shelves for 'pending' (all full), and one for 'unaccountable' (part-full). As Mr. Littlewood searched, the consultant stood beside him, and related a series of carefully-documented and heart-felt incidents about the shortcomings and failures of the new medical records filing section.

The consultant departed to the ward, bearing the records. Mr. Littlewood regarded Mr. Fraser sourly, 'We will meet at nine o'clock today in my office to find out why this has occurred, and what we are going to do about it. Goodnight.'

PART III

Organizational Change

CHAPTER 7

GROWTH, PERFORMANCE AND ORGANIZATION

'Nothing succeeds like success.' Attributed to Talleyrand

Why grow?

This question is being asked by an increasing number of critics of big business and large public bureaucracies. What is the sense, they say, of forever expanding the scale of organizations which then become less and less manageable, and whose policy makers become more remote from the general public in a way that militates against effective accountability? In the business sector, the very dynamic of expansion seems to depend increasingly upon the artificial stimulation of demand through advertising and planned obsolescence in an age of mounting material shortages. Yet managers and public officials alike are reluctant in the extreme to forgo continued growth as a major objective for their organizations. Was Karl Marx right after all when he wrote of accumulation as the inexorable logic of capitalism which would be pursued until the exploitation of people and resources rose to an intolerable and explosive level?

There has been a great deal of debate as to why growth should remain such an important objective for management. One school of thought suggests that managers' prestige, influence, job security and salary levels provide sufficient reason since all these factors tend to increase with the growth of organizations. Others argue that the spirit of entrepreneurship, risk and invention finds its natural outlet in schemes for expansion. For many business managers operating under competitive conditions, sustained growth is simply seen as a necessary basis for survival. If their company's growth of profit falls behind that of its competitors, its ability to reinvest, and hence its long-term competitive position, is threatened. Similarly, if a company's growth in sales falls behind it will lose market share, and may as a consequence lose some bargaining power, attraction to customers, and morale among its marketing personnel – all of which can react unfavourably upon the rate of return that can be achieved.

Another point which has been put forcefully to the author by several senior executives of large British firms is that a record of sustained growth is necessary to attract and retain high quality managers. These top executives take the view that they have a duty to secure the future prosperity of their firm, past their own retirement. For this reason they must make sure that capable younger managers are recruited and groomed to take up senior positions. Without sustained growth, they argue, it would not be possible to attract the most able of these younger men, to give them general management experience and to retain their commitment to the company. This particular argument for the pursuit of growth is one to which present-day leaders of industry appear to attach great importance.

Growth is a consequence of success. If a business firm returns a surplus and this is not wholly distributed, then its assets will inevitably grow so long as the surplus is calculated net of an adequate allowance for depreciation. One of the most fundamental dilemmas of free competition is that it does not remain free once a successful firm has grown to such a point where it can begin to exercise monopolistic power over others. Similarly, in the public sector an agency that is seen to be successful in offering a desired service is likely to face pressures from the public to expand the scope and scale of its activities. Growth that is itself actively pursued as a matter of policy may, of course, not be profitable or received well by the public. Nonetheless, recent studies of business companies demonstrate that there is generally a positive association between profitability and growth.

There are, then, good reasons for growth which have to be matched against the objections of its critics. The apparently overwhelming constraint of an exhaustion of natural resources is still a subject for debate since it is extremely difficult to estimate the potential for substituting new materials and sources of energy. Even if there is zero growth among the totality of institutions, many organizations will probably remain managed by men who adopt growth for their own unit as a major objective. In this chapter, I shall therefore examine the consequences which growth, and the methods of growth, have for the design of organization before proceeding to the more general question of how organizational and managerial characteristics are associated with performance as a whole.

Stages of growth and their implications for organization

It is important to make a distinction between the implications for organizational design of growth itself and the method of growth that is selected. Simply becoming bigger sets up pressures to reorganize in certain ways. If growth, however, is achieved through diversification as opposed to expansion within the organization's original field of activity, or through vertical integration, then further changes in organization structure may become appropriate.

The relevance of size for the design of organization has emerged in each of the areas covered by previous chapters. As organizations that are relatively successful grow larger in size they experience a number of fairly obvious changes. Their total number of employees increases along with other resources. Their activities and functions increase in size, scope and number. Their operating and management problems increase in scale and complexity. Specialization increases among sub-units both at operating and managerial levels, and a greater range of specialist expertise is probably utilized.

We have seen that these concomitants of growth engender pressures towards delegation of authority, towards formalization in terms of standard procedures, systems and documentation, towards methods of integration between functions which do not depend on referral to top management, and towards an increasing number of management levels. Whether these developments are pursued within a functional, divisional, mixed or matrix grouping of activities will generally depend on the method of growth that has been pursued. This point can be analysed with reference to studies of business companies.

Most companies in the earlier period of their development are able to grow on the strength of one successful product. For a while the domestic market alone may provide adequate support for growth, but eventually it becomes necessary to open up foreign markets in order to continue expansion. Up to this stage, the growth of the company will probably have called for some of the organizational adaptations just mentioned, especially an increase in delegation and the addition of specialized functions. All this can, however, usually be encompassed within a relatively simple functional structure to which the company will move following an initial entrepreneurial, 'one man show' stage. Even when the export market is entered it may be quite feasible to serve this with a largely unmodified range of products and through the existing functional organization. At most an overseas department or international division will be required to handle overseas trade if this builds up to a large volume.

In some cases a firm will choose to develop through vertical integration — that is through acquiring its own sources of supply and/or acquiring its own market outlets. A strong incentive in the past for vertical integration has been to secure a monopoly position. Another argument in favour of vertical integration is that it can achieve economies of scale if, say, a multitude of small inefficient customers are thereby amalgamated into more effective units which can be modernized. Both factors have applied in the development of a company like Courtaulds. Vertical integration, if not accompanied by product or geographical diversification, can be contained within a broadly functional type of structure in which it will probably be appropriate to specialize production according to the different stages in the process.

A strategy of vertical integration can confine a company to a single industry at the expense of pursuing better opportunities elsewhere. It may also run foul of anti-monopoly legislation. For reasons such as these, companies which have grown on the basis of vertical integration have not on average performed as well as those which have grown through diversification. Diversification might be stimulated by competitive pressures on existing activities or by a decision to build from the strength of surplus funds or know-how. For example, the Pressed Steel Car Company in the United States diversified because of the declining demand for its original product — railway carriages and wagons. Fitch Lovell, the giant American food firm, has deliberately diversified on a broad front throughout the food business in order to avoid becoming too dependent on any one product area — having its eggs all in one basket. Letraset, in Britain, has been thinking of diversification for just this reason. Many companies have successfully followed a policy of planned diversification, such as Dixon's Photographic, Imperial Tobacco and Warner-Lambert. Others have diversified in a more fortuitous manner, though not always without success as the Rank Organization's move into the Xerox operation illustrates.

The importance of diversification for organization lies in the pressures it establishes for divisionalization. This point has been discussed previously in Chapter 4. Briefly, a divisional structure helps to meet the problem that, with diversification into new products and/or geographical areas, the number of co-ordinating and communication linkages in a functional structure increases more than proportionately. The divisional structure 'uncouples' some of these linkages by building new subsystems (divisions) composed of units which have intense interactions (around common product or geographical needs) and by reducing the number of other links needed to connect one such subsystem to others. These new subsystems appear in the form of product or area divisions, each headed by a general manager to whom is delegated most of the duties of a chief executive in a functional structure including profit responsibility. So long as the boundaries of divisions are drawn in a way that includes people and departments who have to contribute to product or area operations, then this structure will probably be more effective than the functional organization it replaces. A functional structure will normally be adopted within each division, though if divisions are themselves large and diversified they may be broken down into further product or area sub-divisions as, for example, with the confectionery operations of Cadbury-Schweppes.

Finally, if the fields of operation of a company are so diverse as to be mutually unrelated by market or technology then it will normally be appropriate to take sub-unit segregation to the point where the company functions as a holding company with separate subsidiaries. Whereas in a divisional structure certain functional activities will usually remain centralized, a holding company may operate with a small headquarters staff just concerned with the funding of investment and with monitoring subsidiaries' rates of return.

There is now a substantial body of research into larger American and British companies, the results of which suggest that those companies adjusting their organizational forms to the growth strategies pursued have achieved higher levels of financial performance. Some major studies are cited at the close of this chapter. Broadly speaking, it has been found that (a) firms which diversify into product areas related to their previous operations tend to secure higher profitability than those which do not in this sense seek opportunities for 'synergy' and which diversify into unrelated areas, and (b) firms which match their organization structures to their strategies tend to perform somewhat better than those which do not make this match.

Growth and diversification constantly bring into question the balance between centralization and decentralization, because of the problems of maintaining control and co-ordination which tend to arise. While the considerations I have advanced so far suggest that it is appropriate for a large diversified company to operate through a decentralized and divisionalized structure, this can bring problems as the Ozalid company has found. In Ozalid, divisionalization generated a loss of common identity among subsidiary divisions and excessive competition between them. There are business managers who take the view that the decentralization movement of the 1960s went too far and that some recentralization is required in order to maintain control and cohesion. Certain companies, like the Bendix Corporation, have tried to overcome the centrifugal tendencies of diversification and divisionalization by imposing a strict regime of modern corporate planning techniques and centralized, copious and frequently applied financial controls. A number of successful divisionalized companies, such as United Air Lines in the United States, complement their decentralization of profit responsibility and operating decisions with an advanced system of centralized corporate and financial planning, which serves to keep divisional activities in balance and in accord with corporate profit expectations. In other cases, a policy of decentralized divisionalization has run into trouble, as with Trans World Airlines, because the company did not have available a sufficient corpus of managers capable of filling divisional general management positions. This last constraint may help to explain why many European companies have been reluctant to match their diversification with fully divisionalized structures. Another reason has been said to lie in the greater ease with which European companies were able until recently to expand through market agreements and joint ventures which do not set up the same pressures for basic structural change.

In an attempt to pull together the strands of these various logical connections between growth, strategy and structure, authorities such as Alfred D. Chandler and Bruce Scott have advanced the concept of organizational development through a number of distinct stages. These stages link the progression of an organization from its early small and simple state to a mature state of large scale and complexity. All the well-known presentations of this model are illustrated by references to the business firm, but the essentials of the argument can in principle be applied to organizations with non-commercial functions. The model is summarized in Table 7.1. It implies that as a firm grows it will move from Stage 1 (a small owner-run concern) to Stage 2 where it remains undiversified but it has developed a functional organization staffed by 'professional' managers. Stage 2 organizations may develop international divisions, but if they continue to grow through product or geographical diversification they will tend to move to a divisional structure, adopting appropriate control and other systems. This is Stage 3 — the large multi-unit organization, having a general headquarters and decentralized divisions. Some companies like Unilever have grown to the point where their product and geographical diversification is so great that it becomes appropriate to adopt the grid or matrix structure described in Chapter 4. We may call this Stage 4. On the whole Stage 4 has been reached within the last decade and by very large enterprises. Their size and economic power have provoked a measure of social criticism, while their worldwide operation has brought them into areas which are particularly sensitive politically. For these reasons, political considerations assume a more central role in their strategic planning.

Like all models, this is clearly an oversimplification intended to capture the typical path of organizational development. It does not of itself, for example, indicate how far in practice managers adjust structures to suit strategies (as the model implies they do) as opposed to modifying strategies so as to accord with established structures which it may be difficult to change. The model is, nonetheless, useful in the context of our present discussion since it indicates that the scale element in growth is not the sole influence on choice of structure. Stopford and Wells were able to clarify this point through their studies of multinational corporations. They

Table 7.1

The four stages of organizational development

Company characteristics	Stage 1	Stage 2
Product line	Single product or single line	Single product line
Distribution	One channel or set of channels	One set of channels
Organization structure	Little or no formal structure, 'one-man show'	Specialization based on function
Product-service transactions	Not applicable	Integrated pattern of transactions 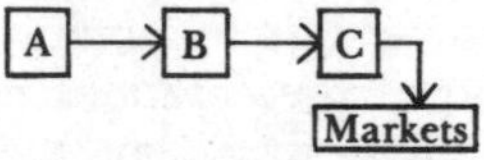 A → B → C → Markets
R & D Organization	Not institutionalized; guided by owner-manager	Increasingly institutionalized search for product or process improvements
Performance measurement	By personal contact and subjective criteria	Increasingly impersonal, using technical and/or cost criteria
Rewards	Unsystematic and often paternalistic	Increasingly systematic, with emphasis on stability and service
Control system	Personal control of both strategic and operating decisions	Personal control of strategic decisions, with increasing delegation of operating decisions through policy
Strategic choices	Needs of owner versus needs of company	Degree of integration; market-share objective; breadth of product-line

Source: Bruce, R. Scott, *Stages of Corporate Development* (Case Clearing House, Harvard Business School).

Description of Stage 4 added by the present writer.

Stage 3	Stage 4
Multiple product lines	Multiple product lines multiple geographical markets
Multiple channels	Multiple channels
Specialization based on product-market relationships	Grid structure based on product-market relationships and regions
Non-integrated pattern of transactions 	Non-integrated product and market transactions 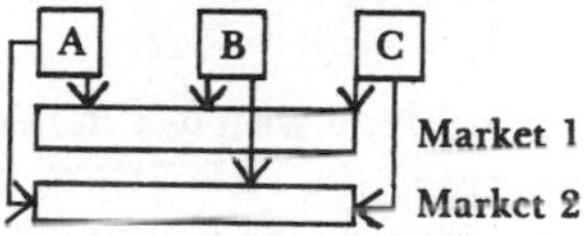
A B C Markets	A B C Market 1 Market 2
Institutionalized search for new products as well as for improvements	Institutionalized search for new products as well as for improvements
Increasingly impersonal using market criteria (return on investment and market share)	Increasingly impersonal, using market criteria (return on investment and market share) but considerations of regional political development also used as criteria.
Increasingly systematic with variability related to performance	Increasingly systematic, with variability related to performance
Delegation of product-market decisions within existing businesses, with indirect control based on analysis of 'results'	Delegation of product-market decisions within existing businesses, with indirect control based on analysis of 'results' and area control of business also delegated
Entry and exit from industries; allocation of resources by industry; rate of growth	Entry and exit from industries; allocation of resources by industry and by region; rate of growth

concluded that the transition from a Stage 1 to a Stage 2 structure in the early period of an organization's growth can be attributed to the increase in its absolute size. 'As the volume of activity increases, the top executive is unable to co-ordinate the enterprise, and an increasing degree of task specialization is required,' *Managing the Multinational Enterprise* (p.71). When, however, one examines the transition from Stage 2 to Stage 3, 'the fact that most of (the) 500 largest firms (in the United States) have Stage 3 structures . . . is not a result of their size but of their diversification,' (p. 72). Within each of the divisions of a Stage 3 structure, the size factor is still very relevant to, for example, the degree of delegation pursued by divisional managers, the number and range of specialists they employ, and the degree of formalization that is developed.

Strategies of development and implications for organizational design

Growth is the most obvious strategy which a management can attempt to pursue as a means for developing the strength of its organization. Growth may take place within the organization's existing fields of activity, or by means of diversification. The structural developments usually associated with growth via diversification have just been discussed, while the implications of increased size *per se* were reviewed in previous chapters. These are summarized in section 1 of Table 7.2.

There are also at least three other strategies which are adopted in order to enhance or safeguard an organization's position within its environment. These are (a) policies aimed at enhancing competitive power or public approval through increased efficiency or through incorporating technological progress; (b) the establishment of a secure operating field through finding protected areas of activity, or negotiating these in the form of joint programmes with other organizations; and (c) developing the organization's ability to react flexibly to any potentially threatening external changes. Each of these strategies has certain implications for organizational design.

1 There has been a great deal of controversy as to the implications technological development has for organizational design. Its effects on the growth of occupational specialisms within organizations, and the consequently increasing specialization of skills, jobs and functions, are reasonably clear. These generate the problems of integrating specialist personnel which were discussed in Chapter 5. Other implications, however, depend on the type of technology which is introduced, and even then there may be some choice as to how jobs and departments are organized for any given work technology. For example, in the past an introduction of mass production techniques has generally led to a removal of planning functions from operatives and also supervisors; specialist

Table 7.2
Summary of relationships between strategies of organizational development and structure

Strategies of organization development	Related structural changes (often assumed to be 'effects')
1 Organizational growth	(a) 1.1 increased vertical differentiation (lengthening hierarchies)
(a) growth in size *per se*	1.2 growing number of jobs and departments (horizontal differentiation)
	1.3 rising formalization
	1.4 increased delegation
	1.5 possible economies in administration, offset by rising problems of administering complexity
(b) growth via diversification	(b) 1.6 increased specialization of skills and functions
	1.7 divisionalization of major sub-units
	1.8 rising formalization, especially of planning and resource allocation procedures
	1.9 increased delegation
2 Technological development	2.1 growth of specialized, professional staff
	2.2 increased specialization of skills and functions
	(other structural concomitants depend on type of technology employed)
3 Acquiring a secure domain through non-competitive means (especially joint programmes)	3.1 establishment of new roles, especially to manage relationships with other organizations
	3.2 increased delegation
	3.3 more active internal communications via lateral relationships
4 Creating organizational flexibility	Depends on methods adopted, but usually associated with:
	4.1 establishment of new specialized roles to service vertical information systems (e.g. computer-based systems) and/or to promote lateral co-ordination
	4.2 more active internal communication via lateral relationships
	4.3 increased delegation

planners have been recruited and procedures devised to substitute planning systems for personal judgement. Today, however, a reaction to this approach has set in, partly because it creates alienation at work, and partly because formal planning systems cannot easily cope with the need for frequent revisions due to unexpected contingencies. So the technology itself is a constraining rather than a determining factor.

Much the same can be said of another significant technological development — the introduction of computers. There has been a considerable debate as to whether computers will increase centralization, because local information can now be more readily transmitted to, and analysed for, top management. In practice, decisions on the degree of centralization have reflected management philosophy on information and control systems rather than the presence of a computer *per se*. There is some evidence, however, that computers can reduce staff numbers in paper-processing clerical organizations or departments. Computers have also made it possible to regroup specialized departments into one because they have rationalized information storage and reduced work volume.

2 An important means of developing an organization is through negotiating joint programmes with another organization. The few studies which have been made of this strategy found that entering into joint programmes led the organizations concerned to hire more specialists, intensify internal communications and delegate decision-making. Changes of this nature have taken place in American welfare and health organizations entering into joint programmes and in Swedish housing firms, and they were remarkably similar despite the contrast in type of organization.

For example, Peter Broden a young Swedish researcher, studied AB Götene Träindustin, a prefabricated housing firm which entered into a joint programme with a large building contractor as a way to ensure further growth. Certain structural developments took place. New specialized jobs were created to deal with contractors both at the policy level and at the operational level where one or two persons in the plant were always available for daily contact with contractors. Communications became more active through the new emphasis on personal contact, especially between the managers of the prefab firm and the contractors. In conjunction with these developments there was more delegation of day-to-day decisions than had previously been the case.

3 In addition to the strategies mentioned, a management may decide that a more flexible mode of operation is required for its organization to remain effective in modern conditions. Chapter 5 discussed the way in which flexibility can be enhanced through structural measures designed to increase integration across different departments. Delegation of decision-making and the grouping together of functions linked by a common contribution to a particular task are also directions of structural development which suit a flexibility strategy. The need to develop a greater measure of flexibility within large bureaucratic organizations is a

pressing one in many spheres of activity today, and it is discussed further in Chapter 9.

The points made in this section are summarized in Table 7.2.

Performance and organization

It emerged from the studies of growth and development just discussed that the strategy adopted by management *and* the degree to which structure is adopted to suit the strategy are both potential influences upon the level of overall performance achieved by an organization. Strategy and the plans by which it is expressed are critical factors because they establish which activities are undertaken. While strategic decisions are likely to reflect the views and interests of top managers, they will also incorporate a response to pressures imposed on managers by various groups within the organization and its environment. The performance of an organization is a function of the value placed upon its activities by customers and clients, and of the cost-effectiveness with which outputs have been produced. Unwanted activities will not secure a good return however efficiently their production is organized — hence the basic importance of choosing a viable strategy

Over the long term, the strategies adopted will help to place an organization into a given configuration of situational contingencies. The environments in which the organization operates, the scale of its operation, its diversity, technology and personnel will all in some degree be the product of previously chosen strategies. The design of structure in the light of these situational contingencies is a major field of decision, and is itself likely to affect the ease and efficiency with which management policies and plans can be carried out. A problem will arise, however, if different contingencies carry conflicting implications since these could create inconsistencies in organizational design. So as well as fitting prevailing contingencies, an important criterion for organizational design is its degree of internal consistency.

The whole gamut of influences upon organizational performance is therefore extremely complex. As Jonathan Boswell said in his *The Rise and Decline of Small Firms*, 'A vast number of influences on performance are at work. Some of these are quantifiable, others aren't; some are external to the firm, others are internal and managerial, and of the latter many are subtly interwoven' (p.38). The quality of management is a pervasive influence which can affect all aspects of organizational behaviour, while the design of structure is likely to have its main impact in specific areas such as information flow, control, co-ordination and morale. The relation of structure and strategy to performance is summarized in Figure 7.1, which employs terminology appropriate to business organizations.

It is clear from Figure 7.1 that performance is not simply a dependent variable. The performance levels achieved by an organization constitute a vital input of information to its managers which is likely to stimulate them to make adjustments in policies and modes of operation. These adjustments may be an attempt to correct a poor level of performance or to accommodate the consequences of good performance, such as a growth in scale, and to sustain the favourable trend. In other words, it is unrealistic to regard performance *only* as a variable dependent on other factors.

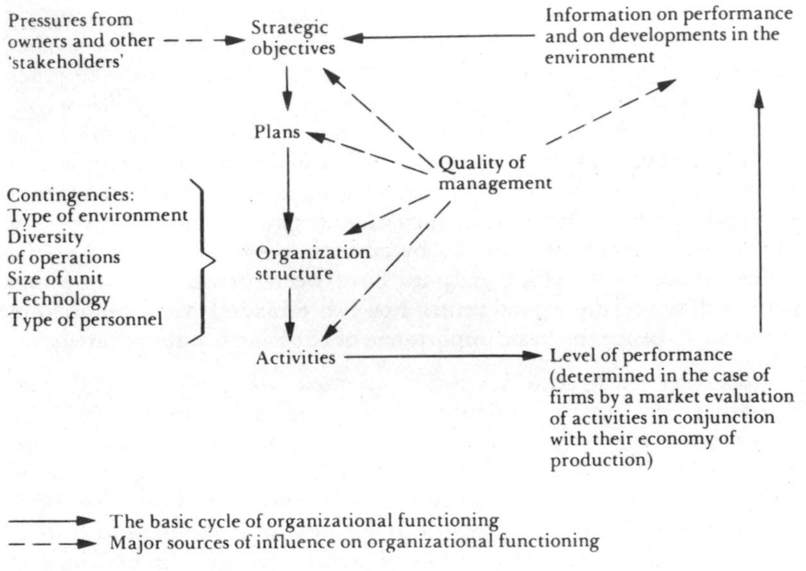

Figure 7.1
Performance in the context of organizational behavior

The practical importance of this point becomes clear when interpreting the type of statistical results produced by most studies so far conducted on management, organization and performance. These generally show that there is an association, in a sample of organizations, between a structural or managerial factor and a performance variable. Cause and effect are not, however, determined and one has by and large to interpret the results in terms of common sense and personal experience.

For example, from research conducted at the Aston Management Centre into 82 British companies, I found that less profitable and slower-growing firms used manpower budgets and other cost controls more than did high performers. The implications of this correlation are ambiguous. To what extent do manpower budgets contribute to lower performance because of their intrinsic inflexibility and because they focus managers' attention onto departmental status rather than onto organization-wide needs? On the other hand, to what extent is manpower budgeting instituted or intensified as a response to poor performance, in an attempt to keep manpower costs to a minimum and to control a staffing situation that may be getting out of hand? There is no question that in practice a period of poor performance often stimulates an intensification of financial controls.

Considerations of contingency: environment, diversity, size, technology and personnel

Most authorities take the view that the design of organization structure most conducive to high performance can only be formulated with contingent circumstances in mind. According to this so-called 'contingency' approach there are no general principles of organization, and managers have to weigh up the implications for structure of the contingencies they happen to face.

This argument has emerged in various forms throughout the preceding chapters and it goes as follows: Contingent factors such as the type of environment or the size of the organization have some direct influence on levels of success. There may, for example, be economies of scale open to the larger organization. Certain environments, such as particular industries, may be more beneficent and provide greater opportunity. Second, it is assumed that a set of structured administrative arrangements consciously adapted to the tasks that are to be done, to the expectations and needs of people performing the tasks, to the scale of the total operation, to its overall complexity, and to the pressures of change being encountered will themselves act to promote a higher level of effectiveness than will a structure ill-suited to these contingencies. Organization structure is seen in this way to modify the effects of contingencies upon performance.

1 Environment

According to contingency theory, different approaches to organizational design are conducive to high performance, depending on whether or not the environment in which the organization is operating is variable and complex in nature, or stable and simple. Variability in the environment refers to the presence of changes that are relatively difficult to predict, involve important departures from previous conditions, and are likely, therefore, to generate considerable uncertainty.

Complexity of the environment is said to be greater the more extensive and diversified the range of an organization's activities, which correspondingly take it into more diverse sectors of the environment. These diverse sectors are all relevant areas of external information that it should monitor. There is evidence that the degree of environmental variability is a more important contributor to uncertainty among managerial decision-makers than is complexity. I shall discuss variability now and return to complexity in a later section on diversity of operations.

The general conclusion which emerges from available research is that, in conditions of environmental variability, successful organizations will tend to employ the following structural characteristics:

(a) Arrangements to reduce uncertainty. These might include staff support for sophisticated search and information processing activities, and attempts to gain greater control over the conditions under which inputs are acquired and outputs disposed of, even to the extent of vertical integration.

(b) A relatively high level of internal differentiation. The critical nature of a variable environment means that an organization is under pressure to employ specialist staff in boundary or interface roles — in positions where they form a link with the outside world, securing and evaluating relevant information. This may well involve the establishment of more specialist departments, which increases the internal differentiation of the organization's structure. With a great deal of external change, there will be some pressure to delegate operational decision-making to the 'men on the spot' who are in a position to respond quickly. This in a sense increases the vertical differentiation of an organization through a dispersion of decision-making.

(c) A relatively intense level of integration, achieved through flexible and participative, rather than formalized, processes. If there are many significant external changes to which an organization has to adapt, and if it becomes internally differentiated through setting up specialized roles to cope with such areas of change, then it will also need to give particular attention to the maintenance of integration among its personnel. These personnel are now organizationally more differentiated from one another and require greater co-ordination, while the context of change itself places a greater burden upon integrative mechanisms because it means that the co-ordinated response to new developments has to be made without undue delay. In a variable environment, contingency theorists conclude, flexible rather than highly formalized or hierarchical methods of co-ordination and information-sharing are appropriate. These generally entail a high level of face-to-face participation in discussions and decision-making, with an emphasis on close lateral relations among members of different departments instead of formal links up and down hierarchies or via periodic formal meetings. This method of working also implies a higher degree of delegation down the hierarchy with operational decisions being left to the people most familiar with relevant information.

Various studies that have examined the performance of organizations in variable environments in relation to their structures have produced sufficiently consistent findings to support the conclusions just presented. Each study, of course, examines the structural elements I have mentioned in more detail. In the United States there is the well-known work of Paul Lawrence and Jay Lorsch as well as studies by Robert Duncan, Pradip Khandwalla, Anant Negandhi, and Bernard Reimann, among others. Of British studies Tom Burns' and G. M. Stalker's is the best known. All are listed at the end of this chapter.

Our own research at the Aston Management Centre has indicated that companies in the variable science-based environments characterizing electronics and pharmaceuticals which were achieving above average levels of growth tended to rely less on formal procedures and documentation than did slow-growing companies. Among firms in more stable environments, high growth companies relied more (but only marginally so) on formalized methods of integration than did less successful firms.

These organizational differences between high and low growth companies located in contrasting environments were most marked in certain areas of management. Within the stable sector, faster growing companies had significantly more formalization in the production area, especially in matters like defining operator tasks, training operators, and recording their performance. The faster growing companies, particularly in variable environments, made less use of formal training procedures and standardized personnel practices, and of formal hierarchical channels for communication.

2 Diversity

We have seen that among large American firms product diversification on a multinational level was adopted as a means for sustaining a path of continued profitable growth. Studies of these companies indicate that organizations which group their basic operations into divisions once these operations become diversified will tend to achieve higher levels of performance.

This proposition expresses the fundamental argument for the divisionalized organizational structure that has become the dominant form among large business firms today and that can also be seen in some large public undertakings. Organizations having a spread of different products or services, and having outlets in a number of regions, operate in a complex total environment. Such organizations are also likely to be large. Because of both their size and their diversity, they will almost certainly experience communications difficulties.

To overcome these problems, it is logical to create decentralized, semi-autonomous operating units or divisions, for these can group formal relationships in a way that reflects the necessities of exchange and co-ordination around common problems. These commonalities usually centre around product groups favouring a product division type of organization, but they may also centre on geographical regions, favouring an area division structure. If both product and regional co-ordination are equally vital, then a mixed, or 'grid' structure may be logical.

The detailed research of Stopford and Wells supports the argument that these divisionalized arrangements work. They found that American multinational corporations which have divisionalized their structures in response to a diversity of activities tend to be superior performers. The more successful firms have in most cases adopted the kind of divisionalization — internal divisions, global area divisions, global product divisions, mixed or grid structures — that considerations such as product diversity and level of involvement in foreign business would logically dictate. Large diversified European firms began to adopt divisionalized structures during the 1960s, partly in emulation of the American example, but mainly because increased competitive pressures forced them to adopt a more effective structural model. However, it should be noted that none of the research so far carried out has demonstrated the presence of a *strong* connection between diversification, structural design *and* performance.

3 Size of organization

The reasons why larger organizations generally employ a greater degree of delegation and formalization than do smaller ones have been examined in previous chapters. This trend towards 'bureaucracy' in larger organizations has often been deplored by critics such as E. F. Schumacher who argue that 'small is beautiful'. The problem of the large organization, they say, lies in the dead weight of bureaucratic administration that it takes on. In an attempt to hold together its many divisions and departments, the large organization emphasizes conformity to rules and systems, a trait which has prompted the observation that 'a new idea has never come out of a large corporation.' Many studies of organization have confirmed that large scale does indeed breed bureaucracy in the form of highly compartmentalized jobs and areas of work, detailed procedural and paperwork systems, long hierarchies, and delegation of routine decisions to lower level managers within precise discretionary limits.

Much as critics may decry bureaucracy, I found that, in the research mentioned, the more profitable and faster growing companies were those that had developed this type of organization in fuller measure with their growth in size above the 2,000 or so employee mark. The larger the company, the greater the association between more bureaucracy and superior performance. At the other end of the scale, among small firms of about 100 employees, the better performers generally managed with very little formal organization. Figure 7.2 illustrates these findings.

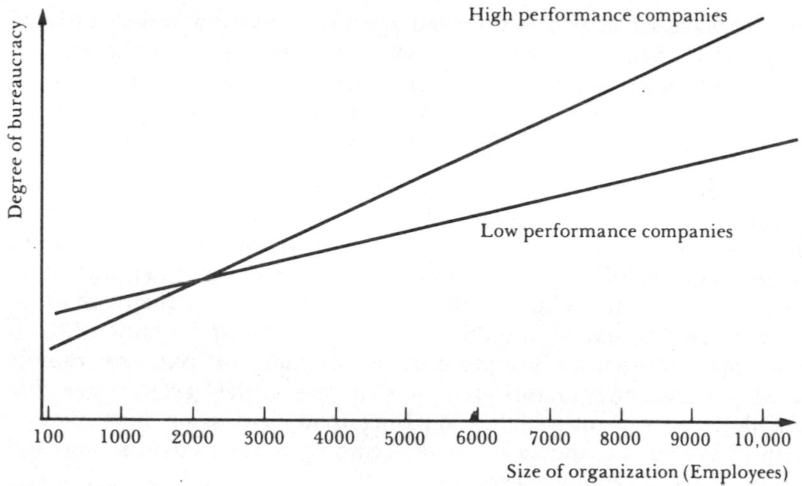

Figure 7.2
Size of organization, bureaucracy and performance

Poorly performing large companies tend to specialize their staff less, to have less developed systems and procedures, and to delegate decision-making less extensively. It is also worth noting that among the poorly performing companies the strength of the association between changes in size and changes in structure is noticeably reduced, compared with that among high performers.

In the faster growing and more profitable companies, as total size increases so the development of specialized roles takes place quite rapidly in the areas of finance and accounting, production control, methods and work study, personnel and general administration. The following systems and procedures tend to be among those used more extensively by high performing companies as they grow larger, as opposed to poor performers: sophisticated financial controls applied to a wide range of activities, a precise definition of operative tasks by management, the application of work study and methods, the use of labour turnover statistics, the planning of recruitment, and the regular updating of company forms and documents.

Comparisons of larger companies within the same industry clearly illustrate this trend. For example, we studied three of the largest British national daily newspaper groups. One was the superior performer by a substantial margin, in terms of growth, return on net assets, and return on combined circulation plus advertising sales. Although this particular group was the smallest of the three big companies in numbers employed, it operated a highly formalized type of organization — it had developed a more elaborate set of procedures and systems covering a wider range of activities than had the other two companies, and it relied heavily on written communication and records. Indeed, its most distinguishing feature lay in this heavier use of documentation, especially job descriptions, manuals, work records, and the like.

The newspaper industry represents a relatively stable environment. When the nature of each organization's environment is taken into account, as well as its size, the association between organization and performance becomes more complicated. The need for companies operating in a more variable environment to keep a check on the formality in their organization, especially its routine enforcing elements, probably explains why it is the successful companies in a more stable environment that most rapidly take on a formal bureaucratic type of structure as they grow larger. We found that the rate at which companies tend to develop bureaucratic structures as their size increases varies according to their environment and performance in the following sequence:

	Rate of development in organizational structuring and delegation as size increases.
1 Below average performers in stable environments	Low
2 Below average performers in variable environments	
3 Above average performers in variable environments	
4 Above average performers in stable environments	High

Managers, it appears from our research, have to take note of multiple contingencies, such as environment plus size, when planning the design of their organization. When there is not much variability in the environment, the need to develop organization to suit size becomes relatively more dominant. In this environment, the better performing companies tend to develop formalized structures at a faster rate as they grow than do poor performers. When the environment is a variable one, however, these differences in structural development are reduced, because the contingency of coping with uncertainty tends to offset the contingency of coping with large scale. We found that in a variable environment, the *rate* of increase in formalization accompanying growth in scale is higher for good performers, but the absolute level of their formalization only reaches that of poor performing companies at a size approaching 10,000 employees. In other words, smaller high performing companies in a variable environment tended to be particularly free of a bureaucratic style of structure: they were highly centralized and without much formalization. The picture is complex indeed, as most practical managers are well aware!

4 Technology

The term 'technology' is employed in almost as many senses as there are writers on the subject. Not very much of the research on links between technology and structure has looked for possible effects upon organizational performance. Joan Woodward's pioneering studies suggested that when organizations make structural arrangements to fit their technologies, they secure a superior level of performance. Woodward's view of technology concentrated upon the physical organization of work flows. Does the organization have heavy plant and a rigid sequence of production, as in automobile assembly? Or does it have fairly light plant and flexible production, as in the manufacture of some electronic equipment and, even more so, in service industries? Unfortunately, neither Woodward nor subsequent investigators adopting her approach have employed precise measures of performance.

Khandwalla, in more recent research conducted among some 79 American manufacturing companies, found that the more profitable firms were those which had in definable respects adjusted their structures according to the 'mass output orientation' of their technology. High performing firms producing large quantities of standardized products (mass production and continuous-process companies in particular) tended to employ sophisticated control systems and also to delegate decision-making. These relationships were not evident among the firms achieving a low annual return on net worth, and Khandwalla's findings therefore draw one's attention to a possible contingency that the standardization of production presents for structural design. Sophisticated controls are more readily applicable under standardized conditions, while delegation (as we saw in Chapter 5) itself requires a framework of formal controls. The potential benefits of controls and delegation are, for these reasons, probably greatest under standardized operating conditions within relatively stable environments.

The research I conducted in Britain indicated that the pattern of specialization in production and ancillary areas such as production control and maintenance was predictable in terms of the technology employed. In addition, the proportion of total employment allocated to some of the ancillary functions varied along with differences in technology. For example, more rigid technologies, such as those of a process type, tend to have relatively few production control specialists and less internal specialization within production control departments where these exist. Most control is actually built into the technology itself.

These associations between technology and the structure of employment lead one to ask whether, along with environment, size, and diversity, there is some logic of adjustment to contingencies here. If there is, does the extent to which organizations adapt to the logic predict differences in their performance?

The closeness of fit between technology and the pattern in which roles were specialized did not vary significantly between good and poor performing companies. What did distinguish the more successful firms, however, was that they tended to vary their investment in manpower devoted to production support activities according to differences in their technology. For instance, among companies using heavy plant and more rigid production systems, the more profitable and faster growing ones had significantly larger percentages of their total employment given over to maintenance activities. In other words, allocation of manpower in relation to technological requirements appears to improve performance.

5 Type of personnel

It is a cornerstone of the behavioural approach to management that organizations which adopt forms of structure consistent with the expectations and perceived needs of their personnel will tend to attract a greater contribution from them towards high performance. Most readers will be familiar with the views on this subject of influential organizational psychologists such as Chris Argyris, Frederick Herzberg, Rensis Likert and Douglas McGregor. They have argued for structures and styles of management that secure a higher degree of commitment to the organization from employees by more adequately meeting their expectations and their needs as mature adults. Only by working towards these structures can personal needs be harnessed to the requirements for effectiveness placed upon the organization as a whole. In a broader context, moves to enrich jobs and the developments in industrial co-determination now under way in Europe also reflect this view since they start from the premise that employees' expectations and perceived needs are not being fulfilled adequately by existing organization forms.

The results of many research studies indicate that the general argument is valid. Indeed, some would call it a truism. While it is unnecessary to review familiar ground, some qualifications are in order. The argument refers to the expectations and perceived needs of personnel. This reference to the perceptual level is important, for whatever the order of man's universal psychological needs, it is clear that different types of people do not have the same requirements of their work at the conscious perceptual level. One has only to compare the professional employee with the manual worker to realize that sociocultural factors are crucial in shaping different expectations as to what constitute legitimate conditions of work. Similarly, comparisons between different countries have indicated that different supervisory styles are effective with employees located in different cultural milieux where different attitudes toward work and authority are evident. Finally, as noted in the discussion on job enrichment in Chapter 2, there are situations in which technology can set limits upon the design of jobs and the structures which shape this. In these situations the costs of investment in a different technology have to be weighed against the likelihood of further motivational contributions to performance.

Managements need to spend time ascertaining the expectations of different groups among their employees if they want to have a reliable idea of which arrangements will secure the willing commitment of those employees. The basic point is that the employees of an organization constitute a major contingency in the design of its structure.

Limitations of the contingency approach

The contingency approach has become the dominant paradigm in the field of organizational design. It is supported by a growing body of research which appears to testify to its validity and practical utility. This picture is, however, somewhat misleading, and there are difficulties and limitations in the contingency approach which the practising manager should bear in mind.

One major limitation of the contemporary contingency approach lies in the lack of conclusive evidence to demonstrate that matching organizational designs to prevailing contingencies contributes *importantly* to performance. There are two problems here. First, the discovery of a simple correlation between organizational design and level of performance does not demonstrate that organization is the causal factor. Second, non-organizational variables may turn out to have higher levels of association with performance. I shall examine these problems in turn.

The problem of causality was mentioned at an earlier point. It qualifies the interpretation which can be placed upon several major contingency studies employing cross-sectional data. For in addition to the possible effects organization has on performance, the performance achieved constitutes a vital feedback of information to managers which may stimulate them to make adjustments to structure. Lawrence and Lorsch, for instance, found that poorer performing organizations failed to develop integrative mechanisms adequate to match their degree of internal differentiation. They argued that inadequate integration led to poor performance. However, in so far as more elaborate integrative mechanisms (co-ordinators, frequent meetings, even matrix systems) are more expensive, it is possible that their non-adoption was partly a reflection of an existing condition of poor performance and low organizational slack. It may also have reflected the tendency to centralize decision-making and to tighten control through insistence on hierarchical referral which is a typical managerial response to poor performance. Both these reactions reduce the intensity of lateral integration.

Another study by Lorsch and Allen found in a comparison between two high performing and two low performing conglomerates that the latter had a more complex set of rules and systems, laying a heavy emphasis upon control and co-ordination but at the same time permitting a relatively low degree of differentiation between headquarters and divisions. The writers interpreted this structural configuration as being dysfunctional for performance in multi-divisional firms, but one could also argue that it is just the kind of recentralizing managerial response to be expected when performance is sub-standard in the first place. A third example of this interpretive problem was given earlier from the author's research: the finding of an association between lower profitability and greater emphasis on cost controls.

Because most studies have been cross-sectional in nature and because few have paid attention to the reasons why particular structures were adopted, it is not possible to conclude as yet that a close matching of organizational design to contingencies is a significant determinant of high performance. Many studies have not even employed precise measures of performance, and even where such indices have been constructed, the proportion of their variance accounted for by a contingency-structure fit is usually relatively modest.

In the area of environmental, strategic and structural relationships, where the contingency approach is most developed, studies such as those by Channon and Rumelt suggest that strategic policies on diversification and growth may of themselves make a far more significant contribution to financial performance than does the degree to which structural forms have moved in line with such strategies. Franko, studying large European business enterprises, all of which had remained viable over many decades, concluded that for the most part structural changes had not closely followed changes in product strategies. Research by Pennings (1975) found, in 40 branch offices of a large United States brokerage organization, that the degree of fit between environmental and structural variables appeared to have little bearing on the effectiveness of the offices. The proportion of variance in effectiveness, both with reference to production and personnel criteria, that was explained was primarily due to organization structure *per se* in isolation from environmental contingencies.

It remains, therefore, very much an open question as to just how significant an influence on organizational performance the organizational design-contingency match really is. One reason for this uncertainty lies in the fact that most research has treated contingencies virtually as God-given constraints. This ignores the possibility that some organizations may be less dependent upon their environments, and in a more secure position with respect to maintaining their target levels of performance than are other organizations.

The variable of dependence is coming to be recognized as a major explanatory factor both for structural and performance variation. An organization, which, for instance, has achieved some degree of monopoly or has found a protected niche in the environment, might well be in a position to control or ignore environmental contingencies. In so far as it has little to fear from the threat of better performing competing organizations, then it can also afford to accept a level of sub-optimal performance if it chooses not to match its structure to suit prevailing contingencies. In other words, expressed in the language of economic theory, whenever there are imperfections in the competitive situation or in the public accountability of organizations, the possible inefficiencies resulting from what contingency theorists would regard as a mis-match between organizational design and contingencies are likely to have limited implications for the survival of that organization.

There are in practice considerable imperfections in the economics of resource allocation and competition, especially for non-business organizations. Even in the business sphere, inefficient organizations often take a long time to die and many survive protected by concentrated ownership, by their location in the interstices or niches which fall between major competitive markets, and so forth. For these reasons, and also because it may be far more significant for performance to achieve certain strategic objectives aimed at manipulating contingencies themselves (dominance in certain markets, economies of scale, standardized production and so forth) than to achieve the optimal structural design, one finds that there is usually some variation in the structures of otherwise comparable organizations. This variation is sometimes sustained over many years without much apparent effect on success or failure.

A further problem has not been recognized sufficiently: that multiple contingencies will be present at the same time. Most researchers have so far failed to adopt a multivariate analysis of contingent or contextual variables in relation to structural design and performance. They have concluded that organizational design should be decided with reference to environment, or with reference to scale, or technology, and so forth. But what happens when a configuration of different contingencies is found, each having distinctive implications for organizational design? A large firm may, for example, be operating in a variable environment. Following the guidelines of the contingency approach, should it set a limit on its levels of internal formalization in order to remain adaptable, or should it allow this to rise as a means of coping administratively with the internal complexity that tends to accompany large scale? This question helps to explain why larger firms frequently experience difficulties in sustaining the rate of innovation required by highly variable environments, and why the quality of their R & D relative to expenditure is often inferior. Another commonly found example of conflicting contingencies concerns job design, in those situations where there is a trade-off between the economics of assembly-line mass production and the social (and sometimes economic) benefits which may accrue from its replacement because of motivational factors.

All organizations function within a context of multiple contingencies. To the extent that considerations of contingency have force, this poses a significant organizational design dilemma because the structural implications of each contingency are unlikely to be the same. The solution usually adopted is an internal differentiation of the organization into separate or semi-separate units. For example, a large organization entering a dynamic environmental field will often create a separate and relatively small subsidiary unit to deal with the new area of operation — the creation of 'venture management' units fits into this category. The small venture subsidiary will find it easier to adopt the flexible, less formalized type of organizational design which is appropriate for an innovative strategy within a new variable environment. Companies such as Motorola have been known to modify technologies in order to permit enriched jobs or autonomous work groups in part of a plant but to retain a traditional form of engineering in other parts where the demand for new job designs was less keenly expressed. One also quite often finds organizations making a differentiation between units employing a mass-output standardized technology to meet a stable environmental demand alongside other units employing a more flexible technology to meet more variable demands.

If adaptations of this kind are made in order to meet multiple contingencies, they are likely to promote intra-organizational structural variation. Several studies have found evidence of such variation between segments of organizations which face different contingencies in regard to routineness of tasks, skills and technologies utilized, and type of personnel employed. Lawrence and Lorsch found that inter-functional differentiation increased in companies operating in dynamic environments, particularly because 'boundary spanning' roles such as marketing and research had to function in a mode more closely adapted to the conditions of their relevant environmental sectors. If adaptation to multiple contingencies takes the form of divisionalization or the creation of separate subsidiaries, the patterning of structural variation is likely to correspond to these sub-unit boundaries possibly combined with an overlay of inter-functional differences.

A major problem with intra-organizational structural variation of any kind is that it is likely to promote internal conflicts, tensions and malcommunication — in short, problems of integration. The main theme contained in the work of Lawrence and Lorsch and their colleagues at the Harvard Business School has, of course, been that a balance needs to be drawn in organizational design between differentiation and integration, which implies that the higher the degree of intra-organizational structure variation, the greater the burden of maintaining integration which is imposed.

Integrating mechanisms generally become more costly of time and managerial overhead as they become elaborate — involving more frequent meetings, the appointment of co-ordinators, project managers, or even a full matrix structure with two or more overlying managerial hierarchies. In addition, internal differentiation within an organization tends to promote or reinforce sub-unit goals and stereotypes which are always a potential source of conflict and its attendant inefficiencies. The inter-group hostility and rivalry which often accompanies differentiation cannot necessarily be dissipated by the introduction of structural mechanisms for integration. It is interesting in this connection to note Rumelt's finding that American corporations diversifying into related fields have generally been superior performers. This may well be due partly to the fact that related diversification does not require radically different forms of structural design in newly established divisions.

To summarize at this point: contingency theorists have not in the main recognized the organizational design difficulties which may result from the presence of multiple contingencies. These difficulties accrue from the structural differences, even incompatibilities, which result when an attempt is made to match the structuring of different functions or divisions to the dominant contingencies which they face. Reconciliation of such structural variations may impose a heavy cost on the organization. The question is raised, therefore, as to how significant an influence on organizational performance is the internal consistency of structural design in addition to the closeness with which it matches prevailing contingencies.

Considerations of consistency

Khandwalla in an examination of the organizational structures of 79 American manufacturing firms was led to conclude that the internal consistency of structural design is significantly associated with levels of organizational performance (*Academy of Management Journal,* September 1973). The structural features assessed in this study were arrangements to reduce uncertainty with respect to the environment, the degree of differentiation within the organization and the extent to which integrating mechanisms were employed.

Khandwalla found that it was the more profitable firms which adopted these three structural features in proportion to each other. In the less profitable firms there was far less consistency between the elements of their structural design. Khandwalla adopted a contingency interpretation of his findings to the extent that he believed that for organizational effectiveness, 'the particular design would depend on, among other factors, whether it is a large firm or not, and how uncertain its external environment is' (p.492). At the same time, however, 'what the findings suggest is that the gestalt or configuration of an organization is likely to be a more potent determinant of its effectiveness than any of the individual components of this configuration' (p.493). If that configuration matches up to the organization's contingencies, then performance should be further enhanced.

For reasons already discussed, it is likely that, taking an organization's structural design as a whole, there will be some conflict between the principle of matching structural arrangements to every contingency and the principle of retaining a high degree of internal consistency. The importance of the consistency factor is still to be researched, but given the limitations of the contingency argument it may prove to be quite significant. This much is suggested by the preliminary work which the author has been undertaking in comparing major airlines. The successful airlines so far studied differ greatly in their approach to organization despite facing many of the same major contingencies. Their organizations are, however, characterized by a high degree of internal consistency. As yet, comprehensive information is only available from a pilot study of four North American airlines carried out in 1974, supplemented by some data from a European airline.

Two of the airlines, which for reasons of confidentiality I shall call A and B, were superior performers on most criteria to the other two airlines C and D. The European airline E was a moderately good performer. Table 7.3 illustrates the contrast with reference to a calculation of profitability and growth.

Table 7.3
Performance of five airlines

	Net profit as % of equity and long-term debt			Change in net profit levels $ million
Airline	**1972**	**1973**	**1974**	**1972-1974**
A	5.62	12.40	11.50	+62
B	0.12	3.03	5.81	+81
C	2.68	1.89	−3.45	−81
D	1.26	0.82	−0.98	−18
E	2.11	4.94	3.79	+9

What distinguished airlines A and B from C and D was not that they adopted similar organization structures but that the structures utilized were internally highly consistent. This characteristic is particularly interesting because the four airlines shared many contingencies. They operated in similar environments and were direct competitors on some routes. They employed similar technologies and had comparable fleet compositions. They were faced with almost identical operating decisions. All were large airlines, with employment ranging from approximately 22,000 to 50,000 personnel. The main contextual difference lay between airline A and the others in that its route structure was geographically somewhat more compact.

Airline A was not divisionalized and had no profit or cost centres. Its planning and managerial time horizons were relatively short. It allowed very little autonomy to its main line management units. It employed centralized but very frequently activated decision-making processes, concentrating these onto a top executive group which met daily. This permitted a rapid response to variance from plans. Overall, this approach enabled the airline to have an economic and flexible managerial structure. It is, nonetheless, a remarkable structure to find in a large corporation. It was probably made viable by the airline's policy of concentration on the domestic airline business, geographical contiguity, a very long service management who had built up considerable trust and understanding of one another, and finally a consciously fostered 'open-door' policy to free-up communications. Conflict was low in this airline and was on the whole settled on an informal interpersonal basis.

The other high performing airline B was a complete contrast, except for the fact that it also operated through a highly consistent structure. This airline had divisionalized by region and by major resource area. It had attached full profit responsibility to its cost centres. It delegated authority on expenditure, staffing and other decisions to its divisions. It employed a highly formalized approach to financial and resource management using sophisticated controls. It planned ahead to a relatively long time horizon, using a powerful corporate planning group to provide co-ordination and review. Conflict resolution was largely by means of direct and open confrontation of issues and was part of the formal decision process. In short, this company was consistent in employing all the main elements of a structure which most authorities would say is appropriate to a large organization having a geographic spread of operations and a range of resource areas.

The two poorly performing airlines C and D (both of which made a loss in 1974) each had a structural framework for decentralized operation, but neither was using this to the full. In particular, both the airlines placed severe restrictions upon delegated decision-making while at the same time retaining the costly paraphernalia of formalization and the staff functions to support it. Airline D, for example, had some elements of regional divisionalization including cost centres, a corporate planning function and a long time horizon, but other elements were missing. It had no profit centres and there was limited delegation whereby, for instance, approval for capital projects was not considered to be authorization for expenditure and several further decision hurdles had to be cleared. Information gathered from branches involved the use of elaborate and highly formalized procedures and was very time-consuming especially as conflicts tended to be resolved not at middle management level but were referred up the hierarchy instead. This airline had a large managerial and staff overhead for the scale of its business (see Table 7.4), yet it remained relatively centralized. By operating an inconsistent structure in this manner it was not deriving the full benefits of any structural model. Staff in both airlines C and D were aware of the problem and advanced reasons for retaining centralization. In airline C it was ascribed to poor quality divisional level management and in airline D to public accountability, but one cannot be certain that either was an overriding consideration.

Table 7.4
Managers and staff-support personnel as a percentage of total employees*

Airline	%
A	15.1
B	18.5
C	18.9
D	23.6
E	9.1

*Staff-support personnel include finance, computer and system services, personnel, corporate planning.

Contrasts between the airlines begin to provide some clues as to why organizational design consistency has an effect on performance. Consistency is likely to make for a lower level of conflict and personal frustration. In airline D, where it was possible to explore issues in greater depth, it was clear that many managers were frustrated and demotivated because there was an inconsistency between those aspects of the system spelling out a decision-making role for them and the hurdles which were placed in the way of activating that role. In the opposite case, an organization in which there is decentralization without framework of procedures for maintaining control and integration is likely to incur penalties of communication breakdown and strains towards sub-unit rather than whole unit goal optimization.

If the structural inconsistency is of the kind found in airline D, then it may manifest two other costs. Managerial overhead will become inflated in so far as additional roles, even whole departments, have been created in order to service a comprehensive set of decision-making procedures. At the same time, however, the overload on top management is not reduced through effective delegation and is actually increased to the extent that an inflated managerial component has the result of widening spans of control. In airline D the chief executive's span of control was eight subordinates, while in the other three airlines it was five or six. In situations like this one in effect finds a 'mock bureaucracy', which fails to gain acceptance or to operate meaningfully, but which nonetheless absorbs time and resources.

The European airline E operated at a similar level of business to airline D, but was financially more successful. It generated approximately the same revenue as D, but with some 6,000 fewel personnel. Its organizational structure reflected some of the economy of airline A, but it had even lower managerial and staff overheads, employing a very flat structure. Its managerial philosophy was consistent with such a structure. Delegation was emphasized, and status based solely on formal job titles and hierarchical position was to a large degree avoided. There was an informal approach to interpersonal relations, with co-ordination and consultation emphasized rather than command. The significant point in the present context is that this philosophy was compatible with the form of organizational structure employed, and no serious inconsistencies were apparent. While data are not available in depth for this airline, they seem to indicate still further that different approaches to organization are viable within the one industry, and that possibly the most critical criterion for their viability is a reasonable degree of internal consistency.

In conclusion, studies conducted within a contingency framework do not demonstrate conclusively that variation in the design of organizations operating in similar situations will have serious consequences for their levels of performance. One reason for this is likely to lie with the conflicting design implications of the multiple contingencies faced by most organizations. The difficulties of satisfying all of these simultaneously could be one reason why organizational structure rarely emerges as a strong correlate of performance levels. The benefits of retaining consistency between the elements of an organizational design may indeed prove to be considerable in their own right.

The most commonly adopted method of coping with conflicting contingencies is to retain as much sub-unit design consistency as possible through segmenting those parts of the organization facing different major contingencies. Divisionalization is the model normally employed. Problems of integration can arise, however, and alternative methods of coping are also available. In particular, organizations may be able to modify some contingencies or they may even be in a position to ignore them for a while at least. These possibilities are not readily incorporated into the contingency approach. They draw attention to the necessity of incorporating the dimensions of strategy (aimed at adjusting contingencies and optimizing their mix) and of dependence/independence which signifies how critical the adaptation of structure to match contingencies is likely to be for organizational survival.

A note on quality of management

In this chapter, as throughout the whole book, I have concentrated on the design of organization structure. When considering the question of performance it would be wrong, however, to ignore the pervasive effects that 'quality of management' may have. Figure 7.1 earlier on suggested that this was the central factor. Management not only establishes (within constraints) an organization's strategic policies; it is also responsible for structural design and the successful implementation of change. In other words, the quality of management will be manifest in the ability of managers to grasp the complexities of organization structure, to devote sufficient thought to the matter and to come up with a solution that is acceptable and works well.

Although the 'good manager' is a keynote of many popular views about the sources of organizational performance, there has been relatively little systematic research on the possible links between managerial characteristics and organizational performance. To some extent, the contingency view has discouraged the idea that there are any qualities of management which promote better performance generally — across a range of different types of organization. Recent investigations have nonetheless pointed to the possibility that such general relationships do occur. These are reviewed in three papers written by the author, and which are referenced at the close of this chapter. What follows is a brief summary.

Several independent studies have now found a connection between company success and younger senior management teams. The difficulty here is to distinguish cause from effect, but younger managers have been found to possess attitudes and to behave in ways which are more innovative and thrustful than their older counterparts. If age and performance are generally linked in this way, then there are some clear implications for career policy. Younger people of proven ability should be given opportunities to advance rapidly to senior positions, while older executives should perhaps be transferred where appropriate into less demanding positions. This is, of course, a more 'American' approach which goes against traditional European practice.

Successful companies also tend to have managements which are better qualified than others. The balance between the fields of qualification held by top executives or directors can relate to success. For example, there is some evidence from British industry that manufacturing companies which are poor performers tend to have a heavy weighting of directors with an engineering or production background, the implication being that in such companies marketing and financial considerations may be less adequately reflected in policy decisions.

The mix of policy objectives is another facet of management which one would expect to have an important bearing on organizational performance. One danger is that effort may be dissipated and conflict generated in trying to achieve too many different aims at once, especially when the cleavage in aims coincides with the internal differentiation of the organization into units and departments, as it is apt to do. Among the eighty British companies which I studied, the more profitable and faster growing ones had chief executives who concentrated on the basic financial objectives of profit and growth to a greater extent than did the heads of poorly performing companies. Concentration on a range of key objectives does not imply that a management utilizes less information in its policy making, but rather that the information is more precisely directed in the evaluation of progress. A comparative study of acquisition behaviour among American companies carried out by Igor Ansoff and his colleagues supports the principle of this argument. It was found that the more successful firms in terms of profit and growth restricted their attention to a more limited range of possible acquisitions, which allowed for a more thorough evaluation of each.

The results of investigations into links between the concentration of ownership with management and company performance have in some cases suggested that owner-controlled firms are more profitable and enjoy higher rates of growth. These studies taken as a whole are not very conclusive. Some more recent research, undertaken by Steve Nyman at Nuffield College, Oxford, has approached the subject in a different way by examining the personal stake (market value of shares) which directors hold in British commercial and industrial companies. Higher levels of stockholding were significantly associated with higher rates of company growth, and there was a weak association with higher profitability too. Given higher growth and higher profitability, it is not surprising that a larger personal stake in ownership was also associated with a higher stock market rating and a higher price earnings ratio. Again there is a problem of cause and effect in interpreting these results, but they suggest that whenever managers have a direct personal stake in the success of an undertaking, its performance will tend to be enhanced.

It is clear, even from this summary account, that the quality of management may in different ways powerfully influence organizational performance. Previous chapters have pointed to the ways in which the design of organization structure can effect the managerial contribution through its influence on motivation, co-ordination and control. Policies designed to improve quality of management directly through career planning and job enrichment will be of benefit if appropriate structural provisions, such as delegation, are also in force.

Summary

This chapter has attempted to place the issues covered in Part II into perspective by reviewing our present state of knowledge on the structural and managerial factors which are associated with different levels of organizational performance. On the whole the structural approaches which lend themselves to good performance appear to vary considerably with the type of organization and the contingencies it faces. Certain managerial qualities, on the other hand, seem to make a positive contribution to performance in most situations.

Despite the severe economic and ecological difficulties which stand in the way of its achievement, growth remains a major objective for most managers. Growth, indeed, is a consequence of good performance whether this is assessed by reference to profit or to the demand for a public service which is being offered. The growing size of an organization and the means employed to sustain growth are both very significant contingencies for the choice of design of its structure. This point has given rise to a theory of growth and structure in which several distinct stages of development are identified. Growth is significant because it usually brings with it changes in major contingencies for organization structure such as new environments, greater diversity of operations, changes in technology and large scale itself. Other strategies of development, such as entering into joint programmes, also set up pressures for changes in structure.

It may be extremely difficult to achieve a design of organization structure which adequately satisfies all contingencies. It is usually within the power of managements to modify the impact of some contingencies through deliberate changes of policy over the course of time. In any case, there is reason to believe that another principle is just as important, namely that the different elements in structure should be consistent, both in themselves and with the overall philosophy of management being employed. Different structures and managerial philosophies can be found within successful companies which operate under broadly similar conditions. These considerations lead one to qualify the popular contingency approach, which a closer examination in any case shows to be scarcely well proven.

Alertness to the complexities of designing an appropriate structure is likely to prove a good indicator of the quality of an organization's management. Available research studies enable us to begin to identify some of the attributes of successful management. These appear to include relative youth, relevant training attested by qualifications, a personal stake in ownership or the success of an undertaking, and a concentration on important objectives.

Reference to growth and development serves to remind us that the design of organization structure takes place in a dynamic setting. The successful introduction of organization change is therefore a prime requirement, and this is the subject of the following chapter.

Suggested further reading

Alfred D. Chandler, Jr., *Strategy and Structure* (M.I.T. Press 1962), illustrates in detail how in the development of large American corporations new strategies gave rise to new forms of organization structure. Bruce R. Scott has presented a formal model of this process in his *Stages of Corporate Development* (Harvard Business School 1971). Derek F. Channon analyses the phenomenon in *The Strategy and Structure of British Enterprise* (Macmillan 1973) covering the period 1950-70. John M. Stopford and Louis T. Wells, Jr., *Managing the Multinational Enterprise* (Longman 1972), examine the development of 187 large American multinational firms, focusing upon changes in their structures and the extent to which the structural designs adopted predicted differences in levels of financial performance. Richard P. Rumelt's *Strategy, Structure and Economic Performance* (Harvard Business School 1974) analyses a sample of 246 large American firms over the period 1949 to 1969. Lawrence G. Franko surveys large European manufacturing firms in 'The Move Toward a Multidivisional Structure in European Organizations', *Administrative Science Quarterly*, December 1974, and in his *The European Multinationals* (Harper and Row 1976). Moving to the other end of the size spectrum, Jonathan Boswell analyses *The Rise and Decline of Small Firms in Britain* (Allen and Unwin 1972) and identifies a number of managerial features which influence their level of success.

Studies which have found that the most effective design of organization structure varies according to the environment include the following: Tom Burns and G. M. Stalker, *The Management of Innovation* (Tavistock 1961), Paul R. Lawrence and Jay W. Lorsch, *Organization and Environment* (Harvard Business School 1967), Robert B. Duncan, 'Multiple Decision-Making Structures in Adapting to Environmental Uncertainty: The Impact on Organizational Effectiveness', *Human Relations*, Vol. 26, 1973, Pradip N. Khandwalla, 'Uncertainty and the Optimal Design of Organizations', *Faculty of Management Working Paper, McGill University, Montreal* 1972, Anant R. Negandhi and Bernard C. Reimann, 'Task Environment, Decentralization and Organizational Effectiveness', *Human Relations*, Vol. 26, 1973. Research into technology as a contingency for organizational design includes Joan Woodward, *Industrial Organization: Theory and Practice* (Oxford University Press 1965) and Pradip N. Khandwalla, 'Mass Output Orientation of Operations Technology and Organizational Structure', *Administrative Science Quarterly*, March 1974. Additional sources mentioned in connection with the contingency approach were (1) Jay W. Lorsch and Stephen A. Allen III, *Managing Diversity and Interdependence* (Harvard Business School 1973), (2) Johannes M. Pennings 'The Relevance of the Structural-Contingency Model for Organizational Effectiveness', *Administrative Science Quarterly*, September 1975, and (3) Pradip N. Khandwalla,

'Viable and Effective Organizational Design of Firms', *Academy of Management Journal*, September 1973.

Further discussion of the structural concomitants of organizational growth and development is contained in John Child and Alfred Kieser, 'The Development of Organizations over Time' to appear in William H. Starbuck (editor), *Handbook of Organizational Design*, volume I (Elsevier 1977). The author's own research into factors associated with performance is reported in John Child, 'Managerial and Organizational Factors Associated with Company Performance', *Journal of Management Studies*, October 1974 and February 1975. Shorter and less academic papers are his 'Why Company A Manages Better', *Management Today*, November 1973, and 'What Determines Organization Performance? The Universals vs. the It-All-Depends', *Organizational Dynamics*, Summer 1974.

Also referred to was H. Igor Ansoff et al. *Acquisition Behaviour of U.S. Manufacturing Firms 1946-1965* (Vanderbilt University Press 1971).

CHAPTER 8

RE-ORGANIZATION—THE NEED FOR STRUCTURAL CHANGE AND PROBLEMS OF ITS IMPLEMENTATION

'Change is the biggest story in the world today, and we are not coping with it adequately.' Warren Bennis, *Organization Development: its Nature, Origins and Prospects*, (Addison-Wesley 1969), p. 1.

Pressures for re-organization

Previous chapters have identified ways in which it is appropriate to shape jobs and design structures so as to suit the circumstances under which organizations carry on their operations. The need to maintain consistency between elements of structure has also been emphasized. As circumstances change, it is therefore incumbent upon the manager to examine the implications of the change for the design of his organization's structures and jobs, and to decide whether any re-organization is required. Change has indeed become so ubiquitous in modern industrial societies that many large business companies in North America and on the continent of Europe have established specialized organization planning departments, giving them the task of constantly monitoring the requirements for structural changes and of devising appropriate schemes to accomplish this. British organizations have, on the whole, been somewhat backward in appreciating the case for treating re-organization as a continuing process in this way.

There are several commonly occuring types of change which set up pressures for re-organization, and these can be analysed in terms of the contingencies identified in the previous chapter.

1 Environment

For most organizations environmental conditions have in recent years been changing with increasing speed. Business companies have generally experienced a heightening of competitive pressures. In many industries, competition in product markets has increased along with the lowering of tariff barriers and the multinational spread of large companies' activities. Competitive pressures have sometimes been increased by a rising rate of product innovation, as in the field of electronics since the early 1960s where micro-circuitry is a prime example.

Quite recently, changes in world economic conditions have substantially shortened the time horizons up to which it is realistic to plan ahead. Commodity prices and supplies have, for example, fluctuated considerably and become more dependent upon political factors. In the case of sugar and cocoa beans, for instance, market fluctuations have greatly increased the uncertainty of management in the confectionery industry. Violent fluctuations in copper prices have had similar consequences for management in the non-ferrous metals industry, and there are many other examples. A rapid rate of price inflation also raises uncertainties about the behaviour of consumers whose patterns of expenditure often begins to exhibit new peaks and troughs of demand in anticipation of and following major price rises. In the field of employment, an increasing flow of new legislation, together with demands for new information sharing arrangements and other aspects of participation, are all contributing further changes in the conditions under which organizations can function.

These environmental changes are recognized well-enough, but they do carry important implications for structural change. When environments become more volatile, with consequently shortened planning time horizons, a premium is placed on adaptability. This means that it is necessary for managers to secure more up-to-date intelligence about events in the outside world, and to evaluate and co-ordinate the information more rapidly for the purpose of deciding how to respond to changing conditions. In structural terms, this implies that management may have to consider increasing its employment of specialists like market researchers, representatives to trade fairs and conferences, commodity buyers and so forth in order to improve its capacity to keep track of external developments. Specialists such as these also provide the expert advice required for management to know how to respond creatively to the opportunities, or threats, new developments bring. Even the use of outside agencies for some of this activity is itself likely to increase the number of specialists employed within the organization, as was noted in Chapter 2. In short, one path of re-organization which appears to follow from contemporary environmental conditions leads towards a more complex and specialized structure.

A complex and differentiated structure is more difficult to co-ordinate and, indeed, the external conditions described make it imperative for organizations to generate an increased capacity for integrating information across different specialized functions and for transmitting the end result effectively to the point of management decision. Circumstances today often change too rapidly to be able to rely upon programmes, plans and referral of exceptions for top level decision as the means of coping with eventualities that arise. These traditional bureaucratic decision and planning mechanisms are likely to be too slow and inflexible. Events are liable to occur too frequently and to present too many novelties. In times of world economic stringency and pressures upon cash flow, it is not usually good sense either to build in flexibility for coping with greater uncertainty through costly higher inventory or through delays, backlogs and other reduced standards of performance.

These limitations imply that in the new conditions organization structures have to be re-examined to see how well they facilitate effective communications laterally between units and functions, and whether full advantage is being taken of aids such as planning staff and computerized information systems which improve the way the vertical flow of information operates. In other words, improved structural mechanisms for both lateral and vertical integration are called for. These might well include some regrouping of activities in order to reduce the complexity of communications and to strengthen links between those functions which need to work together in a particular area.

An example of thinking along these lines is provided by Ian Mangham and his colleagues in their booklet on *Managing Change* (1972). The Petrochemicals Division of ICI, when reviewing its objectives, recognized that in a period of increasing social and technical change one of its highest priorities was to improve the management and capabilities of its people. Success in coping with change was seen to depend upon the contribution employees were prepared to make. The Division's management concluded that this required not only encouragement for individuals to take on greater responsibility, but also a freeing-up of the organization structure so as to increase contact between managers and employees, and the capacity of teams and sections to work in an integrated manner. In this way, the Division's evaluation of strategic requirements led it to embark upon a major effort in the field of organizational change and development.

Competitive pressures provide a major stimulus for re-organization. Many companies in Europe during the mid 1970s attempted to reduce staff and managerial overheads in response to a period of economic stringency. Appropriate re-organization here might encompass a reduction in the number of management levels, using a method of the kind described in Chapter 3. It may be feasible to centralize certain service functions such as purchasing and training, thereby reaping some staff economies. Attention will almost certainly be given to improving the control of expenditure within the organization. This is often interpreted as meaning not only less expenditure but less delegation of discretion on expenditure as well, which in circumstances where a greater capacity to adapt is also required may be counter-productive to the longer-term success of the organization. It is usually more sensible to improve control through obtaining more accurate and up-to-date information on expenditure rather than referring more decisions on expenditure up the hierarchy with inevitable delays because of top executive overload.

The increasing intervention of government and its agencies is another significant change in organizational environments. In Britain at the time of writing, there is regulation of prices and incomes. In the business sector this obliges management to standardize and centrally regulate policies in areas where previously considerable discretion may have been delegated to local operating units. One reason for delegation is, of course, to permit the sub-units of an organization to respond more rapidly to changes in local circumstances. In the public sector too, a trend towards centralization can be observed in recent re-organizations. These centralist tendencies have occasioned the comment that Britain and some other industrial societies are moving towards a corporatist state. If sustained, they are likely to put a brake upon policies of devolution within organizations which are designed to facilitate a more flexible response to environmental change. Leaving aside social or political considerations, the inflexibility which governmental regulation imposes on managerial policies will be a disadvantage in terms of coping with environmental change unless the state itself can remove a substantial amount of uncertainty through effective national planning.

2 Diversification

In the early stages of diversification into a new field of activity, managements quite often make only minor adjustments to organization structure. A special 'co-ordinator' may, for example, be appointed to look after the new operation and left to secure a commitment of time and resources from functional departments as best he can. At a later stage, when the amount of business in the new area builds up to a substantial proportion there are pressures to adopt a divisionalized structure which now allocates resources specifically to the diversification as a major area of business within the organization. The question of at what point an organization moves away from a functional structure, or creates a new division out of an existing one, is a particularly difficult one. Indeed, there is always the choice of not moving over to a fully fledged divisional structure, but instead, grafting a divisional-type split of certain departments like marketing onto a basically functional structure. This type of mixed structure will have to be complemented with clear policies on priorities in order to avoid the problem experienced by the manufacturer of specialist steels cited in Chapter 4, where difficulties arose because of competing claims upon a single production function.

3 Growth

Growth is a familiar source of re-organization which has already been examined in some detail. Pressures for re-organization arise when the top executive or the top team can no longer maintain effective day-to-day control, and when the growth of the organization speaks for a greater specialization between, and broadening in the range of, management functions. Growth generally leads to extended hierarchies and problems of communication. If it occurs on the basis of diversification into many unrelated fields, it can generate serious problems of control and co-ordination. Continued expansion is, in these various ways, a prime source of pressures for re-organization. It is for this reason that size has emerged in so many studies as the major predictor of the type of structure adopted by organizations in practice.

Fisons Limited provides an example of how problems of growth, diversification and competitive pressure led its management to undertake a major re-organization. Fisons had during the 1940s and 1950s diversified away from its vulnerable reliance on a single industry product — fertilizers — into other activities including pharmaceuticals, agrochemicals, industrial chemicals, food products, the assembly of industrial refrigerators and many other products. By the mid-1960s, however, the results of diversifying into so many largely unrelated products had proved to be disappointing. The company's strong position in its basic fertilizer business was being eroded by competition, and difficulties were being experienced in the introduction of new technology for manufacturing intermediates and end-products. Profits in other newer areas appeared to be declining and the company was facing a cash crisis. This was the combination of pressures on Fisons to change direction at the time.

The company decided to clarify its prime corporate objective which was to be continuous growth in earnings per share. It decided upon a concept of its business, in which the connecting thread would be health for humans, animals and plants. This signalled a determination that the company's future growth would come from related and mutually-supporting activities, and all activities which did not fit this concept were disposed of (this also solved the company's cash problem). The re-organization which was undertaken followed from these strategic decisions. In 1967 the company had as many as 53 wholly-owned subsidiaries, each with its own Board, set of accounts, company secretary, accountants and other managers. The complexities of co-ordinating this collection of miscellaneous largely unrelated businesses were forbidding and very wasteful of management energies. In accord with the policy decision to concentrate on only three major activities — Fertilizers, Pharmaceuticals and Agrochemicals — most of these separate companies were wound up and a three-division structure substituted instead. Full profit, capital expenditure and cash flow budgetary responsibility was allocated to the director in charge of each division.

4 Technology

The main thrust of technological change in the last twenty years has concerned the application of electronics in the fields of computers and process automation. The early introduction of computers generally substituted electronic for manual maintenance of files, which had consequences for the employment of clerks but few implications for the structure of the organization as a whole. More recent and advanced computer applications have, however, involved a more fundamental change in which functions can be closely integrated through sharing common computer files as part of specially designed systems which are intended to govern the flow of work across departments. It is only with the coming of the computer that many techniques of systems analysis and operational research have become practical possibilities.

The impact of integrated information systems upon management structures and jobs can be considerable, and may provide a rationale for an elimination of established boundaries both horizontally between departments and vertically between middle and top management. Horizontally, the thrust tends to be away from a functional division of responsibilities and towards matrix or product forms, since these accord with the logic of the major workflows which the stages in information processing must parallel. The possible implication for vertical boundaries can be illustrated by means of an example. In a non-computerized situation a manager of, say, a warehouse will have important decisions to make and re-make on a recurrent basis. He is subject to various constraints such as satisfying delivery promises; he has to choose between competing customer priorities; and he has to satisfy requirements such as minimizing the company's inventory in finished goods. In this situation, the manager is likely to be harassed by the complexities and pressures he faces, and in his defence is able to evade full responsibility by pointing to the impossibility of reconciling the conflicting demands which are placed upon him. When a computer is introduced, this picture can change dramatically. Rules can be established by senior management as to the appropriate trade-off between requirements for customer service, low inventory and other factors, which a computer can apply easily to any given situation, however complex. The computer allows relevant data to be updated continuously and for this information to be passed to top management for review. These data can be easily combined with other relevant facts, on interest rates, on production schedules and so on, to provide both a much broader analysis than before and the capacity for senior management to take decisions itself should it wish.

In situations such as this, the middle manager could disappear from the scene, certainly as a decision-maker. A similar possibility emerges with respect to advanced automation of production or workflow processes, whereby a whole plant is now integrated into the scope of a single control system. This allows for information on items such as output, stocks, costs and manning to pass rapidly up to senior management. A more rapid appraisal of performance becomes possible and decision-making can be transferred from local departmental production managers to top management. These are the reasons why several commentators on the introduction of advanced technology have predicted that it will provide a rationale for quite substantial structural changes, particularly a decrease in the number of middle management levels and a centralization of much operational decision-making. There can be little doubt that middle managers, many of whom are now unionized in Britain, will seek to resist re-organization of this kind.

Computers and automation, despite the more conservative view that is now taken of their potential, introduce the most far-reaching pressures for re-organization out of the whole gamut of technological changes. Other developments such as a move from small batch to mass production are also of relevance since they occasion changes in appropriate systems of production control and in the employment of specialists. Most technological advances, including of course computerization and automation, tend to enhance the numbers and the importance of certain specialist groups. Operational researchers, production controllers and management accountants are three groups whose specialist skills can be greatly enhanced by the use of computers. From a structural point of view, difficulties may arise in the integration of specialists into traditional line hierarchies. It was seen in Chapter 5 that many organizations have therefore experimented with team structures which detach specialists from functional departments and allocate them to teams concerned with the management and servicing of a particular workflow.

5 Personnel

Chapter 2 mentioned the long-term changes in educational levels, distribution of occupational skills, and employee attitudes which have together stimulated interest in job enrichment and participation. At shopfloor and office levels, job enrichment and participation imply changes in the organization of work and in the role of junior management. Employees might take over responsibility for some of the detailed organization of the work, allocation of people to tasks, inspection and routine maintenance of equipment. The burden falling upon the first-line manager is potentially reduced. His control of work could now take the form more of negotiating output targets and less of direct personal supervision. In these ways, the first-line manager can be relieved from having constantly to deal with immediate contingencies. In principle, this should give him the chance to devote more attention to opportunities for longer-term improvements in methods, layout, equipment and employee development.

It is doubtful whether this kind of change will in practice be implemented swiftly or easily. As I have emphasized already, changes in organization at the operative level require modification in procedure, delegation, management style and so forth, at higher levels. In other words top management has to hold a positive philosophy about job enrichment and participation, and to know what they entail, before any change in that direction is likely to succeed. A second problem lies in the doubtful capacity and willingness of all first-line managers to cope with the longer time perspective and the negotiating role that has been described. Third, a lengthening of time horizon upwards from the bottom will increase the overlap between work done at adjacent hierarchical levels unless there is increased delegation right the way down the management hierarchy. Even then, the position may be reached when it is decided to remove a level of management, which may be beneficial in the long term but provoke resistance in the short run. Nonetheless, these comments point to the difficulties of implementing change rather than to the inappropriateness of that change as a response to developments in the personnel field.

At the more global plant or company-wide level, in Europe at least, formal systems of participation have been, or are still being, introduced. Judging by experience in Israel, Yugoslavia and other countries, these developments will also promote structural changes. Many processes of decision-making will become more formalized and a sharper distinction drawn between matters of policy and matters of executive management. Purely *ad hoc* policy making through the medium of executive decisions will become less acceptable. Although the processes of participation can create delays, the bringing of decision-making into a more open and formalized arena may well result in a better co-ordination of information and contributions from the different parts of the organization. The clear separation of policy from executive decisions could also have the effect of relieving executive authority from much of the challenge it currently receives to its legitimacy, as Lord Wilfred Brown has consistently argued in his writings on organization. The strong impression, which I have gained from visiting plants in Israel both in the small-scale co-operative Kibbutz sector and in the larger-scale Histadrut sector where participation is well advanced, is that affording workers the opportunity to share in policy making leads them to accept day-to-day executive authority with little demur.

There are clearly many developments, some long-term and some more immediate, which create pressures for structural change. How then can managers identify the need for change when it arises in their own organization? What are typical warning signals, and what guidelines may help to identify the nature of an organizational problem?

Identifying a need to re-organize

In general terms when any of the major pressures for re-organization just discussed come into play then it is timely to consider whether structural changes are called for. This planned approach to change will help to avoid a situation in which the performance of an organization actually has to decline before an inappropriate structure is identified as a contributory factor. A greater rate of environmental change raises questions of how to ensure adequate innovation in the organization's activities and how to avoid an overload in its decision-making capabilities. Competitive pressures may also require an innovatory response and possibly ways of securing administrative economies as well. Growth and diversification should alert managers to the problem of how to avoid deteriorating communication, control and speed of response in an organization that is becoming more complex. Technological developments signal possible implications for the management of new specialist staff, for the role of middle managers and (in the case of integrated systems) for relations between hitherto separate departments. Participation indicates possible changes in the structure of operative level management and in managerial decision processes.

The need for organizational change does not necessarily arise as a consequence of a major strategic development. Nor is the change required necessarily large-scale. The continual incremental changes in operating conditions, size, technique, personnel and other features at any level down to the work group may generate problems that require some modifications in organization. If performance begins to suffer, once the immediate source has been identified, it often becomes apparent that this is rooted in a more fundamental behavioural failure for which structure has to take some of the blame.

For example, the immediately obvious reason why a company is losing sales is its failure to honour promised delivery dates. Underlying this, however, may be inadequate integration between sales and production departments. Sales are perhaps forcing unplanned 'special' orders onto production. Production may be giving lead-time estimates based on standard runs knowing that delays can be blamed on Sales and their special orders. I have known a situation like this which had deteriorated so much that special orders were regarded by each party as an opportunity to discomfort the other. A structural development such as the SOLD system described in Chapter 5 would be one means of improving matters and of ensuring that sales and production worked to agreed criteria and a common programming system.

There are a number of problems which often have their root in structural deficiencies, and which are on the whole arising more frequently at the present day. These are problems of managerial overload, poor integration, inadequate innovation, weakening control and withdrawal from work. The presence of these problems can serve as a warning that organization structure requires examination.

Warning signs of a structural problem

1 Overload

One common sign of overload among top management is the working of excessive hours. Hard work is not a necessary concomitant of good management. If it signifies overload, the likely consequence will be a deterioration in the quality of decision-making and a slowing down of communication with the rest of the organization. In most cases of overload, the need for greater delegation is signalled with only the clearly strategic issues remaining reserved for top management attention. The achievement of effective delegation may require a series of further changes in structure including the establishment of a framework of indirect controls, the personal development of subordinates and possibly the establishment of more general management positions below the chief executive.

2 Integration

Conflict between managers or between their departments is also a common occurence. Although this problem can have its source in a clash of personalities, it is not unusual to find that it is a sign of structural inadequacy as well. Genuine differences of opinion between departments whose activities are interdependent, such as a conflict between engineers and buyers over the correct balance between quality and price in purchases, have ultimately to be resolved in one form or another since the purchases must be made. A structural mechanism, such as a regular purchasing meeting, would probably offer an opportunity for different opinions to be brought into open confrontation and resolved in a way that elicits the formal agreement of the parties concerned. The alternative is likely to be that the conflict continues to be dealt with on a basis of mistrust and mutual evasion.

Open disagreement between parts of an organization presents one of the more easily identifiable problems in the area of communication and integration. Less obvious, but still very costly, problems can include duplication of effort between units that are not exchanging information adequately, and poor morale among staff who feel that they are not given enough information about changes planned for their areas of work. Supervisors often complain that their authority is undermined by this latter failing. It is true that a complaint about 'communication problems' has often been used by managers as a euphemism for the presence of deep-seated conflicts, but it nevertheless remains the case that communication, in the sense of information processing, is often deficient. Such deficiency could signal the need for some re-organization such as reducing management levels, re-grouping activities or introducing new co-ordinative mechanisms.

3 Innovation

A little verse was once written about one of Britain's largest enterprises, referring to its organization:

> 'Along this tree from foot to crown,
> Ideas flow up and vetoes down.'

A failing capacity to innovate and to be receptive to new ideas is often another sign of structural failure. Innovation of any kind encompasses a multi-stage process in which ideas are generated, selected for further development, and adopted for regular use by the client or beneficiary. The type of structure an organization has can affect this process at any of its stages, but the same structure will not be appropriate for every stage. For example, among the conclusions which emerge from studies of creativity and the generation of ideas is that both are enhanced by (a) freedom to communicate with other people who are a source of ideas inside and outside the research group and by (b) freedom to pursue research without too much distraction or administrative interference. Basically, the requirement at this stage of the process is for the innovators to be able to consider every relevant possibility and avenue of advance. This speaks for a structure which is 'organic' in nature and to some degree self-contained from the everyday operational side of the organization. It also suggests, for instance, that the inventive productivity of scientists is increased when they are not expected to attend too many administrative meetings, which could be time-wasting and distracting for them.

On the other hand, a common reason for the failure of ideas once formulated to gain recognition and practical application lies in the over-separateness of the 'ideas men'. They may be too removed from the level at which decisions on adoption of new developments are made, or lack a sponsor at that level, so one is left with the problem described in the verse.

There may be a failure to integrate the ideas men with members of the organization who are aware of customer or client needs, so that innovations tend to be rejected at the end of the day as not practical or economically attractive. A well-designed structure can assist in the integration and control of the whole innovative process, and repeated failures in this field quite likely signify a structural weakness.

4 Control

One of the essential requirements for the planning and control process to be effective is that people should have a good idea of what they are expected to achieve. A very commonly heard complaint from employees and managers is that they have not been given a clear definition of what their responsibilities or authority are, or that they have not had the opportunity of establishing their work objectives in discussion with management. The classical approach to management, which is still reflected in standard personnel practice, would see this problem as primarily a failure of structural definition, which can be resolved by a clear statement of objectives, responsibilities and authority in job descriptions, manuals of procedure and the like.

Depending on the circumstances, other approaches might be appropriate but these would still require some structural change. For example, job descriptions and other aspects of formalization can be self-defeating in rapidly changing or ambiguous situations. In these cases, it will be more appropriate to keep the definition of people's jobs open to adjustment. Employees, particularly professional and skilled personnel, may resent a managerial attempt to define methods of work to an extent which denies them personal discretion. In these circumstances, the type of structure that is called for could well involve more self-control on the basis of mutually agreed objectives and performance criteria, and the provision of an adequate means for integrating individual efforts through, for instance, grouping all concerned into the same team.

5 Withdrawal from work

It goes without saying that labour turnover, absenteeism and less dramatic manifestations of a withdrawal of employee commitment from work can be extremely costly to an organization. My colleague, David Huber, has for example recently reminded one large British firm that it is having to recruit 15,000 employees each year because of labour turnover alone. Given the costs of recruitment and induction, its labour turnover figure is taking a sizeable proportion out of that company's annual profits. Surveys conducted into labour turnover and employee alienation indicate that structures which create impersonality and a remoteness in personal relationships can contribute to the problem. It is important to qualify this remark by pointing out that it is impossible to generalize without taking employees' expectations of the job, its conditions and prospects, into account. Also, as Huber's as yet unpublished researches demonstrate, external conditions such as local unemployment rates will themselves heavily influence labour turnover by enhancing or diminishing prospects for alternative employment.

Manifestations of high withdrawal from work may signal a partly structural problem. Huber found that among male staff employees in the company mentioned, the failure to provide a regular procedure for reviewing their progress and career plans was a major source of discontent and was cited by many male staff leavers as the main reason for quitting. These employees had clearly thought-out career aspirations. They were on the whole technically trained men whom the company could ill afford to lose. Part of the problem lay in a structural (procedural) inadequacy, which in a sense created unnecessary remoteness between the company and themselves.

Specific questions to ask

Through the use of these examples, I have been trying to make the point that commonly found problems of management are often made worse by structural inadequacies. The presence of such problems serves to warn managers that some change in structure may be necessary. Having said that, it is not of course always easy to decide just where the root of the problem lies, to what degree it arises from poor structure, and at what stage it is worth undertaking the trouble of re-organization. It is impossible to offer any useful generalizations about these matters since they relate entirely to the particular problem and situation. It is possible, though, to suggest a number of questions which may help to sensitize a manager to the nature of an organizational problem, and so provide him with the rudiments of an analytical approach:-

1 What is the scope of the problem?

Sometimes the performance of an organization will be poor along a whole range of dimensions — poor growth, low profit and/or high costs for services provided, lack of innovation and investment, and so on. In other instances the problem may be far more localized. In the event of poor overall performance, if the strategy of management appears to be sound, then it is quite possible that the whole structural framework through which the management is attempting to operate is ill adjusted to prevailing contingencies, is internally out of balance, or is simply more costly compared to that of competitors. In these circumstances a great deal can often be learned about one's own organizational problem by making a direct comparison with more successful competitors. The airline study described in the previous chapter was set up for such a purpose, and it has already led the sponsoring company to make constructive changes in its own organization.

2 What is the source of the problem?

Most localized organizational problems first show up in personal terms. That is, the problem appears to revolve around a particular person or around poor relations between two or more people. There is always a temptation to make a scapegoat for organizational troubles of the person who does not fit in. For example, in one company which had diversified into a technically more sophisticated segment of its industry, the Production Director was blamed for failures in meeting delivery dates. He was a rough diamond in a socially conscious senior management team and, not unexpectedly, reacted to criticism in a highly defensive manner which made no contribution at all towards resolving the problem. In fact, the trouble stemmed at least in part from a structural failing. When the diversification took place a new sales group was established to market the new product lines. The production department was therefore faced with competing demands on its resources from two sales groups. No procedure was laid down to provide the production department with criteria by which to decide on trade-offs between producing the standard and the new lines, both of which required the same plant. No integrative mechanisms were established for collectively discussing problems of priority in scheduling. The need for these was all the more pressing because there were frequent technical failures in producing the new more sophisticated products, and these constantly affected delivery dates.

This, then, is an example of where personal blame was being attached to a man for failures which stemmed in part from structural inadequacy. It is well-known that personal behaviour will tend to become erratic and even aggressive when someone is under strain. This means that a person's natural disposition can become substantially modified when he is placed in a stressful position on account of circumstances which have their root in poor structure or in some other feature of inadequate management. It is always worthwhile asking the question whether structure, management policies or other circumstances could be having an effect on the personal behaviour one first observes to be the problem. It is in any case extremely difficult to change personalities, and unreasonable to expect people to cope with a badly structured situation — it may be much easier to change organization instead. This is not to deny that personal style can create problems of its own which training and development may mitigate, or that inter-personal hostility can be reduced through techniques of confrontation, teambuilding and training-groups. It is, however, important to warn that one should not expect too much from such efforts if there is an underlying structural inadequacy which is not amended as well.

3 Is the problem temporary or permanent, unique or recurrent?

Considerable managerial time and effort is often required to effect a change in organization structure. It is therefore worth making an evaluation of whether the problem at issue, to which one is thinking of applying a structural solution, is only a temporary matter or a more basic problem. Similarly, one has to assess whether the problem is unique or part of a recurrent pattern. If the problem does seem to be temporary and one-off in nature, it will not be worth undertaking a substantial re-organization in order to deal with it. This is the kind of decision which managers face when choosing between the establishment of a temporary task force to bring together a range of contributions to tackle a problem which has arisen or a more permanent team such as one would find within a matrix structure. On the other hand, there is always a temptation to regard a problem as being unique and temporary, in the hope and expectation that it will soon go away or be resolved! It is worth re-examining such problems to see if they do not turn out to be phases of a recurrent difficulty that has so far only been dimly perceived. In fact, if a manager finds he is frequently having to deal with apparently unique problems he may well be deceiving himself about their uniqueness and their temporary nature. In that case, re-organization could be called for.

4 At what level in the organization is the problem located?

For some purposes it is useful to think of organizations as systems of interdependent segments. This helps to remind us that not only are different departments interdependent through their contributions to the same activities and workflows, but so also are the different levels in an organization. We noted back in Chapter 6 how the concentration of decision-making at a high level in the management structure appears to affect behaviour lower down, promoting conformity and an unwillingness to innovate. This is an example of how a problem that appears at one organizational level can have its source at another level.

Most organizations are hierarchical institutions in which it is accepted as legitimate that those at a higher level have executive authority over those lower down. This means that employees and managers will take their cues on many matters from those at the next level above them. If a manager thinks that he has problems among his subordinates he should therefore analyse what contribution he might be making towards them. Is he applying appropriate methods of co-ordination, control, objective setting, assessment and so forth? Is he allowing his subordinates to define and carry out their roles in a way that meets their aspirations and capabilities? Has he assisted them to integrate adequately with other departments? A manager can in various ways structure the roles and behaviour of his subordinates, and so he is partly responsible when these characteristics become problematic.

Formal structural arrangements are an important part of the organization member's work environment. As such they are likely to affect his behaviour and performance either by facilitating the way he carries out his job and his motivation towards it, or by impeding these. To a large extent structure is 'imposed' upon the individual by higher management – the main structural parameters will appear to be established from above. It is for this reason that attempts to develop organizations which focus upon the organization member and his immediate relation to other people and to machinery often do not have as much effect as does a focus upon the context of structural practices, policies and regulations. These structural features in turn need to be understood in relation to the organization's choice of overall strategy and to the contingencies this brings into effect.

Seen in this light, diagnosing the level of an organizational problem and deciding on the appropriate level for any planned change are vital requirements. If it is desired to modify the ways in which people behave and relate or in which work is done, it may be fairly ineffective simply to try to 'develop' the people concerned, *even* if all parties are agreed on the desired direction of change. A tendency to concentrate upon people and to ignore the structural and contingent work environment deriving from a higher level has been one of the reasons for the high rate of failure in the so-called 'Organizational Development' movement.

The practical importance of level in the analysis of requirements for change is illustrated in a paper by Robert Toronto which appeared in the journal *Behavioural Science*, part 3, 1975. He describes change programmes in two functions of a southern U.S.A. oil refinery. These were the shipping function, responsible for the handling of finished products, and a maintenance function responsible for the maintenance of a portion of the refining facilities. The shipping function was subject over a two-year period to changes at the immediate operational level (what Toronto calls the 'system' level). There was no attempt to effect change at a higher ('suprasystem') level involving the wider department of which shipping was part. The trend of performance over this period was erratic. There was a temporary upsurge in the early stage of the change programme, when employees were expecting a significant change for the better. When their expectations were not met, performance fell off, and after some subsequent improvement during the rest of the programme, it then declined sharply. Toronto concludes that 'a gradual improvement cannot sustain itself without supporting changes in the suprasystem' (p.152).

In the case of maintenance, this was subject to changes both at operational and at higher levels. The exact nature of these changes is not specified. Judging maintenance performance in terms of reductions in minor maintenance costs, Toronto concludes that the improvement in that area was more consistent and sustained than in the shipping area. It was also found that a measure of effort given to teambuilding at the level of the function's top management was more closely related to the trend of cost reduction than was effort given to teambuilding at the foreman-employee level. Toronto's data do not permit a causal analysis, but they are highly suggestive in regard to the question of interdependence between levels in organizational change. As Toronto concludes, 'I believe that . . . holistic reasoning is the direction that organization theory and research must take in order to adequately understand and describe the complexity of organizational change' (p.156).

Problems of implementing re-organization

This book concentrates primarily upon the diagnosis of organizational problems. For organization to make a full contribution, however, quality of diagnosis must be complemented by quality of acceptance. Gaining acceptance is the main requirement for a successful introduction of organizational change, and this is the main point that I wish to make in this section. It has important implications for how, in contemporary conditions, managers seek to implement new proposals, for the time that the process of implementation may require and for the use of third parties in the change process. I have space here only to draw attention to these points; they are given detailed consideration in the further reading suggested at the close of the chapter.

1 Method of implementation

As E. A. Johns has said in his book on *The Sociology of Organizational Change*, it is extremely doubtful whether any change introduced today without some measure of consultation would be successful. The reasons for this lie in the capacity of organizational members to resist the introduction of a change or to subvert its operation, and in the value of the positive contributions they can make to the design of a change.

There are various reasons why a re-organization is likely to meet with resistance. It is important for a manager to understand such reasons, for they will help him to appreciate how a change that he regards as rational and even of minor significance may well appear unreasonable and far from trivial to the people directly affected. It is tempting for a manager who does not understand the reasons why people object to change to dismiss their opposition as 'bloody-mindedness' and then make matters worse by attempting to force through changes without any consultation at all. Resistance to change is in fact a universal phenomenon among groups who feel that their interests are threatened. It is found at all levels of organization from boardroom to shopfloor and throughout history from handloom weavers in the early 1800s to motorway protest groups today.

People will resist re-organization if they believe that it is detrimental to aspects of their work life and roles which they value. If the change breaks up established informal social groups, it is likely to be seen as a threat to satisfying social relationships. If it involves a re-arrangement of lines and levels of authority, some people will see in the change a threat to their status within the organization. A change aimed at simplifying an organization structure, maybe through reducing the number of hierarchical levels, will probably be seen by some as a threat to their job security and to their prospects of promotion further up the hierarchy. A change aimed at enriching the jobs of subordinates may be viewed by a manager as a threat to his authority. A re-allocation of functions will be regarded with alarm by some senior managers as a diminution in their territorial rights within the organization. Increased delegation may be received, at least initially, as just an extra burden by some subordinates. A specialist may regard the attempt to re-structure him away from his functional department and into a production or product team as a threat to his professional development and market value. The very process of change itself may be seen as an unwelcome disturbance and interference to a well-established routine. These are just a few of the many reasons why people are likely to react unfavourably to a proposed change in organization structure.

Any decision within organizations is reached and implemented through a political process. Politics is about the use of power, and decisions are a formalization of that use, which will have to be reached through negotiation and compromise when power is spread among several parties. When the decision involves a major change, the political process leading up to it is likely to be all the more active. It is not too difficult to identify the likely major sources of resistance to a proposed change, if one understands the ideology and perceived interests of the groups concerned, and if one can estimate their awareness of their power to influence the change and their propensity to employ it.

The main areas of resistance to change in organizations are reasonably well known by now. Employees will resist changes which they perceive to affect their job security, payment and status differentials, working conditions and methods; on the whole these are the 'hygiene' factors singled out by Herzberg as sources of dissatisfaction when threatened. At the managerial level, a focal point of resistance to change lies in the relationship between specialists and the 'line' manager users of their services. Specialists such as operational researchers, management services staff, and management development personnel, justify their presence by the projects they contribute for improvement and change. They not only seek to promote change, but naturally this is change defined in terms of what is best according to their 'professional' judgement. Their clients often resist such proposals. There is a risk to the maintenance of their routine operations in accepting the disruption of something new. There may be resentment at the implied criticism of having specialists tell them how to manage better.

Because resistance to change is to be expected, and because it is in some degree predictable, Tom Lupton writing in the *Journal of Management Studies* in May 1965 suggested the rudiments of a systematic approach for carrying out such prediction. He saw the management problem to be twofold. First, how to minimize potential disturbances during the period of change. Second how to move quickly to a new stable situation which will produce a satisfactory level of performance. He suggested that those planning the change should:

(a) List all the alternative ways of implementing a change, together with estimated time schedules.

(b) Identify all the sections of the organization, occupational categories or work groups affected by the change, however indirectly.

(c) Calculate the likely reaction of these groups in general terms.

(d) Calculate their likely reaction for specific issues such as wage rates, differentials, promotion prospects, retraining, working practices and redeployment. Securing data of reasonable quality on these issues involves securing the opinion of managers in close contact with all the groups, and even better the direct reaction of the people concerned.

(e) Conclude by estimating in a crude way the overall acceptability of the change and of each approach to change.

Information gathered through applying an approach such as this clearly remains highly subjective. But it is systematically organized and in this respect better than the alternative which is sheer guesswork. One major requirement in assembling information is to ascertain whether spokesmen and sources accurately reflect the views of the people they speak for. This is one of the main considerations in favour of adopting a participative approach in the planning and implementation of change.

If a proposed change is clearly contrary to the interests of those affected by it, there is no point in trying to plan it on a participative basis as a mutual problem. A man who stands to lose his job is only concerned with negotiating the best possible severance terms. In other situations, however, where zero-sum bargaining is not involved and an integration of interests is possible, the involvement of people concerned in the design and implementation of a change will normally offer the best chance of success. One reason is that participation provides an opportunity for the rationale behind the proposed change to be explained and critically examined. This can help to lessen people's fears stemming from a lack of knowledge and a feeling of powerlessness. If people contribute actively towards establishing the new development this helps to create among them a degree of commitment to the change and to making it work. It has been found in American companies, for example, that the probability of operational research projects being successfully implemented is much higher when user departments are fully involved in their design and feel some sense of ownership over them, than in situations where this degree of participation was absent.

A second consideration is that a great deal of the information required as a basis for planning a change — data on present problems, work activities, decision points, time cycles, files, costs, personnel and so forth — will only be known in detail to the people who are affected. Their participation is therefore necessary if the re-organization is to have a grounding in the realities of the situation. The implementation of Mary Parker Follett's 'Law of the Situation' requires participation, as she realized. Thirdly, the process of participation should assist managers to learn about their employees' attitudes, values and perceptions, and this learning experience should assist them to plan further necessary changes in ways that provoke less conflict. Equally, the chance to influence and understand structural change should create an awareness on the part of employees of the need in modern conditions for frequent re-organization, and perhaps eventually a desire to take the initiative in this field through the medium of new participative mechanisms such as planning agreements.

A participative approach, then, is usually appropriate in introducing organizational change, and it offers the best prospect of developing an 'adaptive learning capacity' in organizations. Many people, the writer included, would also maintain that it is ethically the correct procedure for planning changes which affect other people. One can, however, expect too much from it. Participation is a way of confronting the political issues involved in change, not a means of avoiding or smoothing over them. If there is a deep-seated conflict of interest between the parties involved in a proposed change, participation will probably not turn up a mutually acceptable solution. Also if hidden anxieties and hostilities are present, it may be necessary to introduce a skilled third party, a social consultant, to bring these into the open where they can be confronted and dissipated. So long as anxieties and conflicts are present, and not totally recognized, participation is likely to prove an unfruitful exercise.

A participative approach can be difficult for other reasons as well. It is usually very time consuming, the more so in a large-scale organization where participation has to cross so many hierarchical levels to link decisions on change initiated at a senior level to the people affected at a junior level. In some circumstances that time may simply not be available, when a quick reaction to an unexpected event is required. The point is also made by managers that time spent in discussion is time lost to getting on with the job. These are genuine difficulties, though they are to some extent exaggerated by a failure to anticipate new developments in advance to allow time for their discussion, rather than having to react at the last minute. A further problem that is often raised concerns the apparent lack of interest among employees in participation — an unwillingness to devote the effort and share in the responsibility. It is true that some experiments in adopting an American democratic management style have not evoked a positive response in European countries, such as Norway (where one direct replication of an American experiment was made). This, however, does not indicate employee resistance to participation so much as the fact that in Europe this has traditionally been undertaken by union officers and local elected departmental representatives rather than through direct personal relations with managers. I know of no evidence to indicate that members of organizations do not desire to enter discussions on matters of immediate relevance to their jobs and work, be this direct discussion or via representatives. In short, the participative approach to handling change is not an easy one, and is not always functional. The consequences for management of refusing to participate can, however, be most costly where people are in a position to resist or even sabotage change.

If considerable resistance to a proposed change is anticipated, and if it is possible to introduce it first of all on a limited basis, then the use of a 'pilot project' may be helpful. In a pilot project it is agreed that certain specific changes to the existing organization will be made on an experimental basis. After a given period of time, the change is evaluated on the understanding that it will be withdrawn if it is unsuccessful or unacceptable. This approach can have a number of advantages. A favourable situation can be selected for the pilot scheme, perhaps enlisting volunteers. This contributes to the eventual success of the change by getting it over the early period of trial and error in favourable circumstances. Less committed and confident members of the organization may be more prepared to accept the change once the pilot is completed, and this category includes managers who may be wary of committing resources to any new development until they can assess its effects.

Pilot projects do, however, carry risks. They prolong the period of uncertainty which accompanies any change, and if this is a source of considerable anxiety, the result may be to increase rather than lessen hostility to the change. If the pilot scheme is located in too favourable an environment, it may not be possible to replicate any success it has across other parts of the organization. A pilot scheme which excludes people who are less receptive to change may also exclude those with the power to block change. Indeed, the people who hold some power as, say, employee representatives are likely to be particularly cautious about proposed organizational changes because they have a responsibility to work out every possible ramification for their constituent's interests. For this reason it may not be easy to secure the open approval of employee representatives for a pilot scheme. Yet paradoxically by running a change as a pilot scheme, management are in effect placing it on a conditional basis. A change which managers may believe is vital to the continued effectiveness of the organization is in this way made subject to a legitimate, formal veto. Finally, given the inter-connectedness of functions and levels, it will in many situations be impossible to isolate a proposed change in organization and to pilot it on a limited experimental basis.

2 Time required

The implementation of organizational change, because it usually involves a threat to someone's position, is characteristically a lengthy process which is often punctuated by crises between the parties involved. These crises can be quite positive in their consequences since they bring opinions out into the open and make everyone face up to the issues realistically. The participative and discursive approach to implementing change is often blamed for being a time-wasting process, especially by those who maintain that it would be better to decide on a change, impose it and 'be done with it'. Quite apart from the ethics of the matter, we have already seen that resistance to change is likely to attend this kind of policy since people will mostly not accept authoritarianism as legitimate unless there is a real and obvious emergency on their hands. Hugh Marlow, who has had a long experience of re-organization when working for a company manufacturing and introducing computer systems and subsequently for a major consulting firm, has pointed out in his book *Managing Change* that the successful introduction of any change within organizations will take a long time. In his view, changes take place in four phases. These phases can be identified and defined separately, though they tend to overlap in practice. Marlow's opinion is that where re-organization has failed, this has usually been the result of a management attempting to shorten or eliminate one or more of the phases:-

Phase 1 — Personal acceptance. This phase can take at least six months. It involves the gaining of acceptance by the persons who are responsible for introducing an organizational change. More than just personal acceptance is involved here; it also includes acceptance of the function they belong to (systems team, organization department, etc) or of their company if they are outside consultants.

Phase 2 — Expression of resistance to change. During this phase which may last a further six months or so, underlying fears, hostilities and suspicions regarding the proposed changes are brought into the open. Until such views and feelings are expressed openly, no matter how much information is given by management it will not be accepted at its face value.

Phase 3 — Identification with the objectives of the re-organization. It is at the beginning of this phase that the underlying fears encountered in Phase 2 are resolved. The people affected by the change can now begin to see the objectives of the change programme as their objectives and not something imposed on them by higher management. Practical steps towards achieving the objectives of the change can now start to be taken. This phase of active mutual effort towards implementing the change may last for some two years or so in Marlow's experience.

Phase 4 — Building into the organization a facility for continuous critical appraisal. At this stage the re-organization is completed and it is being evaluated. The monitoring of the change and subsequent adjustments should help all concerned to recognize that some organizational modifications have to take place continually. Instead of management waiting until it is forced to adapt to changed circumstances, there could now be a conscious positive effort to anticipate and plan for change. This may become institutionalized in the form of an organization planning or development team. If this stage is reached it is likely to be some three years or so after the original re-organization was first mooted.

This time scale is lengthy indeed, and many managers I have spoken to reject it as being unrealistically so. Their problems just will not wait that long. In practice, a minor re-organization, perhaps establishing a new co-ordinative mechanism such as a regular meeting or a new communications procedure, will take nowhere near as long to plan and implement. A major change, however, such as divisionalization, could well take as long as Marlow suggests. Once an organization has experienced a structural change, it should be possible drastically to reduce the time scale of receptiveness to change so long as the process of critical problem examination and discussion of possible organizational solutions is maintained. While not wishing to advocate change for change's sake, it will assist a management facing the need for frequent adjustments of structure if it can make the process of adjustment and re-organization part of the accepted mode of maintaining long-term equilibrium, rather than introducing change as a relatively infrequent and therefore more traumatic experience. The former approach shortens the time it takes to implement re-organization and also offers a facility for identifying needs for organizational change at an early rather than a late point.

3 Use of third parties

The term 'third party' in the context of organizational change refers to any individual or group who assists in the process of diagnosing problems and implementing solutions, but who is not part of the organization system directly involved in change. Third parties could be outside commercial consultants, academic staff, or members of an organization's development team. The benefits which they can bring include the contribution of analytical technique and experience developed elsewhere, an ability to assist in the resolution of conflicting views by standing outside the conflict, and the acceptability of their advice by virtue of their image as experts and (especially in the case of academics) by virtue of their relatively neutral position with respect to organizational politics. For reasons such as these, third parties have been frequently asked to assist in organizational changes.

The involvement of third parties can create certain problems. Commercial consultants are usually perceived by employees as being committed to top management interests alone, by virtue of their fee payment. There is also some temptation for consultants to apply a standard solution to organizational problems. This is partly because their experience lies largely in the application of standard techniques, and partly because the costs of consultancy can only be borne over a limited time so that a reasonably quick solution is called for. Standardized approaches, however, go against the contingency approach and they are unlikely to be in tune with the unique culture of a particular organization. If, then, management is going to engage commercial consultants in the field of organizational change, it would be well advised to ensure that solutions are not decided upon at the outset, or to the exclusion of other groups concerned in the change.

The staff of management schools are potentially in a better position to enter into long-term collaborative relationships with organizations, and to extend this collaboration over the period of diagnosing and implementing change. It is easier for them to undertake the role of action researcher, which devotes some time to the formation of a consensus on the direction of change through research, feedback and mutual discussion. The typical sequence of events in an action research approach to organizational change would be: (a) research is carried out to provide data for problem diagnosis; (b) this is fed back to relevant management and employee groups; (c) the feedback is evaluated by all concerned; (d) there is then discussion with the researchers regarding options for action; (e) a decision is made on what action to take — a change is made. The effects of the change can then be further investigated by the researcher (possibly doing this together with people from the organization). There is further feedback, discussion, and the cycle continues. The research and feedback stages of the cycle are likely to identify problems and create an awareness of their existence in people's minds — roughly equivalent to going through the first two stages in Marlow's scheme. Discussion of options for action is likely to promote a sense of 'ownership' of the change project and identification with the objectives of the change which are indeed being clarified by the discussion itself (equivalent to Marlow's stage three).

If the organization is large enough to employ its own internal organizational planning and development teams, or internal consulting teams, then they may be able to play the part of action researcher instead. They have, of course, to gain credibility and to be seen as performing a relatively neutral service role. They may also have to rely on outside help for advice on techniques such as those of survey analysis. Internal consultants will, however, enjoy considerable familiarity with the organization's background and management will find them easier to programme than outsiders.

Action research is a lengthy process, and careful control has to be retained over the programming of feedback reports and discussions if valuable time is not to be lost and expectations within the organization disappointed. Management school staff have other demands upon their time, and may not be able to provide the intensity of commitment that is required. Another point is that while such staff with their professional academic standing are more likely to be seen as 'neutral' to the political issues within an organization, the price of this independence will be that the academic feels free to import values of his own into the organization. Managers and employees alike should ascertain what they are taking on when the third party is an independent academic for there is a considerable variation in their values and approaches. Some go so far as to see action research as a means of subverting what they believe are oppressive and exploitative bureaucratic institutions. Others appear to limit themselves purely to a top management perspective, which is also a limitation on their potential contribution as 'third parties' and facilitators of the organizational change process. Many management school staff are, on the other hand, sensitive to the difficulties of playing a role which inevitably brings them into organizational and industrial politics, but feel nevertheless that they have an obligation to offer their services as best they can and to apply their knowledge to practical use.

Bearing in mind that organizational change must gain the positive commitment and understanding of those who have to live with the new arrangements and make them work, it is appropriate that third parties adopt a role which facilitates this. In other words, they are not required to solve organizational problems. Rather, they are required to collaborate with the parties immediately involved in reaching their own solution through activities such as advising on surveys of attitudes, helping people to establish constructive working relationships and promoting the open confrontation of conflicts. Those with experience in this field have pointed out that there are situations in which progress can be made by the third party himself taking on the role of expert problem solver, when for instance a technical matter is concerned. It has even been suggested that a dominant role, backed by top management, can speed up the progress of change. While it is true that to be effective a third party must have some influence, the adoption of a leading or dominant role is unlikely to prove an effective general strategy. Apart from any ethical considerations of power without responsibility, such roles can engender an undue dependence upon the third party. A successful implementation of organizational change in the long-run requires that the people concerned participate actively in the process of working out the new arrangements both as a learning experience and as a basis for generating their personal commitment to the change.

The relationship between third parties and members of an organization is therefore not an easy one to manage. There may be a difference of values and language, different ways of working, different time perspectives. These are compounded when the technical training of the people concerned also varies, as with a behavioural scientist working with engineers on a change in job design, or an organizational expert working with accountants on a change in control procedures. Integration into an effective team can be difficult, but this difficulty is a price that has to be paid for bringing together the people best suited to doing the detailed work on a complex change which involves many different technical facets.

4 Major considerations in the success or failure of organizational change

On the basis of studies which have been made into success and failure in job enrichment and organizational change, it is possible to offer a number of tentative guidelines to the operative factors. On the whole, an organizational change has a better chance of success when the following conditions apply:

(a) The change has the support and understanding of top management, or at least of one influential manager if we are talking of a localized change only. It is therefore treated as a mainstream rather than a peripheral activity.

(b) The change is preceded by a careful diagnosis of the existing situation in order to ascertain the nature and level of the problem, and to isolate the organizational features which are contributing to it.

(c) There is discussion of the problem and possible lines of action with all groups who will be affected, and a willingness to adapt any plans in the light of this discussion. When a change is initiated, it continues to be handled in a participative and adaptive manner.

(d) Partly based on the information gained from participation in discussions, there is an attempt to assess how receptive people are likely to be to the proposed change and to different modes of implementation. This assessment is allowed to influence judgement of how to proceed, and what direct or side effects to expect at each stage.

(e) Training and personal development requirements connected with the change are satisfied before rather than after the event. The staff concerned with carrying through the change are adequately educated and equipped. Not least, senior management is given an understanding of the problems and duration of change so that it has an appreciation of what is likely to happen, and can be quite clear as to the probable costs as well as benefits.

(f) A clear understanding is reached between all parties involved in discussion of the change and any third party as to what the latter's role is expected to be. The momentum of third party contributions is sustained and these are treated as an integral part of the change process.

(g) Attention is given to a systematic monitoring and evaluation of the change and its effects. This is used as a basis for modification when necessary.

Summary

Pressures for re-organization form part and parcel of the changing world in which we now live. There are changes in market conditions involving a greater rate of competition and of innovation, while commodity markets have become less settled. There is an increasing amount of governmental intervention in organizational affairs. Despite recent economic difficulties, organizations continue to grow and diversify. They incorporate new technologies, such as computerized information systems. Their employees are coming from different backgrounds, have higher levels of education and are developing new attitudes. Each of these broad areas of change creates pressures for new structures of organization and of work, because each is changing the contingencies within which management operates.

In this welter of change, it is likely that an organization's structure will quite frequently become inadequate or obsolescent. Problems which commonly arise nowadays of managerial overload, poor integration, difficulties in achieving successful innovation, failures in control or high levels of withdrawal from work, very often have their roots in unsuitable or insufficient structures. The presence of problems such as these should serve to alert managements to the possible need for organizational change, especially if the context of their operations has also changed in important respects. The nature of the problem can be assessed more precisely by asking specific questions about its scope, source, degree of recurrence, and level.

The successful implementation of re-organization requires that it is accepted by those who have to make it work. In the modern world, this involves processes of participative discussion and working through of details. These can be time-consuming and even frustrating for many managers, but failure often attends the attempt to cut them short. Third parties — consultants, external advisors and internal staff groups — can facilitate the implementation of change, as well as the initial diagnosis of its necessity, but their role is normally defined as helping the people directly concerned to work out their own solutions.

Suggested further reading

The Addison-Wesley Publishing Company's series on Organization Development includes some excellent concisely written volumes on the issues raised in this chapter. In particular, R. J. C. Roeber's *The Organization in a Changing Environment* (1973), Richard Beckhard, *Organization Development: Strategies and Models* (1969), and Paul R. Lawrence and Jay W. Lorsch, *Developing Organizations: Diagnosis and Action* (1969). E. A. Johns, *The Sociology of Organizational Change* (Pergamon 1973), provides a good coverage of research findings on problems of changing organization and is well illustrated with case studies. Newton Margulies and John Wallace, *Organizational Change: Techniques and Applications* (Scott, Foresman 1973), examine relevant techniques in some detail. In his *Action Research and Organizational Change* (Harper and Row 1972), Peter A. Clark examines the role of behavioural scientists as third parties contributing to planned organizational change. Hugh Marlow, *Managing Change: A Strategy for Our Time* (Institute of Personnel Management, London 1975), draws upon the author's wide experience and in particular calls attention to the time scale of the change process. Another practical guide with examples drawn from the ICI Petrochemicals Division is I. L. Mangham, D. Shaw and B. Wilson, *Managing Change* (British Institute of Management, London 1972).

Reference was also made to Robert S. Toronto, 'A General Systems Model for the Analysis of Organizational Change', *Behavioural Science*, volume 20, 1975, and to Tom Lupton, 'The Practical Analysis of Change in Organizations', *Journal of Management Studies*, May 1965.

CHAPTER 9

THE FUTURE OF ORGANIZATION—CRISIS AND CHALLENGE

'Without democracy there cannot be any correct centralism, because people's ideas differ, and if their understanding of things lacks unity then centralism cannot be established.' Mao Tse-Tung, Speech of 30th January, 1962.

In this passage, Mao Tse-Tung points to a profound paradox in the role of organization. When a collective enterprise or a community reaches a certain size and level of occupational specialization, some form of organization has to be laid down as a necessary condition for its continued functioning. People's activities require co-ordination. Except in small and simple groups, this cannot be done just on the basis of face-to-face communication; co-ordination has to be achieved through a centralized point of administration. There also has to be a control function in order to secure information as to what is going on, and to maintain individual rights and obligations in the collectivity. These forces create the need for centralism.

The mode of administration which has most often been adopted, from the appointment of estate managers such as the servants of the Pharaoh and freedmen of the early Roman emperors to the salaried manager and government officer of today, is bureaucracy. Bureaucracy is in most societies the basis of administration throughout government, public service, much of industry, many trade unions, the larger churches and other institutions. The process of setting up centralized bureaucratic administration concentrates information, command of resources, and therefore power into a relatively few hands. Whatever official provisions are laid down to control the use of this power, it is always difficult for those outside administration to gain sufficient access to information or to the decision-making process itself. This explains the concern that governmental decisions may not reflect public opinion or that managers may act against the best interests either of shareholders or employees. People who have achieved high office also have an understandable tendency to seek to preserve the *status quo* in which their position is enshrined. They may therefore be unwilling to adopt progressive organizational policies which satisfy new demands and changing conditions.

The paradox of organization lies therefore in the fact that without it democratically expressed wishes and forward progress cannot readily be given any effect, yet with it barriers may come to be placed in the way of the effective expression of democratic views and desires for change. As Mao Tse-Tung pointed out, without an expression of views by the community there is no legitimate basis for organized, centralized action. On the other hand, organizational decisions cannot readily be reached if there is no consensus of views, and an obvious way out of this situation is for managers to impose a view of their own, thus denying the basis of their authority.

While these issues have troubled thinking men for a long time, they pose particularly acute problems for the structure of organizations in contemporary conditions. For in the western world we have moved into an 'anti-organizational' climate of opinion in which centralism, lack of participation and public accountability, inefficiency and inadequate response to change constitute prominent criticisms which are being made against organizations, particularly larger ones. Bureaucracy is identified as the major source of these failings, and it is being examined critically not just in terms of administrative effectiveness but also of political and social acceptability. The question is therefore raised whether, after many centuries of reliance on bureaucracy, we can now find alternative ways of organizing collective effort.

The analysis of organizational choices in Part II of this book was made with bureaucracy as its main point of reference. It examined ways in which managers can modify bureaucratic structures so as to progress a little way towards meeting the pressures and criticisms which are being experienced today. Bureaucracy is, for instance, characterized by the specialization of employment into precisely (and usually narrowly) defined areas of responsibility. Job enrichment involves a move away from this degree of specialization and definition. The expectations that professionally trained specialists have of how they should work also conflicts with a bureaucratic style of job definition, while the idea of incorporating specialists into fairly organic teams in order to integrate their contributions is a further departure from bureaucracy. Similarly with development away from purely departmental to matrix structures, from long to short hierarchies, from control through formalized systems to self-control, and from integration by plan, procedure or referral up the hierarchy to integration through lateral relationships — all these represent in some degree a shift from the now traditional bureaucratic model of organization. Structural changes of this kind have emerged as appropriate responses for developments in regard to environment, diversification, occupational skills, employee expectations and other conditions which at least some, if not many, organizations are experiencing today.

Yet these are only modifications to bureaucracy, often precarious in their experimental status and not as yet really going very far towards resolving the underlying dilemma of organization. Indeed, despite claims that have been made to the effect, a close examination of the present scene cannot lead one to conclude that the 'end of bureaucracy' is really in sight. There are undoubtedly very strong forces making for the preservation of bureaucracy as an organizational way of life. It would be naive to put this down completely to inertia or to the vested interests of well-established bureaucrats. It is, of course, extremely difficult to make major changes to the structure and style of an organization because of internal political resistance, as the previous chapter indicated, but there are also other reasons for the persistence of bureaucracy. It is, as we have seen, probably the most effective way of coping with the administration of large organizations operating under relatively stable conditions. Although environmental conditions are becoming more volatile and less predictable, organizations are continuing to grow larger and are also attempting where possible to preserve some external stability through negotiation with other organizations and national governments. The growing involvement of government in organizations through legislation on matters of employment rights, safety at work and so forth has in fact been another force making for more bureaucracy, though in this case one instigated by a popular demand for universally applicable employment opportunities and rights.

Bureaucracy, then, may be here to stay for a long time. It seems to be a functional administrative response to large scale and complexity. It is a means for the centre to retain control over sub-units, and it is a system run by people who have little reason to see it abolished. It is even to some degree a means of protecting people from arbitrary government or management — the protection afforded by defining proper procedure and individual rights. At the same time, there are new economic and social developments to which bureaucracy in its traditional form is not well suited.

The growing contradiction inherent in this situation is beginning to present us with a crisis in organizational life. The role of organizational design in reconciling technical and economic with political and social requirements will be a challenging one in the future. It is into this broader perspective that I would now like to place the preceding contents of this book. The elements of the problem need to be analysed step by step. First. what continues to sustain bureaucracy and what are the directions of its present development? Second, which contemporary trends speak for a move towards new forms of organization? Third, what is the nature of the growing crisis in organizational life consequent on the continued presence of bureaucracy? Finally, what policies on organizational design may help to resolve the problem in the future?

Development of bureaucracy

A considerable body of research demonstrates how in many fields — business, public service, trade unions and others — bigness and bureaucracy go hand in hand. So long, therefore, as most of our work is done in large organizations, we can expect bureaucracy to remain the typical approach to administration.

The average size of business firms has increased since the Second World War in the United States, Britain, the E.E.C. as a whole, and in Japan. That is to say, the shares taken by the larger firms in output and assets have increased, and the absolute size of these firms has grown markedly. In Britain, for example, the share of the 100 largest companies in net manufacturing output was 22 percent in 1949. By 1970 this had risen to 41 percent. Should present trends continue, the share of the 100 largest companies could be in the region of 70 percent by the end of the century. Expansion of firms has not, of course, been confined to their domestic economies; many have become multinational enterprises.

In the public sector, in Britain, a movement towards larger organizational units has also been underway. On April 1st 1974 some 1400 English and Welsh local government authorities were reduced in numbers to 422. This represents an increase in the average size of these authorities by a factor of over three. In central government there have been amalgamations of separate ministries into giant 'super-ministries' such as those for environment and industry. Individual small departments have been merged, such as the Government Social Survey and the General Register Office, while previously small groups such as the Cabinet Office have grown significantly. The largest rate of increase in tertiary sector employment in Britain in recent years has in fact been in government service. By July 1976, central and local government wages and salaries were accounting for over one-quarter of all U.K. public expenditure. In the health field, following the re-organization of April 1974 the scale and scope of administrative units has also been increased. Reports from other countries such as Sweden and the United States suggest that this trend towards larger scale organization in public administration is evident in many countries.

The size conditions for bureaucracy are therefore quite widespread today, and are increasing. Industrial research suggests that the link between bigness and bureaucracy has its roots in some degree of economic necessity. For it has been found that, while large organizations as such are not on the whole more effective than smaller ones, the more effective large organizations tend to be more bureaucratic than the less effective large units. That is, in terms of structure, they create more specialized posts and departments, they have longer hierarchies, they rely more on following regulations, they have more red tape and formalization. The details of this relationship were described in Chapter 7.

Although other features, such as the kind of environment in which an organization operates, do modify this economic advantage which bureaucracy affords the large organization, it nevertheless suggests that bigness may breed bureaucracy of some necessity. So if we want to minimize bureaucracy we probably have to reduce the size of organizations and of administrative units.

The detail of this link between bigness and bureaucracy would take some time to trace out. Research carried out at Aston University suggests a several stage process shown in Figure 9.1. Growth tends first to generate departmentalism, an accumulation of different jobs each differentiated from the next, and an increase in hierarchical levels. Problems of communication and co-ordination then arise. The traditional administrative response to these problems is to set up rules, procedures, written instructions and systems of records in an attempt to establish a clear definition of what people are supposed to do and who is supposed to communicate with whom, as well as to secure information on what actually takes place. The employment of specialists in new departments and posts encourages the growth of procedures and paperwork, because many of them view the development of new 'systems' for personnel, maintenance, control of workflow and other matters as a major part of their job.

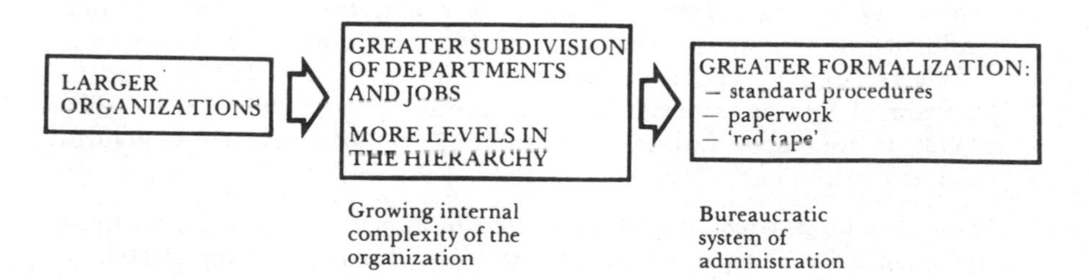

Figure 9.1
The relation of size to bureaucracy

Investigations into the growth of firms over the course of time, as well as some research into American public departments of finance, have confirmed that it is the size factor which exerts a particularly strong push towards bureaucratic organization. I shall note later on how increases in the size of British public authorities seem to be having a similar effect, and one which is attracting considerable criticism. Over and above the size effect, however, it also appears that many organizations become more bureaucratic simply with the passage of time. There is evidence that as organizations become older, even though they do not grow, they tend to become more departmentalized and to employ an increasingly formalized approach to control and communication. The phenomenon of departments multiplying may be due to the operation of Parkinson's Law and the 'strain towards functional autonomy' noted earlier. The development of formalization is partly associated with attempts to delegate and is also a reflection of organizational learning – an attempt to codify over time what experience seems to show is 'good practice'.

Bureaucracy, then, is not only still with us but we seem to be employing it more and more. How well is it likely to accommodate contemporary developments in the world of work?

Elements of organizational crisis

The previous chapter discussed the pressures which oblige management to make changes in the nature of their organizational structures. Many organizations today are faced with an increasingly recurrent need to change their activities and methods, and this places a premium upon their administrative adaptability. There is a search for a form of structure which will facilitate the information processing and co-ordinative effectiveness of an organization seeking to improve its capacity to anticipate and respond to new external developments. Many organizations have, in practice, experienced serious difficulties in adjusting to changes in economic conditions, in adopting improved technologies, and in developing new approaches which satisfy changing expectations among employees and the community at large. These difficulties are manifest in crises of public confidence, in fluctuating levels of corporate performance, in the failures of long-established leaders to adjust policies to signs of failure, and in problems of internal morale. External pressures, particularly when they develop in frequency and intensity, present a requirement for structures which encourage adaptiveness.

At another level, which is perhaps more fundamental since it represents a long-term shift in social attitudes, there is a further current of change which will have profound implications for the structure of organizations. This is the demand that more groups should have access to the arena of organizational decision-making, and the other side of the coin, that the criteria for organizational accountability should be broadened so as to incorporate the interests of employees, the local community and the public at large as consumers or clients of an institution. This growing expectation usually goes under the heading of 'participation' and it is finding widespread public expression today in many western societies, especially in Europe. The British Government for example, set up an official committee of inquiry into participation in August 1975. The E.E.C. Commission's 'Fifth Directive' calls for extensions of employee representation on company boards.

Behind the banner of participation march many causes — the desire of workpeople to have more control over their immediate working environments, the demand of their official representatives to share in the corporate planning process which sets the parameters for their member's working lives, and the impatience of many middle managers and staff personnel with their lack of involvement in the making of significant decisions. The increasing proportion of semi-professional and technically qualified employees within working populations is swelling the numbers of those who not only seek some discretion in their work but also feel they have an expert view which should be taken account of in management decisions. Outside the organization, the notion of 'participation' also encompasses the rights of consumer, community and environmental groups to scrutinize the actions of managers and administrators for evidence of exploitation and lack of social responsibility. All in all, then, participation presents a requirement for organizational structures which facilitate accessibility to information and decision-making.

The presence of a growing requirement for structures which raise both the adaptive capacity and accessibility of organizations has been noted by many commentators and would scarcely be denied. What is perhaps not so widely appreciated is the fact that the continued growth in organizational scale and bureaucracy makes it all the more difficult to achieve the kind of structures which are now called for by these other developments. There is, in fact, a growing contradiction between the pressures for adaptiveness and participation which are being placed upon our major institutions and the direction in which they are currently evolving. The nature of this crisis can be clarified by comparing the main features of bureaucracy with the requirements for organizational adaptiveness and accessibility. This is done in Table 9.1.

In the first column of the Table are some attributes of an organization which has a high capacity for adapting to change. These attributes have been selected on the basis of available research and experience, and the reasoning involved has been developed at various points in previous chapters. It is essentially an organization whose structure encourages a free exchange of ideas, open communications, an awareness of changes in local conditions and a sense of responsibility to various interest groups all of which will from time to time exert pressure for change. In the second column are listed the corresponding attributes of the organization which is participative — accessible to democratic opinion. The attributes are in fact those of a democratic institution. What is interesting is the extent to which they reflect the attributes of an adaptive organization, particularly in provisions for open communication and discussion.

Table 9.1
Adaptiveness, accessibility and bureaucracy

The attributes of an adaptive organization	The attributes of public accessibility and accountability	The attributes of bureaucracy
A sense of responsibility to a network of interest groups	Responsibility to the governed	Responsibility to superiors in the line of command
Participation and involvement in decisions by those concerned with or affected by change	Participation and involvement in decisions	Remoteness of the top of the hierarchy; confidentiality and restriction of information to the public
Exchange of knowledge and open expression of views	The right to dissent	Insistence on conformity to common rules and regulations; maintaining a departmental 'view'
Awareness of changes in local operating environment	Awareness of local and community interests	Geographical centralization of policy making

The third, right-hand column is the quite contrasting profile of bureaucratic organization. This lays emphasis upon responsibility to superiors in the hierarchy and to hierarchical patterns of communication in general. Information is normally treated as highly confidential within bureaucracies and even more so when access by members of the public is concerned. There tends to be an insistence on following the rules and maintaining the 'departmental line' even when an individual has personal reservations. Bureaucracies, moreover, generally centralize their policy making in a headquarters location. This is partly because they are large organizations and the location is frequently the capital city. All these bureaucratic attributes have in the past been thought to characterize sound administration. Yet one can readily appreciate how, point by point, bureaucracy rests upon quite different principles to adaptive and accessible structures.

The least acceptable characteristic of bureaucracy in the context of the 'open society' which many are demanding today is its tendency to remoteness both internally from employees and externally from the public. To emphasize this point, I can do no better than quote an observation of the pioneering sociologist Max Weber who made a long study of the subject:

> Every bureaucracy seeks to increase the superiority of the professionally informed by keeping their knowledge and intentions secret. Bureaucratic administration always tends to be an administration of 'secret sessions': in so far as it can it hides its knowledge and action from criticism.

In this context, a documentary screened by the BBC in April 1974 — 'The Right to Know' — was most significant. It was significant as an expression of public impatience at organizational secrecy. It was significant also for demonstrating with many examples the appalling costs to the community which bureaucratic secrecy on the part of central and local government departments can cover up. One does not need to remind the American reader of Watergate in this respect, which however extreme a case it may have been only represented an accentuation of a general tendency.

There is, then, in my view a growing crisis in organizational life, and it centres around the entrenched position of bureaucracy. I can only illustrate this with first-hand knowledge of events in Britain, although discussions with many colleagues suggest that it is also to be found in other countries. At the time of writing the problem is becoming manifest in various contexts such as debates about industrial participation, protests about the limited rights of objectors in planning enquiries, and concern about the cost of swollen public bureaucracies. Some managers in British industry are aware of the issues involved and are prepared to discuss them openly. Many large firms have started to set up formal participation schemes of their own in advance of impending legislation. Some firms have consciously striven to contain the size of their constituents and plants in an effort to contain bureaucracy and increase flexibility.

In the field of public administration and public services there has been less willingness by British government ministers or senior administrators to recognize that the problem exists. In fact, some official statements have claimed that rather than a trend towards bureaucratic centralism there have been moves in the reverse direction towards devolution and greater public participation. What has been happening in the British public sector provides a good illustration of the organizational problem which is emerging.

Contemporary developments

The background to the organizational crisis, to repeat, is that administrative units are growing in size and becoming more concentrated, often through amalgamation. This growth is justified on the grounds of increasing efficiency, providing a better integration of services and so forth. However, the bigger units are more complex and so correspondingly is their management. With the development of longer and usually more costly managerial hierarchies, policy-making becomes increasingly remote from lay members of the public and from employees of the organizations themselves. This lack of accessibility is in turn likely to reduce the organization's responsiveness to new developments in the environment.

1 Local government

On April 1st 1974 local government was re-organized in England and Wales into larger units. The amalgamation of authorities entailed a centralization of many decisions from local to more distant district authorities.

Considerable concern has been expressed at the consequences of the local government reorganization for ordinary people. In this respect it is instructive to recall the remarks of a Surrey County Councillor who was interviewed for the BBC on the day of re-organization. He admitted that the new larger authorities would be more remote from the people. It would be more difficult for a member of the public to obtain access to local authority officers in order to secure action on specific complaints, and so flexibility as well as accessibility would be reduced. After re-organization it would be virtually impossible to establish the personal relations between local officials and individual members of the public which in the past helped so much to give people a feeling that their particular problem was being recognized and dealt with.

This councillor and others in local government admit that the re-organization is trading accessibility and flexibility for bureaucracy. Their justification for the exchange lies in an increased efficiency of services provided. An objective indicator of greater efficiency in local government would be better services, lower costs and rates, or some balance of the two. Yet in the words of the same councillor, 'by "efficiency" I mean convenience to administrators – whether this is efficiency in any real sense remains to be seen.'

A major item in the efficiency equation is the cost and complexity of administration. The numbers of specialized departments have risen substantially along with the greater size of local authorities. In some fields, such as architecture, civil engineering and planning, the new authorities are now able to operate full departments, in this way saving the cost of contracting work out, and also offering a higher quality of service. Overall, though, the re-organization has substantially increased the staff bill with no clear evidence that this has been reflected in improved services. At the time of re-organization, the number of staff employed in local government rose by about six percent, while salaries climbed by about ten percent. The salary increase is a particularly remarkable comment on increased efficiency to the public, since salaries rose mostly on the basis, not of more responsibility or more work, but merely of the greater population in the new larger local authority areas. The price that rate payers and consumers of local government services were compelled to pay rose far and above the level warranted by the general rate of inflation in Britain. Indeed, the chairman of the new West Midlands Metropolitan County was quoted as saying of the new system that 'I don't think anyone anticipated that it would be anything other than more expensive.'

The increase in British local government employment during the period June 1974 to March 1976 was over 110,000. Some of this increase was accounted for by the provision of new statutory services, but a great deal was administrative overhead and extension of management hierarchy. Mr. Cowley, a Yorkshire farmer, wrote a letter to *The Times* on April 11th 1974 complaining of the local government re-organization and the increase in expenditure it involved. He went on to provide a local illustration of the elaboration in administration which British local government experienced:

> I am one of those who have long pressed for better facilities in my own North Yorks Moors Park – an extra warden and a few more toilets.
>
> We are indeed to get an extra warden, but to administer three wardens in the field and a few car park attendants we are to have a national park officer at over £6,000 per annum with a hierarchy of some thirty principal assistants, and clerical assistants, amounting to a budget of around £150,000.

2 An illustration from central government

In 1974, I received a long letter and some papers from someone who must remain anonymous, but who works in the Social Survey Division of the Office of Population Censuses and Surveys. These documents pass an interesting comment on the issue of size, participation, flexibility and efficiency.

Since its formation during the Second World War, the Government Social Survey had been part of the Central Office of Information. This somewhat anomalous location appeared to suit the Office's top administrators and it left the professional staff of the Social Survey with a considerable degree of autonomy. In 1968 the Social Survey became independent from the C.O.I.; but (I quote) 'the centralist thinkers in the Civil Service could not bear to let small, but relatively efficient and economical, government departments continue an independent life.' Thus, in pursuit of the same path of amalgamation we have already noted in local government, the

Social Survey was merged with the General Register Office at Somerset House, the nature of whose work is quite different.

The consequences of this amalgamation for efficiency and participation by staff were marked. When the Social Survey was a small unit on its own, research officers used to deal directly with heads of specialist branches (sampling, fieldwork, and so on) within the department. The programming staff would participate directly with resource providers in designing and carrying out surveys. With amalgamation and growing size, the administration of the new organization decided to appoint a 'head of specialist branches'. The result is that exactly the same people do the same work as before, except that there is an extra 'level' involved in the communication process, and neither research officers or specialists can participate in decision-making to the same extent as before. So far as efficiency is concerned communication now takes longer and is less effective. It is also costlier. As Robert Townsend has commented in *Up the Organization*, 'each level of management lowers communication effectiveness within the organization by about 25%' – and all the research evidence we have suggests that he is reasonably correct.

3 Development planning

Development planning is closely linked to local government in Britain. Here, the 1971 Town and Country Planning Act, Part II, amended in 1972, introduced a new two-tier system for planning inquiries. A structure plan, which is to be larger and more comprehensive in scope than plans under the old system, deals with issues at the level of policy and general proposals. The lower tier deals with local plans which work out details that have to conform to the principles established at the structure plan inquiry. The status and conduct of structure plan inquiries is therefore of key importance.

Official documents lay considerable emphasis on what is called the 'public participation' and 'examination in public' provided by the new scheme. Yet it is only at the local planning inquiry that members of the public are now permitted to raise objections on the basis of their own local interests. If these objections conflict with the principles of the structure plan, they are likely to be ruled out of order. Under the previous system of planning inquiries individual objectors had the right to a personal hearing. Now, even if they are organized, individual and local communities have no guarantee of a place at a structure plan inquiry. According to the Department of Environment's document on *Structure Plans*, the Secretary of State selects participants according to 'the effectiveness of the contribution which . . . they can be expected to make to the discussion of the matters to be examined.' This criterion could be used to exclude those with basic objections to a given line of official policy, and the provision clearly reduces public access to the planning decision process.

There are undoubtedly good reasons for wishing to streamline the planning process so as, for instance, to reduce periods of uncertainty and planning blight. But to present the new system in a language that implies a greater degree of public participation is to claim the reverse of what has actually happened. In actual fact, the increase in the scale of planning has centralized it into the hands of bureaucracy, limiting public participation and lowering the likelihood that plans will be adapted to suit local interests.

4 National Health Service

The National Health Service was re-organized on April 1st 1974. This particular re-organization has been the subject of fierce controversy, and it provides an especially good illustration of the conflict between bureaucratic and other considerations.

The new health service structure has been influenced by the 'Glacier' approach to organization now expounded mainly by Professor Elliot Jaques and his colleagues at Brunel University. This approach argues for a clear definition of roles and for an executive line of command unimpeded by systems of participation and representation, which should be organized separately. This scheme looks orderly and convincing in Lord Wilfred Brown's writings on how it was intended to operate in the Glacier Metal Company. A management system executes policies which are drawn up by a separate legislative assembly that includes representatives of employees. Yet, in practice when the biggest decision of all came along, namely to sell the company, I am informed by a director of the acquiring firm that this was made without any reference at all to the legislative council or to the body of employees. This suggests that a system of participation which is removed from the real location of information and decision-making is likely to prove quite ineffective.

In the light of this background, it is not altogether surprising that the National Health Service re-organization has been strongly criticized from sources within and outside the service. Criticism has centred on the way that traditional hierarchical management principles are being applied to professional and public service, to the exclusion of effective patient and lay public participation. A further cause of complaint is that the greater flexibility sought from the new organization which integrates community health services has been more than offset by the increase in hierarchical layers and committees which have to be gone through before many decisions can be made.

Space permits me to mention only a few aspects of the NHS re-organization, to illustrate how it conforms to the more general progress of size and bureaucracy which I have been describing. The scale of the new administrative units has been increased, partly by taking in community health services from local authorities and partly because the new Area Health Authorities are normally larger than the Hospital Management Committees they replace.

There is a greater centralization of direction and management under the new system, with fewer authorities now taking decisions. Lay members are far less involved in decision-making. There are now more levels in the hierarchy between hospital patients and the focus of decision-making, so that, for example, in dealing with complaints a far more complex and lengthy procedure has to be gone through.

A major criticism levelled at the new health organization is that it deliberately keeps patients and the public at arms' length. Participation in health service administration is discouraged. As the White Paper on the subject puts it, 'The Government prefer . . . each of the interests . . . management and community . . . to concentrate on its own special function.' But if experience at the Glacier Metal Company is anything to go by, such a separation is highly likely to work at the expense of the community. Do the new arrangements in fact make the health service authorities accountable to the communities which they serve?

Community Health Councils have been set up for expressing local opinion. The Area Health Authorities which they are supposed to monitor actually appoint half their members, and judging by appointments in an area close to Birmingham, the other members are likely to be mainly councillors or other officials. In this area only four out of a total of thirty members are in any way representatives of community or voluntary associations. It is doubtful if many members of the Community Health Councils will come directly from the community at large. The Councils are heavily dependent on the Area Health Authorities for their facilities and goodwill. They only have certain undefined rights of information, visiting and access, and they have no power to take or share in management decisions.

A great deal of the experience embodied in lay members of the former Hospital Management Committees has been lost, because in the words of one such person, most of them were not interested in joining the Community Health Councils. They feel these are likely to become no more than complaints committees. The HMCs used to administer quite considerable financial resources. Naturally, some resentment has been felt at ministerial statements that the involvement of voluntary lay persons in the NHS is as great as before. This could be true regarding their numbers, but it is certainly not true regarding their role in management. What has happened is that lay members of the community taking a share in hospital administration have now been largely superseded by bureaucrats.

Although under the new system the better integration of professional services should be a benefit, there are likely to be a few economies of scale to offset the greater remoteness of decision-making. Benefits of scale in specialized facilities came about under the old system through transfer of patients and general co-operation between different districts. And just as with other re-organizations and increases in scale, the health service is now incurring extra costs arising from increases in administrative staff and office premises required.

On March 9th 1975, a comment on the first year's operation of the re-organized National Health Service appeared in the *Sunday Times* written by Professor Harold Lambert of London University and St. George's Hospital, London. This succinctly expresses the misgivings that professional members of the Service have of the developments I have described. 'Almost a year ago,' wrote Professor Lambert, 'the National Health Service was re-organized; but many of the intended benefits have failed to materialize, and the Service is now being bound in nightmare knots of bureaucracy.' It was hoped that the re-organization would provide an opportunity to break through institutional barriers and open the way to more flexible health care policies. 'From the beginning it was clear that this was not to be. Under the fine phrases of modern management — "maximum delegation downwards, matched by accountability upwards" — could easily be discerned an old-fashioned, pyramidal structure of the most inflexible type, clearly destined to drown the Health Service in bureaucracy.'

Professor Lambert's article goes on to describe in more detail what has gone wrong. For our purposes, it is enough to note that here again is an example of the trend to large scale and bureaucracy which we have discerned across many areas of present-day organization. Clearly, there is growing dissatisfaction with this trend in all walks of activity. The challenge to managers and administrators lies in understanding what is happening and in exploring the possibility of developing alternative organizational policies.

The challenge

The increasing size of organization has been seen to reinforce bureaucracy. This trend reduces opportunities for participation in decisions of consequence, and it is also likely to decrease the adaptability of organizations. If participation and adaptation are becoming two prime requirements for organizations to have, then the challenge must be to find ways of reducing their size, or moving beyond bureaucracy, or both.

1 'Bigness is best' but 'Small is beautiful'

Quite apart from the formality which tends to characterize its administration, the sheer size of large organizations inhibits effective participation or a rapid response to change because of the extended lines of communication which are involved. Although there is considerable interest in the question of participation within British industry, it is doubtful whether any of the schemes formulated so far will achieve complete success in a large company. If there is participation by elected representatives in matters of company policy it is almost impossible for them to maintain adequate communication with their many constituents. Equally, if participation is extended to decisions concerning the way work is done and conditions in the immediate working environment, these will appear remote from decisions on manpower and investment policies affecting people's future working conditions as a whole, when there are many levels in the hierarchy between the two areas of decision-making. Even in a small company employing only 400 persons, I have found that this gap between participation in shopfloor and strategic decisions presented a serious communication problem. The capacity of a large company to adapt to change is also generally inferior to that of a smaller concern, in which lines of communication are shorter and in which it is generally easier to reach a quick decision because fewer people need to be consulted and there is less formalized procedure to be gone through.

The size of organization *per se* is therefore a factor warranting critical examination. Virtually all the research evidence available on the benefits of large scale relates to the industrial field, although the recent experience of British public administration casts doubt on whether size has brought much advantage in that sector. The economic benefits of large-scale industry have on the whole been considerably exaggerated, especially during the merger and rationalization fever which gripped Europe in the 1960s.

The general conclusion which can be drawn from studies of scale in industrial production and in R & D is that, while there may be important economic thresholds for the small organization seeking to become medium sized, these are not on the whole much in evidence for larger units. In some fields scale economies are available in marketing, distribution and international operations. Large size can, of course, bring other benefits — increased bargaining power in markets, a lower cost of raising finance, higher salaries, more security and perhaps greater social prestige for managers — but these are not genuine economies in the sense of increasing the overall social product. Without going into all the details and necessary qualifications of relevant research, five sets of evidence illustrate how doubtful is the argument that 'bigness is best':

(a) Large companies do not in general exhibit higher profitability or appreciably higher growth rates than do small companies — they only achieve a more stable pattern of performance.

(b) Large companies often continue to operate relatively small plants — the concentration of companies is far greater than that of production units. This suggests that arguments for production economies of scale may have been exaggerated.

(c) There is no general association between national economic performance and the average size of firms in a country. Indeed size of plant and national growth rates tend to be inversely related.

(d) In Britain and America, several research studies have demonstrated that there is a high correlation between the size of firms (or of plants) and the intensity of their industrial unrest, levels of labour turnover and other costly manifestations of dissatisfaction. For example, figures for British manufacturing plants over the period 1971 to 1973 show that the time lost through disputes increased with size of plant from 15 days for every 1,000 employees in those employing between 10 and 25 workers to more than 2,000 days in plants employing 1,000 or more people.

(e) Data collected in England and Wales suggested that once farms have reached the three-man unit, there is little further improvement in performance accompanying larger scale. Farm performance is measured by the ratio of the market value of outputs to the cost of inputs (rents, labour and machinery costs, fertilizers, feedstuffs, etc.).

In some industries such as steel, cement and glass bottle manufacturing, there are large technological economies accompanying an increase in scale of production, although in an industry like steel, plant size may be limited in practice by a desire to retain flexibility in type of production. In most fields of work, however, there would appear to be relatively little economies of scale once the cost advantages accruing to the early stages of growth have been gained.

Whatever technological economies of scale that are available to the larger organization will in any case become progressively more counter-balanced by administrative and human diseconomies. Many large organizations recognize the difficulties of communication and control which they incur, and respond to these by setting up costly administrative systems run by non-productive personnel. This additional overhead takes the form of audits, controls, inspections, monthly reports, progress chasers, stock-takings, interim cost statements, elaborate staff assessment schemes, and integrating mechanisms such as formal inter-departmental meetings. Each of these provisions actually increases the complexity of the total communication network. The human diseconomies of scale arise because large bureaucratic organization structures tend to breed anonymity and alienation. People are subject to distant, often impersonal communications and their work tends to be controlled impersonally. As we have seen, their response to this organizational 'distance' often takes the form of a reciprocal withdrawal of commitment in various ways.

Derek Sheane, an internal consultant with ICI, has listed some of the organizational diseconomies which arise in a large organization of that kind when the limits of size and complexity are approached. The complexity of the large organization generates high degrees of interdependence so that one unit may not be able to act independently and respond to important developments in the outside world. In his experience this type of organization also develops a proliferation of political positions and vested interests which can block change and create rigidity in the way the organization functions. A small distribution group could, for example, effectively immobilize a complete manufacturing division. The more complex these power bases become, the more difficult it is for the centre of the organization to hold things together and have adequate effort given to new business opportunities. Centre-division relations tend to become increasingly strained and the proliferation of specialized departments at both levels can leave an individual manager the victim of conflicting pressures and performance criteria. 'For example, a manager may be asked to reduce manpower, pursue growth and manage in a socially responsible manner — all at once.'

Geoffrey Buss, an experienced consultant, has summed up this balance between technical economies and organizational diseconomies of growing size in industry by means of the following diagram:

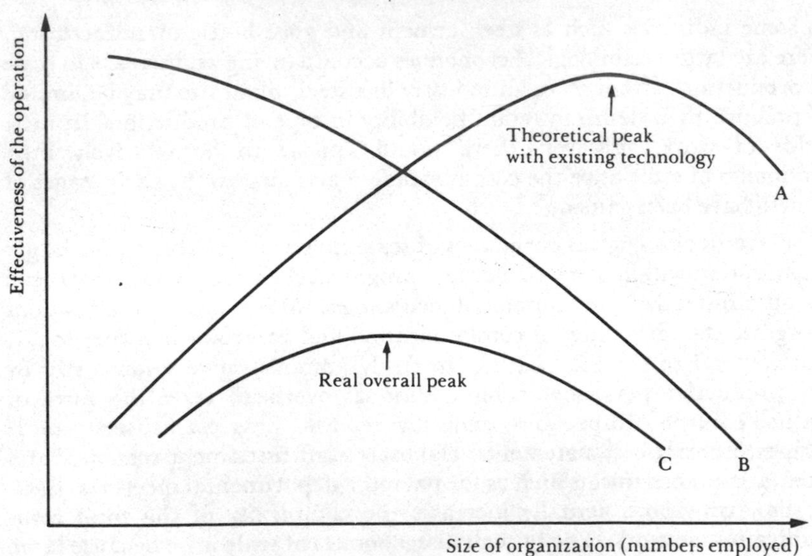

Line A = Technological advantages of scale
Line B = Human and organizational disadvantages of large numbers
Line C = Combined effects of A & B

Figure 9.2
Size and effectiveness

Source: 'Trend Towards Bigger Organizations Must be Reversed', *The Times*, 24th February 1975.

The policy implications of this argument are that wherever possible large-scale organization should be avoided. Even in fields of activity where technological economies of scale are particularly significant, it may be possible to ward off the undesirable effects of bureaucratic organization. If, for example, large plants can be automated then the size of human organization can be kept quite small. Another way in which it may be possible to foster greater adaptability and participation in large units is through devolution. In other words, as an alternative to actually breaking up large organizations, as the United States federal authorities did with Standard Oil and are threatening to do with ITT and IBM, they can be divided into smaller semi-autonomous segments. As E. F. Schumacher has put it in *Small is Beautiful*, 'The fundamental task is to achieve smallness *within* large organization.' These smaller segments can operate less bureaucratically and more flexibly. They can offer more opportunities for their smaller number of members to participate in decisions and influence the segment's policy as a whole.

The National Coal Board, one of the largest commercial undertakings in Europe and one where there is a strong case for running a national industry as a single unit, found it possible to set up smaller quasi-firms for its diversified activities. The Board's primary activity, coal-getting, has itself been organized into seventeen areas each with a high degree of autonomy. In private industry, one sees a similar policy of devolution where companies divisionalize, keeping each division down to a modest size and treating them as independent profit centres. A problem still remains, however, in that some decisions, notably over the allocation of financial resources, will be made at the centre of a large organization so long as that organization continues to operate overall as a single unit. Such decisions will inevitably appear to be remote from employees, and this is particularly true of multinational corporations with headquarters not even within the country in question. One can anticipate a growing demand by unions and other groups within host countries that foreign-owned subsidiaries be subject to local planning agreements and other participative arrangements. This type of pressure may well lead to the further devolution of power to smaller subsidiaries and divisions within large corporations of all kinds.

Large-scale organization has been justified on the grounds of economy, though other more private motives may have sustained the push for growth in the first place. The geographical centralization of corporate headquarters onto a capital city such as London has also been justified on the grounds of an economy in sharing information and the availability of specialized services. Neither of these economies need rule out a deliberate policy designed to achieve the administrative and social advantages of the smaller organization. In many fields, it is possible for small units to achieve external economies of scale through co-operative policies. Farmers, for example, make arrangements to share the same equipment and to market co-operatively. The advantages of geographical centralization can also be exaggerated in an age where ample electronic aids to communication are available.

2 Grafting new provisions onto a bureaucracy

The world is already populated by many large and bureaucratic organizations. Breaking them down into smaller independent units is a relatively drastic social policy which is not yet generally acceptable. Among these large organizations there are some which operate within fairly stable parameters and for which bureaucracy on the whole provides an efficient method of administration. The Inland Revenue in Britain is, for example, primarily concerned with the routine administration of laws and procedures which have to be standardized for reasons of public justice and equity. Bureaucracy is on the whole well suited to the efficient administration of such a function. In a case like this, the adaptability required is limited to accommodating new laws and regulations which are imposed on the organization — its personnel do not have to design new products or programmes of work for themselves. The type of people who are attracted to employment in organizations like the Inland Revenue or banks are, as research studies have demonstrated, on the whole not desirous of too much change and uncertainty in their working lives, and they may even be less enthusiastic than others in their wish for more participation. At one end of the spectrum, then, we have organizations like these where, more than in most other situations, bureaucracy might seem to be reasonably acceptable.

Even where a bureaucratic structure appears well suited to existing contingencies, however, it would be unwise to take a purely static view. The generally increasing rate of change does not leave institutions like the Inland Revenue untouched, as is indicated by recent complaints of its officers that it cannot cope with the spate of new tax legislation. Nor is it likely that the demand for greater participation, and experiments in other institutions designed to satisfy this demand, will pass unnoticed by employees in even the most hallowed of bureaucracies. If these pressures develop, a possible response would be to retain the bureaucracy basically as it stands, and to graft on new provisions aimed at increasing adaptiveness and accessibility. The evidence we have suggests, unfortunately, that this will not work adequately because the bureaucracy itself can in this situation continue more or less unchanged and nullify the new provisions.

If, for example, an idea-generating resource is grafted onto a bureaucracy with the intention of increasing its innovative and hence adaptive capacity, this is likely to encounter all the same blockages to its effectiveness as have been experienced by research and development teams in industry. Investigations into the attributes of successful industrial innovation indicate that it is vital for research or project personnel to be fully integrated into both the operating and power systems of the organization. That is, they must be able to perform their work in close contact with those who can express the needs of the final client or customer to whom new products or services are directed, and they must have the backing of a powerful senior manager for their work to be accepted by the organization as a whole. Simply grafting an idea-generating, forward planning or any other extra resource onto an entrenched bureaucracy is unlikely to satisfy these conditions. The chances are that it will remain isolated from well-established departments, resisting the new threat to the *status quo*. This will therefore not prove to be a very effective way of increasing the organization's adaptive capability.

Much the same conclusion may be drawn from attempts to graft participative mechanisms onto bureaucracies. The German system of co-determination has been criticized, by British managers among others, because it is said not to have had any real effect upon decision-making within the enterprise. If we take the British example of the Glacier Metal Company's participative system, we can see that much the same objection applies. The company attempted to keep its representative system quite separate from its system of management, with the result that it was possible in practice for policy decisions to be taken at a distance from formally constituted representative bodies. The management hierarchy, in other words, carried on much as before. This is an important reason for advocating an organic system of participation in which managerial problems are discussed from the work group upwards, in complete contrast to the separate non-organic system which is merely grafted onto an established bureaucracy. If a separate representative system is required, then representatives themselves will be able to play a more legitimated and informed role with the backing of constituents who are involved in decision-making on an everyday basis. It is important to recognize that whatever neat formal separation of policy making from execution may be shown on organization charts, policy is to an important extent shaped through its mode of execution, and employees cannot but help be well aware of this.

There is, then, some reason to doubt whether the mere grafting of extra structural provisions for innovation and participation onto a basically bureaucratic structure will make a great deal of difference to the way in which it functions. It will be recalled from Chapter 2 that one of the reasons for failure in job enrichment experiments has been a re-assertion of bureaucratic procedures which have encroached on the additional discretion and responsibility given to employees. This provides another example of the staying power of an entrenched bureaucracy. It appears, then, that when bureaucracy becomes inadequate or unacceptable, much more intrinsic changes have to be considered.

3 Post-bureaucratic structures

I have attempted up to this point to develop a perspective on contemporary organizations which recognizes the pressures on them to move away from their traditional structures and administrative systems. I have suggested that mere additions grafted onto a traditionally bureaucratic approach will probably do little, and are likely to be kept at arms length by the unchanged core of the organization. This implies that it is bureaucracy itself which will require increasing modification in the future. I have also taken the view, based on our present state of knowledge, that the factors of large scale and geographical centralization of administrative headquarters – both factors which sustain bureaucracy in very important ways – have had overmuch economic importance attached to them. If this is the case, then it becomes more realistic to give the prospect of moving beyond the bureaucratic model serious attention. I shall conclude therefore with a consideration of the directions this move might take.

Much of the opportunity to free up and open up an entrenched bureaucracy lies in the hands of managers themselves. That is, they can take steps to strengthen the informal network of communication to find out what is happening and to put others in the picture. They can take the initiative of designing systems of work in their areas of responsibility which will devolve decision-making and create opportunities for people to achieve and develop. They can adopt a policy of confronting problems openly and directly rather than allowing 'the system' to take care of them. They can refuse to accept any more bureaucratic procedure. These moves will not alter the fundamentally hierarchical or restrictive nature of modern organization, but they will begin to modify the way in which it operates.

Certain structural developments can help to support this change in managerial behaviour. The need to be adaptive is encouraging some managements to adopt a project team approach for dealing with changes or special problems, to maintain necessary control and co-ordination through agreement on shared objectives, and to adjust structural arrangements progressively over time as new circumstances warrant. It will be seen that these developments move away from traditional bureaucracy and incorporate greater elements of participation in operational decision-making.

One important departure from traditional bureaucratic structure is the use of temporary project teams which draw upon personnel with appropriate knowledge and skills from different departments to deal with a problem. They are staffed not on the basis of hierarchical status but of potential contribution. For this reason the frequent use of project teams offers a greater chance for members of an organization to take part in decision-making processes. Project teams and task forces can handle new and special problems which cannot be dealt with by standing procedures. They therefore add greater flexibility to organization structure and mobilize the most appropriate skills to deal with the task. It is important to note that project teams by drawing upon existing departmental personnel remain integral to the functioning of the organization; they are not in this sense grafted on although their life span may be as short as a few days depending on the nature of the problem.

The project team is more effective than normal standing arrangements based on departments for the non-routine problem to which the organization has to adapt. If and when the new problem becomes of regular occurrence, then standard formal arrangements will probably provide the most economical way of coping with it and the project team can be disbanded. Until it is clear whether or not the problem will become routine, even permanent, in nature, the project team offers a useful way of dealing with it which permits existing standing arrangements to continue as before for routine matters. Moreover, the project team, by drawing upon the services of members from several departments, avoids the need to decide which particular department should take responsibility for the work. This can help management to avoid the opposition to change that comes from departments which feel they are losing out politically, and it allows management to retain command over the complexity of interdepartmental relations rather than being forced into the position of having to adjudicate among rival bureaucratic departments. If an organization is faced with a continuous series of new programmes it may become appropriate to consolidate project teams into a permanent matrix system.

The move to secure a unity of purpose and action through commonly discussed and agreed objectives (self-control) rather than through rigid role definitions and procedures (formalized control) provides a further example of how the bureaucratic structure can be developed to provide more flexibility. This approach sometimes passes under the label of 'management by objectives', though this term has become somewhat discredited because of the plethora of different interpretations it attracts. The significant point is that if managers and employees in different segments of an organization can agree upon joint objectives for a given time period ahead, and if these objectives are reconciled with those of other segments, then each part of the organization can proceed as it sees fit to deal with its problems and contingencies without having to follow a set of standard bureaucratic procedures. This approach should enable members of the organization to devise methods for achieving their objectives and to revise these if circumstances change. Greater flexibility is built into the structure.

In Chapter 8 it was mentioned that many business firms, particularly in North America, are today employing organizational planning teams which are utilized to assist the continuous adjustment of structural elements to suit new requirements. These teams should promote a more open and regular discussion of organizational problems than would otherwise take place, and thus serve as a mechanism for generating gradual rather than discontinuous change. It is a growing practice to try to avoid massive and highly disturbing changes in structure – the global type of reorganization – in favour of making more limited but continuous changes in various parts of the organization. By adjusting the structure as a matter of frequent and normal occurrence, the organization as a whole is usefully assisted in its process of updating and adaptation. The role of the planning unit may be critical here, for as Cyril Sofer has commented, 'this is a living advertisement that the top management does not mean to hold indefinitely to current arrangements, means to move in new directions and will take the necessary steps in those directions' (*Omega*, Vol 2, 1974).

As well as these methods of increasing fluidity into the structures of organizations, complementary changes can be witnessed today in the career structures of personnel such as management specialists. The problem of securing a sufficient degree of integration of specialists, such as management accountants, with line managers so as to provide the quality of control and planning information now required has led to an increasing use of management teams which cut across the traditional boundaries of bureaucratic departments. Urged on by the complaint that there is an inadequate supply of general management recruits, this move towards teamwork is changing the career patterns of some specialist managers, and again in the direction of greater flexibility. Instead of being confined to a career contained within their specialist function, these managers are now acquiring an early understanding of management problems on a broader base, working in teams with line managers and specialists from other areas. This can clearly develop their capacity to handle a wider range of managerial problems.

It will be evident that many of these moves beyond bureaucracy, aimed at providing a more adequate adaptive capacity, also extend the scope of participation in decision-making, at least for staff and managerial employees. I have argued that, in principle, there is no serious conflict between the requirements placed upon structural design by the need for flexibility and for participation. The connection between the two lies in (1) the capacity of employees and other groups to resist changes to which they are not committed, resistance usually activated when they have not been involved in the formulation of the changes, and (2) the need to acquire adequate information and advice on the issues to which a response is required, from all the relevant sections and levels of an organization – again a process of participation is indicated as being functional to adaptation. In contrast to traditional bureaucratic theory, all power and wisdom cannot in these circumstances be assumed to reside at the top of an organization, and a policy of secrecy and closed doors will not be effective. Thus, participation, though it takes time and energy, is on the whole an essential means to adaptability because it forms a necessary part of the process of implementing change.

The modifications to bureaucracy which a development of participation entails have been noted at various points in this book and there is no need to elaborate them again. They include the devolution of decisions from the centre to the smaller segments of an organization, the greater involvement of managers and specialists in planning, the extension of job enrichment and autonomous group working at operative level, and the development of new representative arrangements at board or works council levels. These various elements comprise the kind of movement towards greater participation which is likely to gain further momentum in years to come.

In this book I have used bureaucracy as a major point of reference for organizational design and then discussed alternatives to it. My thesis has been that there is nothing sacrosanct about bureaucracy or any other particular model of organization. The ways in which the various dimensions of structure can be designed are extremely varied. The choice is wide and can suit the circumstances which prevail, as well as the ways in which members of organizations wish to perform their work and relate with colleagues. Given this breadth of organizational choice, it is necessarily an oversimplification to offer any classification scheme which is limited to only a few categories. A classification of organization structures will, nevertheless, help to draw together and summarize some of the main organizational alternatives which have been discussed in this book.

Table 9.2 offers a classification of organization structures, which are distinguished in terms of differences in the approach adopted to control and integration. These two dimensions, control and integration, are singled out because they have the most direct bearing on the way in which the activities and relationships of people in organizations are structured, within the more global framework established by the grouping of activities and the overall shape of the organization.

The classical model of bureaucracy appears in this scheme as the 'mechanistic bureaucracy' (Type 2). The main method of control is through highly formalized definition of people's roles, and integration is achieved through reference up the hierarchy whenever formal plans and procedures are inadequate. This type of organization is usually found in the larger business firm and is also extensively employed in public organizations. Bureaucracy typically replaces a much simpler model of organization once a certain level of scale and complexity of operations is

Table 9.2
A general classification of organization structures

Type of structure	Method of control	Method of co-ordination	Empirical example
1 Centralized, pre-bureaucratic	Direct supervision	Direct supervision	Small firm
2 Mechanistic bureaucracy	Formalization of activities and relationships (role formalization)	Specification in plans and procedures. When inadequate, reference to common superior	Large firm, government ministry
3 Professional bureaucracy	Selection of employees with appropriate qualifications. Sanctions against professional misconduct	Formal meetings (professionals/administrators), informal meetings between professional colleagues	Hospitals, university
4 Team structure	Acceptability of results, achievement of targets	Frequent informal meetings, project leadership	Research team, autonomous work group
5 Implicit structure	Group norms, informal leadership	Informal interpersonal interaction	Small religious sects, communes

reached; this simpler model is a centralized kind (Type 1) in which both control and integration are achieved through the direct intervention of the organization head or a small controlling group of individuals.

At several points in previous chapters, I have discussed the moves beyond bureaucracy which are occasioned by the growing employment of professional staffs, by the increasing need for teamwork between specialized groups, and by pressures to grant people at work more autonomy and opportunity to participate in decisions. There are several models of organization which go some way to satisfying some of these developments, models which are already in wide use. In professional institutions which operate on a large scale, such as hospitals and universities, one finds a form of bureaucracy that is modified in order to allow for the exercise of professional autonomy in the direct work carried out by doctors, nurses and teachers. This is the 'professional bureaucracy' (Type 3). The main methods of control used are the stringent selection of staff, applying criteria of appropriate attested qualification, and sanctions against misconduct in the course of carrying out duties. These controls are largely administered by professional staffs themselves, and external control placed upon them is largely confined to the provision of financial resources. Thus it would be unusual for a university administration to interfere with teaching or a hospital administration to interfere in medical matters; administrators may however have a greater say in the budgets allocated to teaching and medical departments. The integration mechanisms used in this form of organization tend to be formal meetings to cope with the interface between professionals and administrators, and informal meetings or teamwork in the case of working relations between professionals.

The 'team structure' (Type 4) represents another model which is appropriate for relatively small groups of people who have to work together. Task forces and project teams are examples; so also is the autonomous work group at operative level. Managerial control is achieved indirectly through the assessment of how far mutually agreed targets and standards have been met. Integration is informal within the team, though interpersonal relations will generally require leadership directed at maintaining both the progress of the work and also the quality of personal co-operation between team members.

A team organization is formally structured from the outside, as it were, through the conditions and constraints placed upon it by the management of the wider organization in which it is located. An 'implicit structure' (Type 5) is, in a formal sense, completely unstructured. Its structure is implied in the modes of conduct worked out by the organization's members and the objectives they set for themselves. Control is through the pressure of group norms and integration is purely informal. The implicitly structured organization is of interest because it represents the ultimate form of direct participation by members. Its democratic nature distinguishes it from Type 1, the centralized model, though both have little or no formal structure. Whether or not, in the absence of structures defining rights and obligations, implicit structures are vulnerable to centralization through the dominance of one or a few members is an issue deserving further research. Some small religious sects, including the Quakers in their earlier days, and small communes have adopted this relatively 'existential', implicit mode of organization.

The concept of existentialism is by no means irrelevant to the choice that is made between the range of organizational designs covered by the foregoing classificatory scheme. Technological and economic contingencies do, with little question, establish certain limits to the choice of organization which can be made for a given institution if it is to operate efficiently. These limits are, however, broader than some writers have suggested in the past. Within their bounds, the choice that is made will depend ultimately upon the view which we take of ourselves and of our human nature. My own view, moulded by an absorption of research findings as well as by personal philosophy, is that most people respond to an opportunity of exercising more responsibility and of taking part in the determination of their working environments so long as they do not suspect that there is some hidden cost or threat attached to it. There is a wide measure of agreement that considerable energies could be released by a more acceptable organization of work and that this would be quite independent of any further capital investment. The potential is illustrated by the way that, during the 1974 three-day week in Britain, some 80% of normal production was achieved with only 60% of normal power. A more considered and objective examination of existing structures in every organization would play its part in releasing these energies. That is the challenge we face.

Summary

Bureaucracy is, today, the basis of administration in most societies throughout many walks of life. It is a model of organization well suited to the efficient management of large-scale units under relatively stable conditions.

While there has been a steady trend towards large-scale organization, which has promoted bureaucracy, other developments underway in advanced societies are subjecting traditional forms of bureaucracy to increasing criticism and pressure. Environments are becoming more volatile and placing a premium upon organizational adaptability in many fields. Another significant phenomenon lies in the growing demand for participation and social accountability now being placed upon organizations.

Bureaucracy is not well equipped to cope with these new requirements, yet it is still spreading, largely due to the growing scale of organization both in the business and the public authority fields. This contradiction presents us with a contemporary crisis of organization which is not being honestly faced up to by all administrators, though many industrial managers are aware of it. The problem presents a challenge to those who can influence the future shape of organization. Three broad possibilities were examined: containing and even reversing the trend to bigness; grafting new provisions for adaptability and participation onto bureaucracies; and modifying bureaucracy itself in appropriate directions. This last possibility appears to offer the most effective results and has in fact been the rationale for the discussion of organizational design choices discussed in this book.

Suggested further reading

Peter M. Blau and Marshall W. Meyer, *Bureaucracy in Modern Society* (Random House, 2nd edition 1971), discuss the two-faced nature of man's 'greatest social invention': the threat which bureaucracy imposes to freedom, creativity and social progress coupled with its many contributions to effective administration. Warren G. Bennis has written many papers on the future of organization, including 'A Funny Thing Happened on the Way to the Future' in H. J. Leavitt et al. (editors), *Organizations of the Future — Interaction with the External Environment* (Praeger 1974), a collection of papers on the subject. Cyril Sofer discusses ways in which bureaucratic organization can be rendered more flexible and participative in his article, 'Post Bureaucratic Organizations and Managers', *Omega*, Vol. 2, 1974.

The arguments presented in this chapter on the size of organization were drawn from a large number of sources. Two informative sources on size and economic performance are Robin Marris and Adrian Wood (editors), *The Corporate Economy* (Macmillan 1971), and A. P. Jacquemin and M. C. De Lichtbuer, 'Size Structure, Stability and Performance of the Largest British and E.E.C. Firms', *European Economic Review*, Vol. 4, 1973. F. M. Scherer and others present data on technological economies of scale available to different industries in their *The Economics of Multi-Plant Operation* (Harvard University Press 1976). A short readable paper on the size debate is Ted Johns, 'Where Smallness Pays', *Management Today*, July 1976. Derek Sheane's unpublished paper based on his experience at ICI is entitled 'Why do Managers Join Unions?' (1975). S. J. Prais, *The Evolution of Giant Firms in Britain* (Cambridge University Press 1976), studies the growth of firm size and concentration in British manufacturing industry and suggests the need for counteracting policies.

Bibliography

Ansoff, H. Igor et al. *Acquisition Behaviour of U.S. Manufacturing Firms 1946—1965,* Vanderbilt University Press, 1971.

Aguilar, F. J. *Scanning the Business Environment,* Macmillan, 1967.

Argyris, Chris *Personality and Organization,* Harper and Row, 1957.

Barkdull, C. W. 'Span of Control: A Method of Evaluation', *Michigan Business Review,* vol. 15, 1963.

Beckhard, Richard *Organization Development: Strategies and Models,* Addison-Wesley, 1969.

Bennis, Warren G. 'A Funny Thing Happened on the Way to the Future' in H. J. Leavitt et al. (eds.) *Organizations of the Future —Interaction with the External Environment,* Praeger, 1974.

Blau, Peter M. and Meyer, Marshall W. *Bureaucracy in Modern Society,* 2nd edition, Random House, 1971.

Boswell, Jonathan *The Rise and Decline of Small Firms in Britain,* Allen and Unwin, 1972.

Burns, Tom and Stalker, G. M. *The Management of Innovation,* Tavistock, 1961.

Caplan, Robert et al. *Job Demands and Worker Health,* U.S. Department of Health, Education and Welfare, 1975.

Carlisle, Howard M. 'A Contingency Approach to Decentralization', *Advanced Management Journal,* July 1974.

Chandler, Alfred D. Jr. *Strategy and Structure,* M.I.T. Press, 1962.

Channon, Derek F. *The Strategy and Structure of British Enterprise,* Macmillan, 1973.

Child, John 'Strategies of Control and Organizational Behaviour', *Administrative Science Quarterly,* March 1973.

Child, John 'Parkinson's Progress: Accounting for the Number of Specialists in Organizations', *Administrative Science Quarterly,* September 1973.

Child, John 'Why Company A Manages Better', *Management Today,* November 1973.

Child, John and Ellis, Tony 'Predictors of Variation in Managerial Roles', *Human Relations,* vol. 26, 1973.

Child, John 'What Determines Organization Performance? The Universals vs. the It-All-Depends', *Organizational Dynamics,* Summer 1974.

Child, John 'Managerial and Organizational Factors Associated with Company Performance", *Journal of Management Studies,* October 1974 and February 1975.

Child, John and Kieser, Alfred 'The Development of Organizations over Time' in William H. Starbuck (ed.) *Handbook Organizational Design,* Vol. 1, Elsevier, 1977.

Clark, Peter A. *Organizational Design: Theory and Practice,* Tavistock, 1972.

Clark, Peter A. *Action Research and Organizational Change,* Harper and Row, 1972.

Davis, Louis and Taylor, James (eds.) *The Design of Jobs,* Penguin, 1972.

Davis, Michael 'Current Experiments and Trends in Management Structure', in Smith, Brian et al. *Renewing the Management Structure*, British Institute of Management, 1972.

Duncan, Robert B 'Multiple Decision-Making Structures in Adapting to Environmental Uncertainty: The Impact on Organizational Effectiveness', *Human Relations,* vol. 26, 1973.

Filley, Alan C. *Interpersonal Conflict Resolution,* Scott Foresman, 1975.

Filley, Alan C., House, Robert J. and Kerr, Steven *Managerial Process and Organizational Behavior,* 2nd edition, Scott Foresman, 1976.

Franko, Lawrence G. 'The Move Toward a Multidivisional Structure in European Organizations', *Administrative Science Quarterly,* December 1974.

Franko, Lawrence G. *The European Multinationals,* Harper and Row, 1976.

Freeman, C., Robertson, A. et al. *Success and Failure in Industrial Innovation,* University of Sussex Science Policy Research Unit, February 1972.

Galbraith, Jay *Designing Complex Organizations,* Addison-Wesley, 1973.

Greenwood, Ronald G. *Managerial Decentralization,* Lexington Books, 1974.

Hackman, J. Richard 'On the Coming Demise of Job Enrichment' in *Man and Work in Society,* Van Nostrand-Rheinhold, 1975.

Heron, R. P. and Friesen, D. 'Organizational Growth and Development', *University of Alberta, Edmonton, Canada, Working Paper,* March 1976.

International Labour Office *Final Report on A Study of the Effects of Group Production Methods on the Humanization of Work,* 1975.

Jacquemin, A. P. and De Lichtbuer, M. C. 'Size Structure, Stability and Performance of the Largest British and E.E.C. Firms', *European Economic Review,* vol. 4, 1973.

Jaques, Elliot 'Grading and Management Organization in the Civil Service', *O & M Bulletin,* August 1972.

Johns, E. A. *The Sociology of Organizational Change,* Pergamon, 1973.

Johns, E. A. 'Where Smallness Pays', *Management Today,* July 1976.

Khandwalla, Pradip N. 'Uncertainty and the "Optimal" Design of Organizations', *Faculty of Management Working Paper, McGill University, Montreal,* 1972.

Khandwalla, Pradip N. 'Viable and Effective Organizational Design of Firms', *Academy of Management Journal,* September 1973.

Khandwalla, Pradip N. 'Mass Output Orientation of Operations Technology and Organizational Structure', *Administrative Science Quarterly,* March 1974.

Kingdon, Donald Ralph *Matrix Organization,* Tavistock, 1973.

Knight, Kenneth 'Matrix Organization — A Review', *Journal of Management Studies,* May 1976.

Lawrence, Paul R. and Lorsch, J. W. *Organization and Environment,* Harvard Business School, 1967.

Lawrence, Paul R. and Lorsch, J. W. *Developing Organizations: Diagnosis and Action,* Addison-Wesley, 1969.

Leavitt, H. J. et al. (eds.) *Organizations of the Future—Interaction with the External Environment,* Praeger, 1974.

Lorsch, J. W. and Lawrence, Paul R. (eds.) *Studies in Organizational Design,* Irwin-Dorsey, 1970.

Lorsch, J. W. 'Introduction to the Structural Design of Organizations' in Gene W. Dalton, Paul R. Lawrence and J. W. Lorsch (eds.) *Organizational Structure and Design,* Irwin-Dorsey, 1970.

Lorsch, J. W. and Allen, Stephen A., III *Managing Diversity and Interdependence,* Harvard Business School, 1973.

Lupton, Tom 'The Practical Analysis of Change in Organizations', *Journal of Management Studies,* May 1965.

Margulies, Newton and Wallace, John *Organizational Change: Techniques and Applications,* Scott Foresman, 1973.

Marlow, Hugh *Managing Change: A Strategy for Our Time,* Institute of Personnel Management, London, 1975.

Mangham, I. L., Shaw, D. and Wilson, B. *Managing Change,* British Institute of Management, London, 1972.

Marris, Robin and Wood Adrian (eds.) *The Corporate Economy,* Macmillan, 1971.

Mintzberg, Henry *The Nature of Managerial Work,* Harper and Row, 1973.

Negandhi, Anant R. and Reimann, Bernard C. 'Task Environment, Decentralization and Organizational Effectiveness', *Human Relations,* vol. 26, 1973.

Parke, E. Lauck and Tausky, Curt. 'The Mythology of Job Enrichment', *Personnel,* September-October 1975.

Pennings, Johannes M. 'The Relevance of the Structural-Contingency Model for Organizational Effectiveness', *Administrative Science Quarterly,* September 1975.

Pettigrew, Andrew M. 'Strategic Aspects of the Management of Specialist Activity', *Personnel Review,* vol. 4, 1975.

Porter, Lyman W. and Lawler, Edward E., III 'Properties of Organization Structure in Relation to Job Attitudes and Job Behavior', *Psychological Bulletin,* July 1965.

Prais, S. J. *The Evolution of Giant Firms in Britain,* Cambridge University Press, 1976.

Roeber, R. J. C. *The Organization in a Changing Environment,* Addison-Wesley, 1973.

Rumelt, Richard P. *Strategy, Structure and Economic Performance,* Harvard Business School, 1974.

Sadler, Philip, Webb, Terry and Lansley, Peter *Management Style and Organization Structure in the Smaller Enterprise,* Ashridge College, Management Research Unit, 1974.

Scherer, F. M. et al. *The Economics of Multi-Plant Operation,* Harvard University Press, 1976.

Scott, Bruce R. *Strategies of Corporate Development,* Harvard Business School, 1971.

Sheane, Derek 'Why do Managers Join Unions?", Unpublished paper, 1975.

Sofer, Cyril 'Post Bureaucratic Organizations and Managers', *Omega,* vol. 2, 1974.

Stieglitz, H. 'Optimizing Span of Control', *Management Record,* vol. 24, 1962.

Stopford, John M. and Wells, Louis T., Jr. *Managing the Multinational Enterprise,* Longman, 1972.

Strauss, George 'Tactics of Lateral Relationship: The Purchasing Agent', *Administrative Science Quarterly,* September 1962.

Swedish Employers' Confederation *Job Reform in Sweden,* English version 1975.

Sykes, A. J. M. and Bates, J. 'Study of Conflict Between Formal Company Policy and the Interests of Informal Groups', *Sociological Review,* November 1962.

Thompson, James D. *Organizations in Action,* McGraw-Hill, 1967.

Thorsrud, Einar 'Democratization of Work as a Process of Change Towards Non-Bureaucratic Types of Organization' in Geert Hofstede and M. Sami Kassem (eds.) *European Contributions to Organization Theory,* Van Gorcum, Assen, 1976.

Toronto, Robert S. 'A General Systems Model for the Analysis of Organizational Change', *Behavioural Science,* vol. 20, 1975.

Van de Ven, Andrew, Delbecq, Andre L. and Koenig, Richard, Jr. 'Determinants of Coordination Modes within Organizations', *American Sociological Review,* April 1976.

Vision, 'Job Enrichment: No Real Future in Sight', *Vision,* November 1973.

Walker, Arthur H. and Lorsch, Jay W. 'Organizational Choice: Product vs. Function', *Harvard Business Review,* November-December 1968.

Webber, Ross A. 'Red Tape versus Chaos', *Business Horizons,* April 1969.

Wild, Ray *Work Organization: A Study of Manual Work and Mass Production,* Wiley, 1975.

Woodward, Joan *Industrial Organization: Theory and Practice,* Oxford University Press, 1965.

Worthy, James 'Organization Structure and Employee Morale', *American Sociological Review,* April 1950.

Zimpel, Lloyd *Man Against Work,* Eerdmans, 1974.

Index of Names

Index of Subjects